1965

HENRY
JAMES

Seven Stories
and
Studies

GOLDENTREE BOOKS

R. C. BALD, SAMUEL H. BEER & WILLIAM C. DEVANE
Series Editors

C. DAY LEWIS, Editor
English Lyric Poems, 1500–1900

DANIEL G. HOFFMAN and SAMUEL HYNES, Editors
English Literary Criticism (3 vols.): *The Renaissance;
Restoration and 18th Century; Romantic and Victorian*

KATHERINE LEVER
The Novel and the Reader

MILTON MARX
The Enjoyment of Drama, 2nd Edition

HAROLD OREL, Editor
The World of Victorian Humor

ROBERT L. PETERS, Editor
Victorians on Literature & Art

EDWARD STONE, Editor
Henry James: Seven Stories and Studies

EDWARD STONE
Ohio University
EDITOR

1638

HENRY JAMES

Seven Stories

and

Studies

New York
APPLETON-CENTURY-CROFTS, Inc.

For

FANNIE STONE

Ah! certè extremùm licuisset tangere dextram,
Et bene compositos placidè morientis ocellos,
Et dixisse "Vale! nostri memor ibis ad astra."

PREFACE

THERE IS A RECENT TREND in publishing toward making available to students and teachers in one volume both the primary materials of an important literary work and a substantial part of the wealth of interpretation such a work always inspires. This tradition (Controlled Materials, Guided Research, Casebooks, or Sourcebooks), originating with the Harvey T. Lyon, *Keats' Well-Read Urn*, has been laudably continued with such collections as the Lettis-McDonnell-Morris, *The Red Badge of Courage* and the Gerald Willen, *A Casebook on Henry James's "Turn of the Screw"* (there are others on Shakespeare, Conrad, and Literary Symbolism).

The present collection is in this category and, like Willen's, offers homage to Henry James's art and to the men and women who have attempted to interpret it. It contains a baker's half-dozen of his maturest, most challenging (as opposed to merely teasing or vexing) stories. With them are fifty or so commentaries, ranging in space from a sentence to 2500 words and in time from James's own notebook jottings in the 1880's to an article which appeared shortly before this book went to press. The seven Stories have been arranged according to my own opinion of the degree of effort required for their comprehension. Accordingly, the Studies accompanying them progress from the meagerness of the first ones, for which very little more commentary was available than James's own, to the last two or three Studies, which, bulky as they are, had to be most selective. The contents of each Study have been chronologically arranged.

Where selection was possible or necessary, the Study materials have been selected on the basis of their usefulness in classroom discussion. If, therefore, superficiality or even perverseness appears on occasion back to back with brilliance or profundity, the propinquity is deliberate and functional. As some of these materials demonstrate, a student of James can profitably explore not only the surface but the depth of a James story by thorough examination of that story alone. But classroom experience has convinced me that: (1) More often than not, James will daunt even good students, and without wiser (or at least older) heads to help them, they will lose interest and fall back upon the capsule commentaries of literary handbooks and histories. With such help as is here provided, however, they can observe James's fiction in the light of various critical minds and even at times be inspired to formulate their own impressions. (2) Some of the most enlightening interpretations of James's stories are those which seek or find parallels or contrasts with other stories, either of James's or of other writers. A number of the Study materials, it will be seen, employ this approach, and there has been added at the end of the volume a list of "References for Further Reading and Writing," containing hints, proposals, or extended analyses linking the Seven Stories with others of James's and with stories by writers ranging from Poe and Hawthorne to Mann and Joyce.

The title of each of James's stories is followed by the date, in parenthesis, of its first book-form publication. The text of each story is identical with that found in the publication cited at the foot of the first page.

In compiling this volume I drew heavily on the time and resources of the staff of the Chubb Memorial Library of Ohio University, particularly Miss Catherine Nelson, and of the Alderman Library of the University of Virginia, whose Mr. John C. Wyllie and Misses Roy Land, Katherine Beville, Helena Koiner, and Ann Freudenberg provided both environmental coolness and spiritual warmth during the past summer. I shall be forever indebted to Professors Maurice Beebe and William T. Stafford for their "Criticism of Henry James: a Selected Checklist . . . ," appearing in the Spring, 1957, number of *Modern Fiction Studies*. And I am grateful for his encouragement and suggestions to Professor Marius Bewley, a stranger to me but far from a stranger to Jamesians.

Athens, Ohio   EDWARD STONE

CONTENTS

The Marriages

[1891]

I

"WON'T YOU STAY A LITTLE LONGER?" the hostess said, holding the girl's hand and smiling. "It's too early for every one to go; it's too absurd." Mrs. Churchley inclined her head to one side and looked gracious; she held up to her face, in a vague, protecting, sheltering way, an enormous fan of red feathers. Everything about her, to Adela Chart, was enormous. She had big eyes, big teeth, big shoulders, big hands, big rings and bracelets, big jewels of every sort and many of them. The train of her crimson dress was longer than any other; her house was huge; her drawing-room, especially now that the company had left it, looked vast, and it offered to the girl's eyes a collection of the largest sofas and chairs, pictures, mirrors, and clocks that she had ever beheld. Was Mrs. Churchley's fortune also large, to account for so many immensities? Of this Adela could know nothing, but she reflected, while she smiled sweetly back at their entertainer, that she had better try to find out. Mrs. Churchley had at least a high-hung carriage drawn by the tallest horses, and in the Row she was to be seen perched on a mighty hunter. She was high and expansive herself, though not exactly fat; her bones were big, her limbs were long, and she had a loud, hurrying voice like the bell of a steamboat. While she spoke to his daughter she had the air of hiding from Colonel Chart, a little shyly, behind the wide ostrich fan. But Colonel Chart was not a man to be either ignored or eluded.

"Of course every one is going on to something else," he said. "I believe there are a lot of things to-night."

"And where are *you* going?" Mrs. Churchley asked, dropping her fan and turning her bright, hard eyes on the Colonel.

"Oh, I don't do that sort of thing!" he replied, in a tone of re-

FROM *The Lesson of the Master* (New York, Macmillan & Co., 1892).

sentiment just perceptible to his daughter. She saw in it that he
thought Mrs. Churchley might have done him a little more justice.
But what made the honest soul think that she was a person to look
to for a perception of fine shades? Indeed the shade was one that
it might have been a little difficult to seize—the difference between "going on" and coming to a dinner of twenty people. The
pair were in mourning; the second year had not lightened it for
Adela, but the Colonel had not objected to dining with Mrs.
Churchley, any more than he had objected, at Easter, to going
down to the Millwards', where he had met her, and where the girl
had her reasons for believing him to have known he should meet
her. Adela was not clear about the occasion of their original meeting, to which a certain mystery attached. In Mrs. Churchley's exclamation now there was the fullest concurrence in Colonel Chart's
idea; she didn't say, "Ah, yes, dear friend, I understand!" but this
was the note of sympathy she plainly wished to sound. It immediately made Adela say to her, "Surely you must be going on
somewhere yourself."

"Yes, you must have a lot of places," the Colonel observed,
looking at her shining raiment with a sort of invidious directness.
Adela could read the tacit implication: "You're not in sorrow, in
desolation."

Mrs. Churchley turned away from her at this, waiting just a
moment before answering. The red fan was up again, and this time
it sheltered her from Adela. "I'll give everything up—for *you*," were
the words that issued from behind it. "*Do* stay a little. I always
think this is such a nice hour. One can really talk," Mrs. Churchley
went on. The Colonel laughed; he said it wasn't fair. But their
hostess continued, to Adela, "Do sit down; it's the only time to
have any talk." The girl saw her father sit down, but she wandered
away, turning her back and pretending to look at a picture. She
was so far from agreeing with Mrs. Churchley that it was an hour
she particularly disliked. She was conscious of the queerness, the
shyness, in London, of the gregarious flight of guests, after a dinner,
the general *sauve qui peut* and panic fear of being left with the
host and hostess. But personally she always felt the contagion,
always conformed to the flurry. Besides, she felt herself turning
red now, flushed with a conviction that had come over her and
that she wished not to show.

Her father sat down on one of the big sofas with Mrs. Churchley;

fortunately he was also a person with a presence that could hold its own. Adela didn't care to sit and watch them while they made love, as she crudely formulated it, and she cared still less to join in their conversation. She wandered further away, went into another of the bright, "handsome," rather nude rooms—they were like women dressed for a ball—where the displaced chairs, at awkward angles to each other, seemed to retain the attitudes of bored talkers. Her heart beat strangely, but she continued to make a pretense of looking at the pictures on the walls and the ornaments on the tables, while she hoped that, as she preferred it, it would be also the course that her father would like best. She hoped "awfully," as she would have said, that he wouldn't think her rude. She was a person of courage, and he was a kind, an intensely good-natured man; nevertheless, she was a good deal afraid of him. At home it had always been a religion with them to be nice to the people he liked. How, in the old days, her mother, her incomparable mother, so clever, so unerring, so perfect—how in the precious days her mother had practiced that art! Oh, her mother, her irrecoverable mother! One of the pictures that she was looking at swam before her eyes. Mrs. Churchley, in the natural course, would have begun immediately to climb staircases. Adela could see the high bony shoulders and the long crimson tail and the universal coruscating nod wriggle their business-like way through the rest of the night. Therefore she *must* have had her reasons for detaining them. There were mothers who thought every one wanted to marry their eldest son, and the girl asked herself if *she* belonged to the class of daughters who thought every one wanted to marry their father. Her companions left her alone; and though she didn't want to be near them, it angered her that Mrs. Churchley didn't call her. That proved that she was conscious of the situation. She would have called her, only Colonel Chart had probably murmured, "Don't." That proved that he also was conscious. The time was really not long—ten minutes at the most elapsed—when he cried out, gayly, pleasantly, as if with a little jocular reproach, "I say, Adela, we must release this dear lady!" He spoke, of course, as if it had been Adela's fault that they lingered. When they took leave she gave Mrs. Churchley, without intention and without defiance, but from the simple sincerity of her anxiety, a longer look into the eyes than she had ever given her before. Mrs. Churchley's onyx pupils reflected the question; they seemed to say: "Yes, I *am*, if that's what you want to know!"

What made the case worse, what made the girl more sure, was the silence preserved by her companion in the brougham, on their way home. They rolled along in the June darkness from Prince's Gate to Seymour Street, each looking out of a window in conscious dumbness; watching without seeing the hurry of the London night, the flash of lamps, the quick roll on the wood of hansoms and other broughams. Adela had expected that her father would say something about Mrs. Churchley; but when he said nothing, it was, strangely, still more as if he had spoken. In Seymour Street he asked the footman if Mr. Godfrey had come in, to which the servant replied that he had come in early and gone straight to his room. Adela had perceived as much, without saying so, by a lighted window in the third story; but she contributed no remark to the question. At the foot of the stairs her father halted a moment, hesitating, as if he had something on his mind; but what it amounted to, apparently, was only the dry "Good-night" with which he presently ascended. It was the first time since her mother's death that he had bidden her good-night without kissing her. They were a kissing family, and after her mother's death the habit had taken a fresh spring. She had left behind her such a general passion of regret that in kissing each other they seemed to themselves a little to be kissing her. Now, as, standing in the hall, with the stiff watching footman (she could have said to him angrily, "Go away!") planted near her, she looked with unspeakable pain at her father's back while he mounted, the effect was of his having withheld from other and still more sensitive lips the touch of his own.

He was going to his room, and after a moment she heard his door close. Then she said to the servant, "Shut up the house" (she tried to do everything her mother had done, to be a little of what she had been, conscious only of mediocrity), and took her own way upstairs. After she had reached her room she waited, listening, shaken by the apprehension that she should hear her father come out again and go up to Godfrey. He would go up to tell him, to have it over without delay, precisely because it would be so difficult. She asked herself, indeed, why he should tell Godfrey when he had not taken the occasion—their drive home was an occasion—to tell herself. However, she wanted no announcing, no telling; there was such a horrible clearness in her mind that what she now waited for was only to be sure her father wouldn't leave his room. At the end of ten minutes she saw that this particular danger was over, upon which she came out and made her way to Godfrey. Exactly what she wanted to say to him first, if her father counted on the boy's greater indulgence, and before he could say anything, was, "Don't forgive him; dont, don't!"

He was to go up for an examination, poor fellow, and during these weeks his lamp burned till the small hours. It was for the diplomatic service, and there was to be some frightful number of competitors; but Adela had great hopes of him—she believed so in his talents, and she saw, with pity, how hard he worked. This would have made her spare him, not trouble his night, his scanty rest, if anything less dreadful had been at stake. It was a blessing, however, that one could count upon his coolness, young as he was—his bright, good-looking discretion. Moreover he was the one who would care most. If Leonard was the eldest son—he had, as a matter of course, gone into the army and was in India, on the staff, by good luck, of a governor-general—it was exactly this that would make him comparatively indifferent. His life was elsewhere, and his father and he had been in a measure military comrades, so that he would be deterred by a certain delicacy from protesting; he wouldn't have liked his father to protest in an affair of *his*. Beatrice and Muriel would care, but they were too young to speak, and this was just why her own responsibility was so great.

Godfrey was in working-gear—shirt and trousers and slippers and a beautiful silk jacket. His room felt hot, though a window was open to the summer night; the lamp on the table shed its studious light over a formidable heap of text books and papers, and the bed showed that he had flung himself down to think out a problem. As soon as she got in she said to him: "Father's going to marry Mrs. Churchley!"

She saw the poor boy's pink face turn pale. "How do you know?"

"I've seen with my eyes. We've been dining there—we've just come home. He's in love with her—she's in love with him; they'll arrange it."

"Oh, I say!" Godfrey exclaimed, incredulous.

"He will, he will, he will!" cried the girl; and with this she burst into tears.

Godfrey, who had a cigarette in his hand, lighted it at one of

the candles on the mantelpiece as if he were embarrassed. As Adela,
who had dropped into his armchair, continued to sob, he said,
after a moment: "He oughtn't to—he oughtn't to."

"Oh, think of mamma—think of mamma!" the girl went on.

"Yes, he ought to think of mamma"; and Godfrey looked at the
tip of his cigarette.

"To such a woman as that, after *her!*"

"Dear old mamma!" said Godfrey, smoking.

Adela rose again, drying her eyes. "It's like an insult to her; it's
as if he denied her." Now that she spoke of it, she felt herself tremendously exalted. "It's as if he rubbed out at a stroke all the years
of their happiness."

"They were awfully happy," said Godfrey.

"Think what she was—think how no one else will ever again be
like her!" the girl cried.

"I suppose he's not very happy now," Godfrey continued vaguely.

"Of course he isn't, any more than you and I are; and it's dreadful of him to want to be."

"Well, don't make yourself miserable till you're sure," the young
man said.

But his sister showed him confidently that she *was* sure, from
the way the pair had behaved together and from her father's attitude on the drive home. If Godfrey had been there he would have
seen everything; it couldn't be explained, but he would have felt.
When he asked at what moment the girl had first had her suspicion,
she replied that it had all come at once, that evening; or that at
least she had had no conscious fear till then. There had been signs
for two or three weeks, but she hadn't understood them—ever
since the day Mrs. Churchley had dined in Seymour Street. Adela
had thought it odd then that her father had wished to invite her,
in the quiet way they were living; she was a person they knew so
little. He had said something about her having been very civil to
him, and that evening, already, she had guessed that he had been
to Mrs. Churchley's oftener than she had supposed. To-night it had
come to her clearly that he had been to see her every day since the
day she dined with them; every afternoon, about the hour she
thought he was at his club. Mrs. Churchley was his club,—she was
just like a club. At this Godfrey laughed; he wanted to know what
his sister knew about clubs. She was slightly disappointed in his
laugh, slightly wounded by it, but she knew perfectly what she

meant: she meant that Mrs. Churchley was public and florid, promiscuous and mannish.

"Oh, I dare say she's all right," said Godfrey, as if he wanted to get on with his work. He looked at the clock on the mantelshelf; he would have to put in another hour.

"All right to come and take darling mamma's place—to sit where *she* used to sit, to lay her horrible hands on *her* things?" Adela was appalled—all the more that she had not expected it—at her brother's apparent acceptance of such a prospect.

He coloured; there was something in her passionate piety that scorched him. She glared at him with her tragic eyes as if he had profaned an altar. "Oh, I mean nothing will come of it."

"Not if we do our duty," said Adela.

"Our duty?"

"You must speak to him—tell him how we feel; that we shall never forgive him, that we can't endure it."

"He'll think I'm cheeky," returned Godfrey, looking down at his papers, with his back to her and his hands in his pockets.

"Cheeky, to plead for *her* memory?"

"He'll say it's none of my business."

"Then you believe he'll do it?" cried the girl.

"Not a bit. Go to bed!"

"*I'll* speak to him," said Adela, as pale as a young priestess.

"Don't cry out till you're hurt; wait till he speaks to *you*."

"He won't, he won't!" the girl declared. "He'll do it without telling us."

Her brother had faced round to her again; he started a little at this, and again, at one of the candles, lighted his cigarette, which had gone out. She looked at him a moment, then he said something that surprised her.

"Is Mrs. Churchley very rich?"

"I haven't the least idea. What has that to do with it?"

Godfrey puffed his cigarette. "Does she live as if she were?"

"She has got a lot of showy things."

"Well, we must keep our eyes open," said Godfrey. "And now you *must* let me get on." He kissed his sister, as if to make up for dismissing her, or for his failure to take fire; and she held him a moment, burying her head on his shoulder. A wave of emotion surged through her; she broke out with a wail:

"Ah, why did she leave us? Why did she leave us?"

"Yes, why indeed?" the young man sighed, disengaging himself with a movement of oppression.

II

ADELA was so far right as that by the end of the week, though she remained certain, her father had not made the announcement she dreaded. What made her certain was the sense of her changed relations with him—of there being between them something unexpressed, something of which she was as conscious as she would have been of an unhealed wound. When she spoke of this to Godfrey, he said the change was of her own making, that she was cruelly unjust to the governor. She suffered even more from her brother's unexpected perversity; she had had so different a theory about him that her disappointment was almost an humiliation and she needed all her fortitude to pitch her faith lower. She wondered what had happened to him and why he had changed. She would have trusted him to feel right about anything, above all about such a matter as this. Their worship of their mother's memory, their recognition of her sacred place in their past, her exquisite influence in their father's life, his fortunes, his career, in the whole history of the family and welfare of the house—accomplished, clever, gentle, good, beautiful and capable as she had been, a woman whose soft distinction was universally proclaimed, so that on her death one of the Princesses, the most august of her friends, had written Adela such a note about her as princesses were understood very seldom to write: their hushed tenderness over all this was a kind of religion, and also a sort of honour, in falling away from which there was a semblance of treachery. This was not the way people usually felt in London, she knew; but, strenuous, ardent, observant girl as she was, with secrecies of sentiment and dim originalities of attitude, she had already made up her mind that London was no place to look for delicacies. Remembrance there was hammered thin, and to be faithful was to be a bore. The patient dead were sacrificed; they had no shrines, for people were literally ashamed of mourning. When they had hustled all sensibility out of their lives, they invented the fiction that they felt too much to utter. Adela said nothing to her sisters; this reticence was part of the virtue it was her system to exercise for them. *She* was to be their mother, a direct deputy and representative. Before the vision of that other woman parading in such a character, she felt capable of ingenuities and subtleties. The foremost of these was tremulously to watch her father. Five days after they had dined together at Mrs. Churchley's he asked her if she had been to see that lady.

"No indeed, why should I?" Adela knew that he knew she had not been, since Mrs. Churchley would have told him.

"Don't you call on people after you dine with them?" said Colonel Chart.

"Yes, in the course of time. I don't rush off within the week."

Her father looked at her, and his eyes were colder than she had ever seen them, which was probably, she reflected, just the way her own appeared to him. "Then you'll please rush off to-morrow. She's to dine with us on the 12th, and I shall expect your sisters to come down."

Adela stared. "To a dinner party?"

"It's not to be a dinner party. I want them to know Mrs. Churchley."

"Is there to be nobody else?"

"Godfrey, of course. A family party."

The girl asked her brother that evening if *that* was not tantamount to an announcement. He looked at her queerly, and then he said, "*I've* been to see her."

"What on earth did you do that for?"

"Father told me he wished it."

"Then he *has* told you?"

"Told me what?" Godfrey asked, while her heart sank with the sense that he was making difficulties for her.

"That they're engaged, of course. What else can all this mean?"

"He didn't tell me that, but I like her."

"*Like* her!" the girl shrieked.

"She's very kind, very good."

"To thrust herself upon us when we hate her? Is that what you call kind? Is that what you call decent?"

"Oh, *I* don't hate her," Godfrey rejoined, turning away as if his sister bored him.

She went the next day to see Mrs. Churchley, with a vague plan of breaking out to her, appealing to her, saying, "Oh, spare us! have mercy on us! let him alone! go away!" But that was not easy when they were face to face. Mrs. Churchley had every intention of getting, as she would have said—she was perpetually using the expression—into touch; but her good intentions were as depressing as a tailor's misfits. She could never understand that they had no place for her vulgar charity; that their life was filled with a fragrance of perfection for which she had no sense fine enough. She was as undomestic as a shop-front and as out of tune as a parrot. She would make them live in the streets, or bring the streets into their lives—it was the same thing. She had evidently never read a book, and she used intonations that Adela had never heard, as if she had been an Australian or an American. She understood everything in a vulgar sense; speaking of Godfrey's visit to her and praising him according to her idea, saying horrid things about him—that he was awfully good-looking, a perfect gentleman, the kind she liked. How could her father, who was after all, in everything else, such a dear, listen to a woman, or endure her, who thought she was pleasing when she called the son of his dead wife a perfect gentleman? What would he have been, pray? Much she knew about what any of them were! When she told Adela she wanted her to like her, the girl thought for an instant her opportunity had come—the chance to plead with her and beg her off. But she presented such an impenetrable surface that it would have been like giving a message to a varnished door. She wasn't a woman, said Adela; she was an address.

When she dined in Seymour Street, the "children," as the girl called the others, including Godfrey, liked her. Beatrice and Muriel stared shyly and silently at the wonders of her apparel (she was brutally overdressed!) without, of course, guessing the danger that tainted the air. They supposed her, in their innocence, to be amusing, and they didn't know, any more than she did herself that she patronised them. When she was upstairs with them, after dinner, Adela could see her looking round the room at the things she meant to alter; their mother's things, not a bit like her own and not good enough for her. After a quarter of an hour of this, our young lady felt sure she was deciding that Seymour Street wouldn't do at all, the dear old home that had done for their mother for twenty years. Was she plotting to transport them all to her horrible Prince's Gate? Of one thing, at any rate, Adela was certain: her father, at that moment, alone in the dining-room with Godfrey, pretending to drink another glass of wine to make time, was coming to the point, was telling the news. When they came upstairs, they both, to her eyes, looked strange: the news had been told.

She had it from Godfrey before Mrs. Churchley left the house, when, after a brief interval, he followed her out of the drawing-room on her taking her sisters to bed. She was waiting for him at the door of her room. Her father was then alone with his fiancée (the word was grotesque to Adela); it was already as if it were her home.

"What did you say to him?" the girl asked, when her brother had told her.

"I said nothing." Then he added, colouring (the expression of her face was such), "There was nothing to say."

"Is that how it strikes you?" said Adela, staring at the lamp.

"He asked me to speak to her," Godfrey went on.

"To speak to her?"

"To tell her I was glad."

"And did you?" Adela panted.

"I don't know. I said something. She kissed me."

"Oh, how *could* you?" shuddered the girl, covering her face with her hands.

"He says she's very rich," said Godfrey simply.

"Is that why you kissed her?"

"I didn't kiss her. Good-night," and the young man, turning his back upon her, went out.

When her brother was gone Adela locked herself in, as if with the fear that she should be overtaken or invaded, and during a sleepless, feverish, memorable night she took counsel of her un-compromising spirit. She saw things as they were, in all the indignity of life. The levity, the mockery, the infidelity, the ugliness, lay as plain as a map before her; it was a world *pour rire,* but she cried about it, all the same. The morning dawned early, or rather it seemed to her that there had been no night, nothing but a sickly, creeping day. But by the time she heard the house stirring again she had determined what to do. When she came down to the breakfast-room her father was already in his place, with news-papers and letters; and she expected the first words he would utter to be a rebuke to her for having disappeared, the night before, without taking leave of Mrs. Churchley. Then she saw that he wished to be intensely kind, to make every allowance, to conciliate and console her. He knew that she knew from Godfrey, and he got

up and kissed her. He told her as quickly as possible, to have it
over, stammering a little, with an "I've a piece of news for you
that will probably shock you," yet looking even exaggeratedly
grave and rather pompous, to inspire the respect he didn't deserve.
When he kissed her she melted, she burst into tears. He held her
against him, kissing her again and again, saying tenderly, "Yes,
yes, I know, I know." But he didn't know, or he could never have
done it. Beatrice and Muriel came in, frightened when they saw
her crying, and still more scared when she turned to them with
words and an air that were terrible in their comfortable little lives:
"Papa's going to be married; he's going to marry Mrs. Churchley!"
After staring a moment and seeing their father look as strange, on
his side, as Adela, though in a different way, the children also began
to cry, so that when the servants arrived, with tea and boiled eggs,
these functionaries were greatly embarrassed with their burden,
not knowing whether to come in or hang back. They all scraped
together a decorum, and as soon as the things had been put on
the table the Colonel banished the men with a glance. Then he
made a little affectionate speech to Beatrice and Muriel, in which
he assured them that Mrs. Churchley was the kindest, the most
delightful, of women, only wanting to make them happy, only
wanting to make him happy, and convinced that he would be if
they were and that they would be if he was.

"What do such words mean?" Adela asked herself. She declared
privately that they meant nothing, but she was silent, and every
one was silent, on account of the advent of Miss Flynn, the governess, before whom Colonel Chart preferred not to discuss the
situation. Adela recognized on the spot that, if things were to go
as he wished, his children would practically never again be alone
with him. He would spend all his time with Mrs. Churchley till
they were married, and then Mrs. Churchley would spend all her
time with him. Adela was ashamed of him, and that was horrible—
all the more that every one else would be, all his other friends,
every one who had known her mother. But the public dishonour
to that high memory should not be enacted; he should not do as
he wished.

After breakfast her father told her that it would give him pleasure
if, in a day or two, she would take her sisters to see Mrs. Churchley,
and she replied that he should be obeyed. He held her hand a
moment, looking at her with an appeal in his eyes which presently

hardened into sternness. He wanted to know that she forgave him, but he also wanted to say to her that he expected her to mind what she did, to go straight. She turned away her eyes; she was indeed ashamed of him.

She waited three days, and then she took her sisters to see Mrs. Churchley. That lady was surrounded with callers, as Adela knew she would be; it was her "day" and the occasion the girl preferred. Before this she had spent all her time with her sisters, talking to them about their mother, playing upon their memory of her, making them cry and making them laugh, reminding them of certain hours of their early childhood, telling them anecdotes of her own. None the less she assured them that she believed there was no harm at all in Mrs. Churchley, and that when the time should come she would probably take them out immensely. She saw with smothered irritation that they enjoyed their visit in Prince's Gate; they had never been at anything so "grown up," nor seen so many smart bonnets and brilliant complexions. Moreover, they were considered with interest, as if, as features of Mrs. Churchley's new life, they had been described in advance and were the heroines of the occasion. There were so many ladies present that Mrs. Churchley didn't talk to them much; but she called them her "chicks" and asked them to hand about teacups and bread and butter. All this was highly agreeable and indeed intensely exciting to Beatrice and Muriel, who had little round red spots in *their* cheeks when they came away. Adela quivered with the sense that her mother's children were now Mrs. Churchley's "chicks" and features of Mrs. Churchley's life.

It was one thing to have made up her mind, however; it was another thing to make her attempt. It was when she learned from Godfrey that the day was fixed, the 20th of July, only six weeks removed, that she felt the importance of prompt action. She learned everything from Godfrey now, having determined that it would be hypocrisy to question her father. Even her silence was hypocritical, but she couldn't weep and wail. Her father showed extreme tact; taking no notice of her detachment, treating her as if it were a moment of *bouderie* which he was bound to allow her and which would pout itself away. She debated much as to whether she should take Godfrey into her confidence; she would have done so without hesitation if he had not disappointed her. He was so strange and so perversely preoccupied that she could explain it only by the high pressure at which he was living, his anxiety about his "exam." He was in a fidget, in a fever, putting on a spurt to come in first; skeptical moreover about his success and cynical about everything else. He appeared to agree to the general axiom that they didn't want a strange woman thrust into their home, but he found Mrs. Churchley "very jolly as a person to know." He had been to see her by himself; he had been to see her three times. He said to his sister that he would make the most of her now; he should probably be so little in Seymour Street after these days. What Adela at last determined to say to him was that the marriage would never take place. When he asked her what she meant and who was to prevent it, she replied that the interesting couple would give it up themselves, or that Mrs. Churchley at least would after a week or two back out of it.

"That will be really horrid then," Godfrey rejoined. "The only respectable thing, at the point they've come to, is to put it through. Charming for poor father to have the air of being 'chucked.'"

This made her hesitate two days more, but she found answers more valid than any objections. The many-voiced answer to everything—it was like the autumn wind around the house—was the backward affront to her mother. Her mother was dead, but it killed her again. So one morning, at eleven o'clock, when Adela knew her father was writing letters, she went out quietly and, stopping the first hansom she met, drove to Prince's Gate. Mrs. Churchley was at home, and she was shown into the drawing-room with the request that she would wait five minutes. She waited, without the sense of breaking down at the last, the impulse to run away, which was what she had expected to have. In the cab and at the door her heart had beat terribly, but now, suddenly, with the game really to play, she found herself lucid and calm. It was a joy to her to feel later that this was the way Mrs. Churchley found her; not confused, not stammering nor prevaricating, only a little amazed at her own courage, conscious of the immense responsibility of her step and wonderfully older than her years. Her hostess fixed her at first with the waiting eyes of a cashier, but after a little, to Adela's surprise, she burst into tears. At this the girl cried herself, but with the secret happiness of believing they were saved. Mrs. Churchley said she would think over what she had been told, and she promised Adela, freely enough and very firmly, not to betray the secret of her visit to the Colonel. They were saved—they were saved: the words sung themselves in the girl's soul as she came downstairs. When the door was opened for her she saw her brother on the step, and they looked at each other in surprise, each finding it on the part of the other an odd hour for Prince's Gate. Godfrey remarked that Mrs. Churchley would have enough of the family, and Adela answered that she would perhaps have too much. None the less the young man went in, while his sister took her way home.

III

ADELA CHART saw nothing of her brother for nearly a week; he had more and more his own time and hours, adjusted to his tremendous responsibilities, and he spent whole days at his crammer's. When she knocked at his door, late in the evening, he was not in his room. It was known in the house that he was greatly worried; he was horribly nervous about his ordeal. It was to begin on the 23d of June, and his father was as worried as himself. The wedding had been arranged in relation to this; they wished poor Godfrey's fate settled first, though it was felt that the nuptials would be darkened if it should not be settled right.

Ten days after her morning visit to Mrs. Churchley Adela began to perceive that there was a difference in the air; but as yet she was afraid to exult. It was not a difference for the better, so that there might be still many hours of pain. Her father, since the announcement of his intended marriage, had been visibly pleased with himself, but that pleasure appeared to have undergone a check. Adela had the impression which the passengers on a great steamer receive when, in the middle of the night, they hear the engines stop. As this impression resolves itself into the general sense that something serious has happened, so the girl asked herself what had happened now. She had expected something serious; but it was as if she couldn't keep still in her cabin—she wanted to go up and see. On the 20th, just before breakfast, her maid brought her a message from her brother. Mr. Godfrey would be obliged if she would speak to him in his room. She went straight up to him, dreading to find him ill, broken down on the eve of his formidable week. This was not the case, however, inasmuch as he appeared to be already at work, to have been at work since dawn. But he was very white, and his eyes had a strange and new expression. Her beautiful young brother looked older; he looked haggard and hard.

He met her there as if he had been waiting for her, and he said immediately: "Please to tell me this, Adela: what was the purpose of your visit, the other morning, to Mrs. Churchley—the day I met you at her door?"

She stared—she hesitated. "The purpose? What's the matter? Why do you ask?"

"They've put it off—they've put it off a month."

"Ah, thank God!" said Adela.

"Why do you thank God?" Godfrey exclaimed roughly.

His sister gave a strained, intense smile. "You know I think it's all wrong."

He stood looking at her up and down. "What did you do there? How did you interfere?"

"Who told you I interfered?" she asked, flushing.

"You said something—you did something. I knew you had done it when I saw you come out."

"What I did was my own business."

"Damn your own business!" cried the young man.

She had never in her life been so spoken to, and in advance, if she had been given the choice, she would have said that she would rather die than be so spoken to by Godfrey. But her spirit was high, and for a moment she was as angry as if some one had cut at her with a whip. She escaped the blow, but she felt the insult. "And *your* business, then?" she asked. "I wondered what that was when I saw *you*."

He stood a moment longer frowning at her; then, with the exclamation "You've made a pretty mess!" he turned away from her and sat down to his books.

They had put it off, as he said; her father was dry and stiff and official about it. "I suppose I had better let you know that we have thought it best to postpone our marriage till the end of the summer—Mrs. Churchley has so many arrangements to make": he was not more expansive than that. She neither knew nor greatly cared whether it was her fancy or a reality that he watched her obliquely, to see how she would take these words. She flattered herself that, thanks to Godfrey's preparation, cruel as the form of it had been, she took them very cleverly. She had a perfectly good conscience, for she was now able to judge what odious elements Mrs. Churchley, whom she had not seen since the morning in Prince's Gate, had already introduced into their relations with each other. She

was able to infer that her father had not concurred in the postpone-
ment, for he was more restless than before, more absent, and
distinctly irritable. There was of course still the question of how
much of this condition was to be attributed to his solicitude about
Godfrey. That young man took occasion to say a horrible thing to
his sister: "If I don't pass it will be your fault." These were dreadful
days for the girl, and she asked herself how she could have borne
them if the hovering spirit of her mother had not been at her side.
Fortunately, she always felt it there, sustaining, commending,
sanctifying. Suddenly her father announced to her that he wished
her to go immediately, with her sisters, down to Overland, where
there was always part of a household and where for a few weeks
they would be sufficiently comfortable. The only explanation he
gave of this desire was that he wanted them out of the way. "Out
of the way of what?" she queried, since, for the time, there were
to be no preparations in Seymour Street. She was willing to believe
that it was out of the way of his nerves.

She never needed urging, however, to go to Overland, the dearest
old house in the world, where the happiest days of her young life
had been spent and the silent nearness of her mother always
seemed greatest. She was happy again, with Beatrice and Muriel
and Miss Flynn, and the air of summer, and the haunted rooms,
and her mother's garden, and the talking oaks and the nightingales.
She wrote briefly to her father, to give him, as he had requested,
an account of things; and he wrote back that, since she was so
contented (she didn't remember telling him that), she had better
not return to town at all. The rest of the season was not important
for her, and he was getting on very well. He mentioned that Godfrey had finished his exam; but, as she knew, there would be a
tiresome wait before they could learn the result. Godfrey was
going abroad for a month with young Sherard—he had earned a
little rest and a little fun. He went abroad without a word to Adela,
but in his beautiful little hand he took a chaffing leave of Beatrice.
The child showed her sister the letter, of which she was very proud
and which contained no message for Adela. This was the worst
bitterness of the whole crisis for that young lady—that it exhibited
so strangely the creature in the world whom, after her mother, she
had loved best.

Colonel Chart had said he would "run down" while his children
were at Overland, but they heard no more about it. He only wrote

two or three times to Miss Flynn, upon matters in regard to which
Adela was surprised that he should not have communicated with
herself. Muriel accomplished an upright little letter to Mrs. Churchley—her eldest sister neither fostered nor discouraged the performance—to which Mrs. Churchley replied, after a fortnight, in
a meagre and, as Adela thought, illiterate fashion, making no
allusion to the approach of any closer tie. Evidently the situation
had changed; the question of the marriage was dropped, at any
rate for the time. This idea gave the girl a singular and almost
intoxicating sense of power; she felt as if she were riding a great
wave of responsibility. She had chosen and acted, and the greatest
could do no more than that. The grand thing was to see one's
results, and what else was she doing? These results were in important and opulent lives; the stage was large on which she moved
her figures. Such a vision was exciting, and as they had the use of
a couple of ponies at Overland she worked off her excitement by a
long gallop. A day or two after this, however, came news of which
the effect was to rekindle it. Godfrey had come back, the list had
been published, he had passed first. These happy tidings proceeded
from the young man himself; he announced them by a telegram
to Beatrice, who had never in her life before received such a
missive and was proportionately inflated. Adela reflected that she
herself ought to have felt snubbed, but she was too happy. They
were free again, they were themselves, the nightmare of the previous weeks was blown away, the unity and dignity of her father's
life were restored, and, to round off her sense of success, Godfrey
had achieved his first step toward high distinction. She wrote to
him the next day, as frankly and affectionately as if there had been
no estrangement between them; and besides telling him that she
rejoiced in his triumph, she begged him in charity to let them know
exactly how the case stood with regard to Mrs. Churchley.

Late in the summer afternoon she walked through the park to
the village with her letter, posted it and came back. Suddenly, at
one of the turns of the avenue, halfway to the house, she saw
a young man looking toward her and waiting for her—a young
man who proved to be Godfrey, on his march, on foot, across from
the station. He had seen her, as he took his short cut, and if he had
come down to Overland it was not, apparently, to avoid her. There
was none of the joy of his triumph in his face, however, as he came

a very few steps to meet her; and although, stiffly enough, he let her kiss him and say, "I'm so glad—I'm so glad!" she felt that this tolerance was not quite the calmness of the rising diplomatist. He turned toward the house with her and walked on a short distance, while she uttered the hope that he had come to stay some days.

"Only till to-morrow morning. They are sending me straight to Madrid. I came down to say good-bye; there's a fellow bringing my portmanteau."

"To Madrid? How awfully nice! And it's awfully nice of you to have come," Adela said, passing her hand into his arm.

The movement made him stop, and, stopping, he turned on her, in a flash, a face of something more than suspicion—of passionate reprobation. "What I really came for—you might as well know without more delay—is to ask you a question."

"A question?" Adela repeated with a beating heart.

They stood there, under the old trees, in the lingering light, and, young and fine and fair as they both were, they were in complete superficial accord with the peaceful English scene. A near view, however, would have shown that Godfrey Chart had not come down to Overland to be superficial. He looked deep into his sister's eyes and demanded: "What was it you said that morning to Mrs. Churchley?"

Adela gazed at the ground a moment; then, raising her eyes: "If she has told you, why do you ask?"

"She has told me nothing. I've seen for myself."

"What have you seen?"

"She has broken it off—everything's over—father's in the depths."

"In the depths?" the girl quavered.

"Did you think it would make him jolly?" asked her brother.

"He'll get over it; he'll be glad."

"That remains to be seen. You interfered, you invented something, you got round her. I insist on knowing what you did."

Adela felt that she could be obstinate if she wished, and that if it should be a question of organizing a defense she should find treasures of perversity under her hand. She stood looking down again a moment, and saying to herself, "I could be dumb and dogged if I chose, but I scorn to be." She was not ashamed of what she had done, but she wanted to be clear. "Are you absolutely certain it's broken off?"

"He is, and she is; so that's as good."

"What reason has she given?"

"None at all—or half a dozen; it's the same thing. She has changed her mind—she mistook her feelings—she can't part with her independence; moreover, he has too many children."

"Did he tell you this?" said Adela.

"Mrs. Churchley told me. She has gone abroad for a year."

"And she didn't tell you what I said to her?"

"Why should I take this trouble if she had?"

"You might have taken it to make me suffer," said Adela. "That appears to be what you want to do."

"No, I leave that to *you;* it's the good turn you've done me!" cried the young man, with hot tears in his eyes.

She stared, aghast with the perception that there was some dreadful thing she didn't know; but he walked on, dropping the question angrily and turning his back to her as if he couldn't trust himself. She read his disgust in his averted face, in the way he squared his shoulders and smote the ground with his stick, and she hurried after him and presently overtook him. She accompanied him for a moment in silence; then she pleaded: "What do you mean? What in the world have I done to you?"

"She would have helped me; she was all ready to do it," said Godfrey.

"Helped you in what?" She wondered what he meant; if he had made debts that he was afraid to confess to his father and—of all horrible things—had been looking to Mrs. Churchley to pay. She turned red with the mere apprehension of this and, on the heels of her guess, exulted again at having perhaps averted such a shame.

"Can't you see that I'm in trouble? Where are your eyes, your senses, your sympathy, that you talk so much about? Haven't you seen these six months that I've a cursed worry in my life?"

She seized his arm, she made him stop, she stood looking up at him like a frightened little girl. "What's the matter, Godfrey—what *is* the matter?"

"You've vexed me so—I could strangle you!" he growled. This idea added nothing to her dread; her dread was that he had done some wrong, was stained with some guilt. She uttered it to him with clasped hands, begging him to tell her the worst; but, still more passionately, he cut her short with his own cry: "In God's name, satisfy me! What infernal thing did you do?"

"It was not infernal; it was right. I told her mamma had been wretched," said Adela.

"Wretched? You told her such a lie?"

"It was the only way, and she believed me."

"Wretched how—wretched when—wretched where?" the young man stammered.

"I told her papa had made her so, and that *she* ought to know it. I told her the question troubled me unspeakably, but that I had made up my mind it was my duty to initiate her." Adela paused, with the light of bravado in her face, as if, though struck while she phrased it, with the monstrosity of what she had done, she was incapable of abating a jot of it. "I notified her that he had faults and peculiarities that made mamma's life a long worry—a martyr-dom that she hid wonderfully from the world, but that we saw and that I had often pitied. I told her what they were, these faults and peculiarities; I put the dots on the *i*'s. I said it wasn't fair to let another person marry him without a warning. I warned her; I satisfied my conscience. She could do as she liked. My responsibility was over."

Godfrey gazed at her; he listened, with parted lips, incredulous and appalled. "You invented such a tissue of falsities and calumnies, and you talk about your conscience? You stand there in your senses and proclaim your crime?"

"I would have committed any crime that would have rescued us."

"You insult and defame your own father?" Godfrey continued.

"He'll never know it; she took a vow she wouldn't tell him."

"I'll be damned if *I* won't tell him!" Godfrey cried.

Adela felt sick at this, but she flamed up to resent the treachery, as it struck her, of such a menace. "I did right—I did right!" she vehemently declared. "I went down on my knees to pray for guid-ance, and I saved mamma's memory from outrage. But if I hadn't, if I hadn't"—she faltered for an instant—"I'm not worse than you, and I'm not so bad, for you've done something that you're ashamed to tell me."

Godfrey had taken out his watch; he looked at it with quick intensity, as if he were not hearing nor heeding her. Then, glancing up with his calculating eye, he fixed her long enough to exclaim, with unsurpassable horror and contempt: "You raving maniac!" He turned away from her; he bounded down the avenue in the direction from which they had come, and, while she watched him, strode away across the grass, toward the short cut to the station.

IV

GODFREY's portmanteau, by the time Adela got home, had been brought to the house, but Beatrice and Muriel, who had been informed of this, waited for their brother in vain. Their sister said nothing to them about having seen him, and she accepted, after a little, with a calmness that surprised herself, the idea that he had returned to town to denounce her. She believed that would make no difference now—she had done what she had done. She had somehow a faith in Mrs. Churchley. If Mrs. Churchley had broken off she wouldn't renew. She was a heavy-footed person, incapable of further agility. Adela recognized too that it might well have come over her that there were too many children. Lastly the girl fortified herself with the reflection, grotesque under the circumstances and tending to prove that her sense of humor was not high, that her father, after all, was not a man to be played with. It seemed to her, at any rate, that if she *had* prevented his marriage she could bear anything—bear imprisonment and bread and water, bear lashes and torture, bear even his lifelong reproach. What she could bear least was the wonder of the inconvenience she had inflicted on Godfrey. She had time to turn this over, very vainly, for a succession of days—days more numerous than she had expected, which passed without bringing her from London any summons to come up and take her punishment. She sounded the possible, she compared the degrees of the probable; feeling however that, as a cloistered girl she was poorly equipped for speculation. She tried to imagine the calamitous things young men might do, and could only feel that such things would naturally be connected either with money or with women. She became conscious that after all she knew almost nothing about either subject. Meanwhile there was no reverberation from Seymour Street—only a sultry silence.

At Overland she spent hours in her mother's garden, where she had grown up, where she considered that she was training for old age, for she meant not to depend upon whist. She loved the place as, had she been a good Catholic, she would have loved the smell of her parish church; and indeed there was in her passion for flowers something of the respect of a religion. They seemed to her the only things in the world that really respected themselves, unless one made an exception for Nutkins, who had been in command all through her mother's time, with whom she had had a real friendship, and who had been affected by their pure example. He was the person left in the world with whom, on the whole, she could talk most intimately about her mother. They never had to name her together—they only said "she", and Nutkins freely conceded that she had taught him everything he knew. When Beatrice and Muriel said "she" they referred to Mrs. Churchley. Adela had reason to believe that she should never marry, and that some day she should have about a thousand a year. This made her see in the far future a little garden of her own, under a hill, full of rare and exquisite things, where she would spend most of her old age on her knees, with an apron and stout gloves, a pair of shears and a trowel, steeped in the comfort of being thought mad.

One morning, ten days after her scene with Godfrey, upon coming back into the house shortly before lunch, she was met by Miss Flynn with the notification that a lady in the drawing-room had been waiting for her for some minutes. "A lady" suggested immediately Mrs. Churchley. It came over Adela that the form in which her penalty was to descend would be a personal explanation with that misdirected woman. The lady had not given her name, and Miss Flynn had not seen Mrs. Churchley; nevertheless the governess was certain that Adela's surmise was wrong.

"Is she big and dreadful?" the girl asked.

Miss Flynn, who was circumspection itself, hesitated a moment. "She's dreadful, but she's not big." She added that she was not sure she ought to let Adela go in alone; but this young lady felt throughout like a heroine, and it was not for a heroine to shrink from any encounter. Was she not, every instant, in transcendent contact with her mother? The visitor might have no connection whatever with the drama of her father's frustrated marriage; but everything, to-day, to Adela, was a part of that.

Miss Flynn's description had prepared her for a considerable shock, but she was not agitated by her first glimpse of the person who awaited her. A youngish, well-dressed woman stood there, and silence was between them while they looked at each other. Before either of them had spoken, however, Adela began to see what Miss Flynn had intended. In the light of the drawing-room window the lady was five-and-thirty years of age and had vivid yellow hair. She also had a blue cloth suit with brass buttons, a stick-up collar like a gentleman's, a necktie arranged in a sailor's knot, with a golden pin in the shape of a little lawn-tennis racket, and pearl-grey gloves with big black stitchings. Adela's second impression was that she was an actress; her third was that no such person had ever before crossed that threshold.

"I'll tell you what I've come for," said the apparition. "I've come to ask you to intercede." She was not an actress; an actress would have had a nicer voice.

"To intercede?" Adela was too bewildered to ask her to sit down.

"With your father, you know. He doesn't know, but he'll have to." Her "have" sounded like "'ave." She explained, with many more such sounds, that she was Mrs. Godfrey, that they had been married seven mortal months. If Godfrey was going abroad she must go with him, and the only way she could go with him would be for his father to do something. He was afraid of his father—that was clear; he was afraid even to tell him. What she had come down for was to see some other member of the family face to face ("fice to fice" Mrs. Godfrey called it), and try if he couldn't be approached by another side. If no one else would act, then she would just have to act herself. The Colonel would have to do something—that was the only way out of it.

What really happened Adela never quite understood; what seemed to be happening was that the room went round and round. Through the blur of perception accompanying this effect the sharp stabs of her visitor's revelation came to her like the words heard by a patient "going off" under ether. She denied passionately, afterwards, even to herself, that she had done anything so abject as to faint; but there was a lapse in her consciousness in relation to Miss Flynn's intervention. This intervention had evidently been active, for when they talked the matter over, later in the day, with bated breath and infinite dissimulation for the schoolroom quarter, the governess had more information, and still stranger, to impart than to receive. She was at any rate under the impression that she had athletically contended, in the drawing-room, with the yellow hair, after removing Adela from the scene and before inducing Mrs. Godfrey to withdraw. Miss Flynn had never known a more thrilling day, for all the rest of it too was pervaded with agitations and conversations, precautions and alarms. It was given out to Beatrice and Muriel that their sister had been taken suddenly ill, and the governess ministered to her in her room. Indeed Adela had never found herself less at ease; for this time she had received a blow that she couldn't return. There was nothing to do but to take it, to endure the humiliation of her wound.

At first she declined to take it; it was much easier to consider that her visitor was a monstrous masquerader. On the face of the matter, moreover, it was not fair to believe till one heard; and to hear in such a case was to hear Godfrey himself. Whatever his sister had tried to imagine about him she had not arrived at anything so belittling as an idiotic secret marriage with a dyed and painted hag. Adela repeated this last word as if it gave her some comfort; and indeed where everything was so bad fifteen years of seniority made the case little worse. Miss Flynn was portentous, for Miss Flynn had had it out with the wretch. She had cross-questioned her and had not broken her down. This was the most important hour of Miss Flynn's life; for whereas she usually had to content herself with being humbly and gloomily in the right, she could now be magnanimously and showily so. Her only perplexity was as to what she ought to do—write to Colonel Chart or go up to town to see him. She bloomed with alternatives, never having known the like before. Toward evening Adela was obliged to recognise that Godfrey's worry, of which he had spoken to her, had appeared bad enough to consist even of a low wife, and to remember that, so far from its being inconceivable that a young man in his position should clandestinely take one, she had been present, years before, during her mother's lifetime, when Lady Molesley declared gayly, over a cup of tea, that this was precisely what she expected of her eldest son. The next morning it was the worst possibilities that seemed the clearest; the only thing left with a tatter of dusky comfort being the ambiguity of Godfrey's charge that his sister's action had "done" for him. That was a matter by itself, and she racked her brains for a connecting link between Mrs. Churchley and Mrs. Godfrey. At last she made up her mind that they were related by blood; very likely, though differing in fortune, they were cousins or even sisters. But even then what did her brother mean?

Arrested by the unnatural fascination of opportunity, Miss Flynn received before lunch a telegram from Colonel Chart—an order for dinner and a vehicle; he and Godfrey were to arrive at six o'clock. Adela had plenty of occupation for the interval, for she was pitying her father when she was not rejoicing that her mother had gone too soon to know. She flattered herself she discerned the providential reason of that cruelty now. She found time however still to wonder for what purpose, under the circumstances, Godfrey was to be brought down. She was not unconscious, it is true, that she had little general knowledge of what usually was done with young men in that predicament. One talked about the circumstances, but the circumstances were an abyss. She felt this still more when she found, on her father's arrival, that nothing, apparently, was to happen as she had taken for granted it would. There was a kind of inviolable hush over the whole affair, but no tragedy, no publicity, nothing ugly. The tragedy had been in town, and the faces of the two men spoke of it, in spite of themselves; so that at present there was only a family dinner, with Beatrice and Muriel and the governess, and almost a company tone, the result of the desire to avoid publicity. Adela admired her father; she knew what he was feeling, if Mrs. Godfrey had been at him, and yet she saw him positively gallant. He was very gentle, he never looked at his son, and there were moments when he seemed almost sick with sadness. Godfrey was equally inscrutable and therefore wholly different from what he had been as he stood before her in the park. If he was to start on his career (with such a wife!—wouldn't she utterly blight it?) he was already professional enough to know how to wear a mask.

Before they rose from table the girl was wholly bewildered, so little could she perceive the effects of such large causes. She had nerved herself for a great ordeal, but the air was as sweet as an anodyne. It was constantly plain to her that her father was deadly sad—as pathetic as a creature jilted. He was broken, but he showed no resentment; there was a weight on his heart, but he had lightened it by dressing as immaculately as usual for dinner. She asked herself what immensity of a row there could have been in town to have left his anger so spent. He went through everything, even to sitting with his son after dinner. When they came out together he invited Beatrice and Muriel to the billiard-room; and as Miss Flynn discreetly withdrew Adela was left alone with Godfrey, who was completely changed and not in a rage any more. He was broken, too, but he was not so pathetic as his father. He was only very correct and apologetic; he said to his sister, "I'm awfully sorry *you* were annoyed; it was something I never dreamed of."

She couldn't think immediately what he meant; then she grasped the reference to the yellow hair. She was uncertain, however, what tone to take; perhaps his father had arranged with him that they were to make the best of it. But she spoke her own despair in the way she murmured: "O Godfrey, Godfrey, is it true?"

"I've been the most unutterable donkey—you can say what you like to me. You can't say anything worse than I've said to myself."

"My brother, my brother!" his words made her moan. He hushed her with a movement, and she asked, "What has father said?"

Godfrey looked over her head. "He'll give her six hundred a year."

"Ah, the angel!"

"On condition she never comes near me. She has solemnly promised; and she'll probably leave me alone, to get the money. If she doesn't—in diplomacy—I'm lost." The young man had been turning his eyes vaguely about, this way and that, to avoid meeting hers; but after another instant he gave up the effort, and she had the miserable confession of his glance. "I've been living in hell," he said.

"My brother, my brother!" she repeated.

"I'm not an idiot; yet for her I've behaved like one. Don't ask me—you musn't know. It was all done in a day, and since then, fancy my condition—fancy my work!"

"Thank God you passed!" cried Adela.

"I would have shot myself if I hadn't. I had an awful day yesterday with father; it was late at night before it was over. I leave England next week. He brought me down here for it to look well—so that the children sha'n't know."

"He's wonderful!" she murmured.

"He's wonderful!" said Godfrey.

"Did *she* tell him?" the girl asked.

"She came straight to Seymour Street from here. She saw him alone first; then he called me in. *That* luxury lasted about an hour."

Adela said, "Poor, poor father!" to this; on which her brother remained silent. Then, after he had remarked that it had been the scene he had lived in terror of all through his cramming, and she had stammered her pity and admiration at such a mixture of anxieties and such a triumph of talent, she demanded: "Have you told him?"

"Told him what?"

"What you said you would—what *I* did."

Godfrey turned away as if at present he had very little interest in that inferior tribulation. "I was angry with you, but I cooled off. I held my tongue."

Adela clasped her hands. "You thought of mamma!"

"Oh, don't speak of mamma," said the young man tenderly.

It was indeed not a happy moment; and she murmured: "No; if you *had* thought of her"—

This made Godfrey turn back at her, with a little flare in his eyes. "Oh, *then* it didn't prevent. I thought that woman was good. I believed in her."

"Is she *very* bad?" his sister inquired.

"I shall never mention her to you again," Godfrey answered, with dignity.

"You may believe that *I* won't speak of her. So father doesn't know?" she added.

"Doesn't know what?"

"That I said that to Mrs. Churchley."

"I don't think so, but you must find out for yourself."

"I shall find out," said Adela. "But what had Mrs. Churchley to do with it?"

"With *my* misery? I told her. I had to tell some one."

"Why didn't you tell me?"

Godfrey hesitated. "Oh, you take things so beastly hard—you make such rows." Adela covered her face with her hands, and he went on: "What I wanted was comfort—not to be lashed up. I thought I should go mad. I wanted Mrs. Churchley to break it to father, to intercede for me and help him to meet it. She was awfully kind to me; she listened and she understood; she could fancy how it had happened. Without her I shouldn't have pulled through. She liked me, you know," Godfrey dropped. "She said she would do what she could for me; she was full of sympathy and resource; I really leaned on her. But when you cut in, of course it spoiled everything. That's why I was so angry with you. She couldn't do anything then."

Adela dropped her hands, staring; she felt that she had walked in darkness. "So that he had to meet it alone?"

"*Dame!*" said Godfrey, who had got up his French tremendously.

Muriel came to the door to say papa wished the two others to join them, and the next day Godfrey returned to town. His father remained at Overland, without an intermission, the rest of the summer and the whole of the autumn, and Adela had a chance to find out, as she had said, whether he knew that she had interfered. But in spite of her chance she never found out. He knew that Mrs. Churchley had thrown him over and he knew that his daughter rejoiced in it, but he appeared not to have divined the relation between the two facts. It was strange that one of the matters he was clearest about—Adela's secret triumph—should have been just the thing which, from this time on, justified less and less such a confidence. She was too sorry for him to be consistently glad. She watched his attempts to wind himself up on the subject of shorthorns and drainage, and she favoured to the utmost of her ability his intermittent disposition to make a figure in orchids. She wondered whether they mightn't have a few people at Overland; but when she mentioned the idea her father asked what in the world there would be to attract them. It was a confoundedly stupid house, he remarked, with all respect to *her* cleverness. Beatrice and Muriel were mystified; the prospect of going out immensely had faded so utterly away. They were apparently not to go out at all. Colonel Chart was aimless and bored; he paced up and down and went back to smoking, which was bad for him, and looked drearily out of windows, as if on the bare chance that something might arrive. Did he expect Mrs. Churchley to arrive, to relent? It was Adela's belief that she gave no sign. But the girl thought it really remarkable of her not to have betrayed her ingenious young visitor. Adela's judgment of human nature was perhaps harsh, but she believed that many women, under the circumstances, would not have been so forbearing. This lady's conception of the point of honour presented her as rather a higher type than one might have supposed.

Adela knew her father found the burden of Godfrey's folly very heavy to bear and was incommoded at having to pay the horrible woman six hundred a year. Doubtless he was having dreadful letters from her; doubtless she threatened them all with a hideous exposure. If the matter should be bruited Godfrey's prospects would collapse on the spot. He thought Madrid very charming and curious, but Mrs. Godfrey was in England, so that his father had

to face the music. Adela took a dolorous comfort in thinking that
her mother was out of *that*—it would have killed her; but this
didn't blind her to the fact that the comfort for her father would
perhaps have been greater if he had had some one to talk to about
his trouble. He never dreamed of doing so to her, and she felt that
she couldn't ask him. In the family life he wanted utter silence about
it. Early in the winter he went abroad for ten weeks, leaving her
with her sisters in the country, where it was not to be denied that
at this time existence had very little savour. She half expected that
her sister-in-law would descend upon her again; but the fear was
not justified, and the quietude of such a personage savoured
terribly of expense. There were sure to be extras. Colonel Chart
went to Paris and to Monte Carlo and then to Madrid to see his
boy. Adela wondered whether he would meet Mrs. Churchley
somewhere, since, if she had gone for a year, she would still be on
the Continent. If he should meet her perhaps the affair would
come on again: she caught herself musing over this. Her father
brought back no news of her, and seeing him after an interval,
she was struck afresh with his jilted and wasted air. She didn't
like it; she resented it. A little more and she would have said that
that was no way to treat such a man.

They all went up to town in March, and on one of the first days
of April she saw Mrs. Churchley in the park. She herself remained
apparently invisible to that lady—she herself and Beatrice and
Muriel, who sat with her in their mother's old bottle-green landau.
Mrs. Churchley, perched higher than ever, rode by without a
recognition; but this didn't prevent Adela from going to her before
the month was over. As on her great previous occasion she went
in the morning, and she again had the good fortune to be admitted.
But this time her visit was shorter, and a week after making it—
the week was a desolation—she addressed to her brother at Madrid
a letter which contained these words:

"I could endure it no longer—I confessed and retracted; I explained to her as well as I could the falsity of what I said to her
ten months ago and the benighted purity of my motives for saying
it. I besought her to regard it as unsaid, to forgive me, not to
despise me too much, to take pity on poor *perfect* papa and come
back to him. She was more good-natured than you might have
expected; indeed, she laughed extravagantly. She had never believed me—it was too absurd; she had only, at the time, disliked

me. She found me utterly false (she was very frank with me about this), and she told papa that she thought I was horrid. She said she could never live with such a girl, and as I would certainly never marry I must be sent away; in short she quite loathed me. Papa defended me, he refused to sacrifice me, and this led practically to their rupture. Papa gave her up, as it were, for me. Fancy the angel, and fancy what I must try to be to him for the rest of his life! Mrs. Churchley can never come back—she's going to marry Lord Dovedale."

STUDY

≈§§≈

The Notebooks of Henry James

F. O. MATTHIESSEN AND KENNETH B. MURDOCK (eds.) *

[Entry dated January 12, 1887]

A. mentions in a letter that Sir J. R. is to marry the Dowager Lady T— that "he blushes whenever her name is mentioned, and that Mrs. S. C. says it is simply forty years of her mother's life wiped out." There is a little drama here—at least a possible one—between a father and daughter on such an occasion; especially—I mean—when the 1st married life has been a happy one—the 2 have cherished the memory of the wife and mother together. The daughter's sense of the want of dignity of her father's act—as an old, or elderly, man—of the difference between her mother and the new love, etc. It sickens her—she goes to the fiancée, etc. She must have—to make her opposition natural—the worship of her mother's memory—and a kind of horror. I am not sure that there is much of a subject—but a short tale might be made of it. The father may be affected by his daughter's opposition so much as to repent of his engagement. . . . [H]e is ashamed of it, he wishes

* FROM *The Notebooks of Henry James,* edited by F. O. Matthiessen and Kenneth B. Murdock. Copyright, 1947, by Oxford University Press Inc. Reprinted by permission.

to retreat. But he tells her it is there and that he can't get out of it. "Very well," says she. . . . SHE goes to the fiancée again and there she tells her something about the father—a pure fabrication— she swears her to secrecy—which she flatters herself will prevent the woman from wishing to go on with the marriage. (*What* she tells her is a delicate point—to be settled; and of course it must be under the empire of a passionate *idée fixe*.) This communication has its effect—the intended wife shortly afterwards lets the father know that she repents of the engagement and that she releases him. He is pleased at first—pleased that he has pleased his daughter—and she (the daughter) is delighted at what she has done. Before long, however, she begins to see a change in her father—he is sad, brooding, sombre—he looks at her in a different way. In fact, he is beginning to wonder *how* she affected the lady— what she did, what arts she used—and to suspect that she *did* say something that was injurious to him. She perceives this change in him—that he is resentful and unhappy—and suddenly, weary of the whole thing, she gives up her opposition. She determines to go to the lady and tell her that everything she said before was false. She does so, and the latter replies—"I am very sorry—but I have just become engaged to Mr. So-and-So!" It may be represented—to make the daughter's action a little less odious—that the intended wife has not really believed what she said—has seen through it as a manoeuvre—but *has* thought that the father has lent himself to it and despises him accordingly. It wouldn't be a very "sympathetic" tale.

        ❖   ❖   ❖

This is the kind of story in which a later writer would not have skirted the "unsympathetic" element, and would have probed more deeply into the sexual pathology latent in the theme.

Daisy Miller and Other Tales

HENRY JAMES*

Preface [1907–1909]

[O]ne has never to go far afield to speculate on the possible pangs of filial piety in face of the successor . . . to either lost parent, but perhaps more particularly to the lost mother, often inflicted on it by the parent surviving. . . . [I]t's but a question of "first catching" the example of piety intense enough. . . . [T]he drama is all there—all in the consciousness, the fond imagination, the possibly poisoned and inflamed judgement, of the suffering subject. . . .

"Europe"

[1899]

❦

I

"OUR FEELING IS, you know, that Becky *should* go." That earnest
little remark comes back to me, even after long years, as the first
note of something that began, for my observation, the day I went
with my sister-in-law to take leave of her good friends. It's a
memory of the American time, which revives so at present—under
some touch that doesn't signify—that it rounds itself off as an
anecdote. That walk to say good-bye was the beginning; and the
end, so far as I was concerned with it, was not till long after; yet
even the end also appears to me now as of the old days. I went, in
those days, on occasion, to see my sister-in-law, in whose affairs,
on my brother's death, I had had to take a helpful hand. I continued to go, indeed, after these little matters were straightened
out, for the pleasure, periodically, of the impression—the change
to the almost pastoral sweetness of the good Boston suburb from the
loud, longitudinal New York. It was another world, with other
manners, a different tone, a different taste; a savour nowhere so
mild, yet so distinct, as in the square white house—with the pair
of elms, like gigantic wheat-sheaves in front, the rustic orchard not
far behind, the old-fashioned door-lights, the big blue and white
jars in the porch, the straight, bricked walk from the high gate—
that enshrined the extraordinary merit of Mrs. Rimmle and her
three daughters.

These ladies were so much of the place and the place so much of
themselves that, from the first of their being revealed to me, I
felt that nothing else at Brookbridge much mattered. They were
what, for me, at any rate, Brookbridge had most to give: I mean
in the way of what it was naturally strongest in, the thing that we
called in New York the New England expression, the air of Puritan-

FROM *The Soft Side* (New York, Macmillan & Co., 1900).

ism reclaimed and refined. The Rimmles had brought it down to a wonderful delicacy. They struck me even then—all four almost equally—as very ancient and very earnest, and I think theirs must have been the house, in all the world, in which "culture" first came to the aid of morning calls. The head of the family was the widow of a great public character—as public characters were understood at Brookbridge—whose speeches on anniversaries formed a part of the body of national eloquence spouted in the New England schools by little boys covetous of the most marked, though perhaps the easiest, distinction. He was reported to have been celebrated, and in such fine declamatory connexions that he seemed to gesticulate even from the tomb. He was understood to have made, in his wife's company, the tour of Europe at a date not immensely removed from that of the battle of Waterloo. What was the age, then, of the bland, firm antique Mrs. Rimmle at the period of her being first revealed to me? That's a point I'm not in a position to determine—I remember mainly that I was young enough to regard her as having reached the limit. And yet the limit for Mrs. Rimmle must have been prodigiously extended; the scale of its extension is, in fact, the very moral of this reminiscence. She was old, and her daughters were old, but I was destined to know them all as older. It was only by comparison and habit that—however much I recede—Rebecca, Maria, and Jane were the "young ladies."

I think it was felt that, though their mother's life, after thirty years of widowhood, had had a grand backward stretch, her blandness and firmness—and this in spite of her extreme physical frailty—would be proof against any surrender not overwhelmingly justified by time. It had appeared, years before, at a crisis of which the waves had not even yet quite subsided, a surrender not justified by anything, that she should go, with her daughters, to Europe for her health. Her health was supposed to require constant support; but when it had at that period tried conclusions with the idea of Europe, it was not the idea of Europe that had been insidious enough to prevail. She had not gone, and Becky, Maria, and Jane had not gone, and this was long ago. They still merely floated in the air of the visit achieved, with such introductions and such acclamations, in the early part of the century; they still, with fond glances at the sunny parlour-walls, only referred, in conversation, to divers pictorial and other reminders of it. The Miss Rimmles had quite been brought up on it, but Becky, as the most literary, had most

mastered the subject. There were framed letters—tributes to their
eminent father—suspended among the mementoes, and of two or
three of these, the most foreign and complimentary, Becky had
executed translations that figured beside the text. She knew already, through this and other illumination, so much about Europe
that it was hard to believe, for her, in that limit of adventure which
consisted only of her having been twice to Philadelphia. The others
had not been to Philadelphia, but there was a legend that Jane had
been to Saratoga. Becky was a short, stout, fair, person with round,
serious eyes, a high forehead, the sweetest, neatest enunciation,
and a miniature of her father—"done in Rome"—worn as a breastpin. She had written the life, she had edited the speeches, of the
original of this ornament, and now at last, beyond the seas, she
was really to tread in his footsteps.

Fine old Mrs. Rimmle, in the sunny parlour and with a certain
austerity of cap and chair—though with a gay new "front" that
looked like rusty brown plush—had had so unusually good a winter
that the question of her sparing two members of her family for an
absence had been threshed as fine, I could feel, as even under that
Puritan roof any case of conscience had ever been threshed. They
were to make their dash while the coast, as it were, was clear, and
each of the daughters had tried—heroically, angelically, and for the
sake of each of her sisters—not to be one of the two. What I encountered that first time was an opportunity to concur with enthusiasm in the general idea that Becky's wonderful preparation
would be wasted if she were the one to stay with their mother.
They talked of Becky's preparation—they had a sly old-maidish
humour that was as mild as milk—as if it were some mixture, for
application somewhere, that she kept in a precious bottle. It had
been settled, at all events, that, armed with this concoction and
borne aloft by their introductions, she and Jane were to start. They
were wonderful on their introductions, which proceeded naturally
from their mother and were addressed to the charming families
that, in vague generations, had so admired vague Mr. Rimmle.
Jane, I found at Brookbridge, had to be described, for want of
other description, as the pretty one, but it would not have served
to identify her unless you had seen the others. *Her* preparation was
only this figment of her prettiness—only, that is, unless one took
into account something that, on the spot, I silently divined: the
lifelong, secret, passionate ache of her little rebellious desire. They

were all growing old in the yearning to go, but Jane's yearning was the sharpest. She struggled with it as people at Brookbridge mostly struggled with what they liked, but fate, by threatening to prevent what she *dis*liked, and what was therefore duty—which was to stay at home instead of Maria—had bewildered her, I judged, not a little. It was she who, in the words I have quoted, mentioned to me Becky's case and Becky's affinity as the clearest of all. Her mother, moreover, on the general subject had still more to say.

"I positively desire, I really quite insist that they shall go," the old lady explained to us from her stiff chair. "We've talked about it so often, and they've had from me so clear an account—I've amused them again and again with it—of what is to be seen and enjoyed. If they've had hitherto too many duties to leave, the time seems to have come to recognise that there are also many duties to *seek*. Wherever we go we find them—I always remind the girls of that. There's a duty that calls them to those wonderful countries, just as it called, at the right time, their father and myself—if it be only that of laying up for the years to come the same store of remarkable impressions, the same wealth of knowledge and food for conversation as, since my return, I have found myself so happy to possess." Mrs. Rimmle spoke of her return as of something of the year before last, but the future of her daughters was, somehow, by a different law, to be on the scale of great vistas, of endless after tastes. I think that, without my being quite ready to say it, even this first impression of her was somewhat upsetting; there was a large, placid perversity, a grim secrecy of intention, in her estimate of the ages.

"Well, I'm so glad you don't delay it longer," I said to Miss Becky before we withdrew. "And whoever should go," I continued in the spirit of the sympathy with which the good sisters had already inspired me, "I quite feel, with your family, you know, that *you* should. But of course I hold that every one should." I suppose I wished to attentuate my solemnity; there was something in it, however, I couldn't help. It must have been a faint foreknowledge.

"Have you been a great deal yourself?" Miss Jane, I remember, enquired.

"Not so much but that I hope to go a good deal more. So perhaps we shall meet," I encouragingly suggested.

I recall something—something in the nature of susceptibility to encouragement—that this brought into the more expressive brown eyes to which Miss Jane mainly owed it that she was the pretty one. "Where, do you think?"

I tried to think, "Well, on the Italian lakes—Como, Bellaggio, Lugano." I liked to say the names to them.

"'Sublime, but neither bleak nor bare—nor misty are the mountains there!'" Miss Jane softly breathed, while her sister looked at her as if her familiarity with the poetry of the subject made her the most interesting feature of the scene she evoked.

But Miss Becky presently turned to me. "Do you know everything—?"

"Everything?"

"In Europe."

"Oh yes," I laughed, "and one or two things even in America."

The sisters seemed to me furtively to look at each other. "Well, you'll have to be quick—to meet *us*," Miss Jane resumed.

"But surely when you're once there you'll stay on."

"Stay on?"—they murmured it simultaneously and with the oddest vibration of dread as well as of desire. It was as if they had been in the presence of a danger and yet wished me, who "knew everything," to torment them with still more of it.

Well, I did my best. "I mean it will never do to cut it short."

"No, that's just what I keep saying," said brilliant Jane. "It would be better, in that case, not to go."

"Oh don't talk about not going—at this time!" It was none of my business, but I felt shocked and impatient.

"No, not at *this* time!" broke in Miss Maria, who, very red in the face, had joined us. Poor Miss Maria was known as the flushed one; but she was not flushed—she only had an unfortunate surface. The third day after this was to see them embark.

Miss Becky, however, desired as little as any one to be in any way extravagant. "It's only the thought of our mother," she explained.

I looked a moment at the old lady, with whom my sister-in-law was engaged. "Well—your mother's magnificent."

"*Isn't* she magnificent?"—they eagerly took it up.

She *was*—I could reiterate it with sincerity, though I perhaps mentally drew the line when Miss Maria again risked, as a fresh ejaculation: "I think she's better than Europe!"

"Maria!" they both, at this, exclaimed with a strange emphasis: it was as if they feared she had suddenly turned cynical over the deep domestic drama of their casting of lots. The innocent laugh with which she answered them gave the measure of her cynicism.

We separated at last, and my eyes met Mrs. Rimmle's as I held for an instant her aged hand. It was doubtless only my fancy that her calm, cold look quietly accused me of something. Of what *could* it accuse me? Only, I thought, of thinking.

II

I LEFT BROOKBRIDGE the next day, and for some time after that had no occasion to hear from my kinswoman; but when she finally wrote there was a passage in her letter that affected me more than all the rest. "Do you know the poor Rimmles never, after all, 'went'? The old lady, at the eleventh hour, broke down; everything broke down, and all of *them* on top of it, so that the dear things are with us still. Mrs. Rimmle, the night after our call, had, in the most unexpected manner, a turn for the worse—something in the nature (though they're rather mysterious about it) of a seizure; Becky and Jane felt it—dear devoted stupid angels that they are—heartless to leave her at such a moment, and Europe's indefinitely postponed. However, they think they're still going— or *think* they think it—when she's better. They also think—or think they think—that she *will* be better. I certainly pray she may." So did I—quite fervently. I was conscious of a real pang —I didn't know how much they had made me care.

Late that winter my sister-in-law spent a week in New York; when almost my first inquiry on meeting her was about the health of Mrs. Rimmle.

"Oh she's rather bad—she really is, you know. It's not surprising that at her age she should be infirm."

"Then what the deuce *is* her age?"

"I can't tell you to a year—but she's immensely old."

"That of course I saw," I replied—"unless you literally mean so old that the records have been lost."

My sister-in-law thought. "Well, I believe she wasn't positively young when she married. She lost three or four children before these women were born."

We surveyed together a little, on this, the "dark backward."
"And they were born, I gather, *after* the famous tour? Well then,
as the famous tour was in a manner to celebrate—wasn't it?—
the restoration of the Bourbons——" I considered, I gasped. "My
dear child, what on earth do you make her out?"

My relative, with her Brookbridge habit, transferred her share
of the question to the moral plane—turned it forth to wander,
by implication at least, in the sandy desert of responsibility. "Well,
you know, we all immensely admire her."

"You can't admire her more than I do. She's awful."

My interlocutress looked at me with a certain fear. "She's *really*
ill."

"Too ill to get better?"

"Oh no—we hope not. Because then they'll be able to go."

"And *will* they go, if she should?"

"Oh, the moment they should be quite satisfied. I mean *really*,"
she added.

I'm afraid I laughed at her—the Brookbridge "really" was a
thing so by itself. "But if she shouldn't get better?" I went on.

"Oh, don't speak of it! They want so to go."

"It's a pity they're so infernally good," I mused.

"No—don't say that. It's what keeps them up."

"Yes, but isn't it what keeps *her* up too?"

My visitor looked grave. "Would you like them to kill her?"

I don't know that I was then prepared to say I should—though
I believe I came very near it. But later on I burst all bounds, for
the subject grew and grew. I went again before the good sisters
ever did—I mean I went to Europe. I think I went twice, with
a brief interval, before my fate again brought round for me a
couple of days at Brookbridge. I had been there repeatedly, in
the previous time, without making the acquaintance of the Rimmles; but now that I had had the revelation I couldn't have it too
much, and the first request I preferred was to be taken again to
see them. I remember well indeed the scruple I felt—the real
delicacy—about betraying that *I* had, in the pride of my power,
since our other meeting, stood, as their phrase went, among romantic scenes; but they were themselves the first to speak of
it, and what, moreover, came home to me was that the coming
and going of their friends in general—Brookbridge itself having

even at that period one foot in Europe—was such as to place constantly before them the pleasure that was only postponed. They were thrown back, after all, on what the situation, under a final analysis, had most to give—the sense that, as every one kindly said to them and they kindly said to every one, Europe would keep. Every one felt for them so deeply that their own kindness in alleviating every one's feelings was really what came out most. Mrs. Rimmle was still in her stiff chair and in the sunny parlour, but if *she* made no scruple of introducing the Italian lakes my heart sank to observe that she dealt with them, as a topic, not in the least in the leave-taking manner in which Falstaff babbled of green fields.

I'm not sure that, after this, my pretexts for a day or two with my sister-in-law weren't apt to be a mere cover for another glimpse of these particulars: I at any rate never went to Brookbridge without an irrepressible eagerness for our customary call. A long time seems to me thus to have passed, with glimpses and lapses, considerable impatience and still more pity. Our visits indeed grew shorter, for, as my companion said, they were more and more of a strain. It finally struck me that the good sisters even shrank from me a little, as from one who penetrated their consciousness in spite of himself. It was as if they knew where I thought they ought to be, and were moved to deprecate at last, by a systematic silence on the subject of that hemisphere, the criminality I fain would fix on them. They were full instead—as with the instinct of throwing dust in my eyes—of little pathetic hypocrisies about Brookbridge interests and delights. I dare say that as time went on my deeper sense of their situation came practically to rest on my companion's report of it. I think I recollect, at all events, every word we ever exchanged about them, even if I have lost the thread of the special occasions. The impression they made on me after each interval always broke out with extravagance as I walked away with her.

"*She* may be as old as she likes—I don't care. It's the fearful age the 'girls' are reaching that constitutes the scandal. One shouldn't pry into such matters, I know; but the years and the chances are really going. They're all growing old together—it will presently be too late; and their mother meanwhile perches over them like a vulture—what shall I call it?—calculating. Is she waiting for them successively to drop off? She'll survive them each and all. There's something too remorseless in it."

"Yes; but what do you want her to do? If the poor thing *can't* die, she can't. Do you want her to take poison or to open a blood-vessel? I dare say she would prefer to go."

"I beg your pardon," I must have replied; "you daren't say anything of the sort. If she would prefer to go she *would* go. She would feel the propriety, the decency, the necessity of going. She just prefers *not* to go. She prefers to stay and keep up the tension, and her calling them 'girls' and talking of the good time they'll still have is the mere conscious mischief of a subtle old witch. They won't have *any* time—there isn't any time to have! I mean there's, on her own part, no real loss of measure or of perspective in it. She *knows* she's a hundred and ten, and she takes a cruel pride in it."

My sister-in-law differed with me about this; she held that the old woman's attitude was an honest one and that her magnificent vitality, so great in spite of her infirmities, made it inevitable she should attribute youth to persons who had come into the world so much later. "Then suppose she should die?"—so my fellow student of the case always put it to me.

"Do you mean while her daughters are away? There's not the least fear of that—not even if at the very moment of their departure she should be *in extremis*. They'd find her all right on their return."

"But think how they'd feel not to have been with her!"

"That's only, I repeat, on the unsound assumption. If they would only go to-morrow—literally make a good rush for it—they'll be with her when they come back. That will give them plenty of time." I'm afraid I even heartlessly added that if she *should*, against every probability, pass away in their absence, they wouldn't have to come back at all—which would be just the compensation proper to their long privation. And then Maria would come out to join the two others, and they would be—though but for the too scanty remnant of their career—as merry as the day is long.

I remained ready, somehow, pending the fulfilment of that vision, to sacrifice Maria; it was only over the urgency of the case for the others respectively that I found myself balancing. Sometimes it was for Becky I thought the tragedy deepest—sometimes, and in quite a different manner, I thought it most dire for Jane.

It was Jane, after all, who had most sense of life. I seemed in fact dimly to descry in Jane a sense—as yet undescried by herself or by any one—of all sorts of queer things. Why didn't *she* go? I used desperately to ask; why didn't she make a bold personal dash for it, strike up a partnership with some one or other of the traveling spinsters in whom Brookbridge more and more abounded? Well, there came a flash for me at a particular point of the grey middle desert: my correspondent was able to let me know that poor Jane at last *had* sailed. She had gone of a sudden —I liked my sister-in-law's view of suddenness—with the kind Hathaways, who had made an irresistible grab at her and lifted her off her feet. They were going for the summer and for Mr. Hathaway's health, so that the opportunity was perfect, and it was impossible not to be glad that something very like physical force had finally prevailed. This was the general feeling at Brookbridge, and I might imagine what Brookbridge had been brought to from the fact that, at the very moment she was hustled off, the doctor, called to her mother at the peep of dawn, had considered that *he* at least must stay. There had been real alarm—greater than ever before; it actually did seem as if this time the end had come. But it was Becky, strange to say, who, though fully recognising the nature of the crisis, had kept the situation in hand and insisted upon action. This, I remember, brought back to me a discomfort with which I had been familiar from the first. One of the two had sailed, and I was sorry it wasn't the other. But if it had been the other I should have been equally sorry.

I saw with my eyes, that very autumn, what a fool Jane would have been if she had again backed out. Her mother had of course survived the peril of which I had heard, profiting by it indeed as she had profited by every other; she was sufficiently better again to have come downstairs. It was there that, as usual, I found her, but with a difference of effect produced somehow by the absence of one of the girls. It was as if, for the others, though they had not gone to Europe, Europe had come to them: Jane's letters had been so frequent and so beyond even what could have been hoped. It was the first time, however, that I perceived on the old woman's part a certain failure of lucidity. Jane's flight was clearly the great fact with her, but she spoke of it as if the fruit had now been plucked and the parenthesis closed. I don't know what sinking sense of still further physical duration I gathered, as a menace, from this first hint of her confusion of mind.

"My daughter has been; my daughter has been——" She kept saying it, but didn't say where; that seemed unnecessary, and she only repeated the words to her visitors with a face that was all puckers and yet now, save in so far as it expressed an ineffaceable complacency, all blankness. I think she wanted us a little to know that she had not stood in the way. It added to something—I scarce knew what—that I found myself desiring to extract privately from Becky. As our visit was to be of the shortest, my opportunity—for one of the young ladies always came to the door with us—was at hand. Mrs. Rimmle, as we took leave, again sounded her phrase, but she added this time: "I'm so glad she's going to have always——"

I knew so well what she meant that, as she again dropped, looking at me queerly and becoming momentarily dim, I could help her out. "Going to have what *you* have?"

"Yes, yes—my privilege. Wonderful experience," she mumbled. She bowed to me a little as if I would understand. "She has things to tell."

I turned, slightly at a loss, to Becky. "She has then already arrived?"

Becky was at that moment looking a little strangely at her mother, who answered my question. "She reached New York this morning—she comes on to-day."

"Oh, then—!" But I let the matter pass as I met Becky's eye—I saw there was a hitch somewhere. It was not she but Maria who came out with us; on which I cleared up the question of their sister's reappearance.

"Oh, no, not to-night," Maria smiled; "that's only the way mother puts it. We shall see her about the end of November—the Hathaways are so indulgent. They kindly extend their tour."

"For *her* sake? How sweet of them!" my sister-in-law exclaimed.

I can see our friend's plain, mild old face take on a deeper mildness, even though a higher colour, in the light of the open door. "Yes, it's for Jane they prolong it. And do you know what they write?" She gave us time, but it was too great a responsibility to guess. "Why, that it has brought her out."

"Oh, I knew it *would!*" my companion sympathetically sighed.

Maria put it more strongly still. "They say we wouldn't know her."

This sounded a little awful, but it was, after all, what I had expected.

III

MY CORRESPONDENT in Brookbridge came to me that Christmas, with my niece, to spend a week; and the arrangement had of course been prefaced by an exchange of letters, the first of which from my sister-in-law scarce took space for acceptance of my invitation before going on to say: "The Hathaways are back—but without Miss Jane!" She presented in a few words the situation thus created at Brookbridge, but was not yet, I gathered, fully in possession of the other one—the situation created in "Europe" by the presence there of that lady. The two together, at any rate, demanded, I quickly felt, all my attention, and perhaps my impatience to receive my relative was a little sharpened by my desire for the whole story. I had it at last, by the Christmas fire, and I may say without reserve that it gave me all I could have hoped for. I listened eagerly, after which I produced the comment: "Then she simply refused——"

"To budge from Florence? Simply. She had it out there with the poor Hathaways, who felt responsible for her safety, pledged to restore her to her mother's, to her sisters' hands, and showed herself in a light, they mention under their breath, that made their dear old hair stand on end. Do you know what, when they first got back, they said of her—at least it was *his* phrase—to two or three people?"

I thought a moment. "That she had 'tasted blood'?"

My visitor fairly admired me. "How clever of you to guess! It's exactly what he did say. She appeared—she continues to appear, it seems—in a new character."

I wondered a little. "But that's exactly—don't you remember? —what Miss Maria reported to us from them; that we 'wouldn't know her.'"

My sister-in-law perfectly remembered. "Oh, yes—she broke out from the first. But when they left her she was worse."

"Worse?"

"Well, different—different from anything she ever *had* been, or —for that matter—had had a chance to be." My interlocutress hung fire a moment, but presently faced me. "Rather strange and free and obstreperous."

"Obstreperous?" I wondered again.

"Peculiarly so, I inferred, on the question of not coming away. She wouldn't hear of it and, when they spoke of her mother, said she had given her mother up. She had thought she should like Europe, but didn't know she should like it so much. They had been fools to bring her if they expected to take her away. She was going to see what she could—she hadn't yet seen half. The end of it, was, at any rate, that they had to leave her alone."

I seemed to see it all—to see even the scared Hathaways. "So she *is* alone?"

"She told them, poor thing, it appears, and in a tone they'll never forget, that she was, at all events, quite old enough to be. She cried—she quite went on—over not having come sooner. That's why the only way for her," my companion mused, "*is*, I suppose, to stay. They wanted to put her with some people or other—to find some American family. But she says she's on her own feet."

"And she's still in Florence?"

"No—I believe she was to travel. She's bent on the East."

I burst out laughing. "Magnificent Jane! It's most interesting. Only I feel that I distinctly *should* 'know' her. To my sense, always, I must tell you, she had it in her."

My relative was silent a little. "So it now appears Becky always felt."

"And yet pushed her off? Magnificent Becky!"

My companion met my eyes a moment. "You don't know the queerest part. I mean the way it has *most* brought her out."

I turned it over; I felt I should like to know—to that degree indeed that, oddly enough, I jocosely disguised my eagerness. "You don't mean she has taken to drink?"

My visitor hesitated. "She has taken to flirting."

I expressed disappointment. "Oh, she took to *that* long ago. Yes," I declared at my kinswoman's stare, "she positively flirted —with *me!*"

The stare perhaps sharpened. "Then you flirted with *her?*"

"How else could I have been as sure as I wanted to be? But has she means?"

"Means to flirt?"—my friend looked an instant as if she spoke literally. "I don't understand about the means—though of course they have something. But I have my impression," she went on. "I think that Becky—" It seemed almost too grave to say.

But *I* had no doubts. "That Becky's backing her?"

She brought it out. "Financing her."

"Stupendous Becky! So that morally then——"

"Becky's quite in sympathy. But isn't it too odd?" my sister-in-law asked.

"Not in the least. Didn't we know, as regards Jane, that Europe was to bring her out? Well, it has also brought out Rebecca."

"It has indeed!" my companion indulgently sighed. "So what would it do if she were there?"

"I should like immensely to see. And we *shall* see."

"Why, do you believe she'll still go?"

"Certainly. She *must*."

But my friend shook it off. "She won't."

"She shall!" I retorted with a laugh. But the next moment I said: "And what does the old woman say?"

"To Jane's behaviour? Not a word—never speaks of it. She talks now much less than she used—only seems to wait. But it's my belief she thinks."

"And—do you mean—knows?"

"Yes, knows she's abandoned. In her silence there she takes it in."

"It's her way of making Jane pay?" At this, somehow, I felt more serious. "Oh, dear, dear—she'll disinherit her!"

When, in the following June, I went on to return my sister-in-law's visit the first object that met my eyes in her little white parlour was a figure that, to my stupefaction, presented itself for the moment as that of Mrs. Rimmle. I had gone to my room after arriving, and, on dressing, had come down; the apparition I speak of had arisen in the interval. Its ambiguous character lasted, however, but a second or two—I had taken Becky for her mother because I knew no one but her mother of that extreme age. Becky's age was quite startling; it had made a great stride, though, strangely enough, irrecoverably seated as she now was in it, she had a wizened brightness that I had scarcely yet seen in her. I remember indulging on this occasion in two silent observations: one to the effect that I had not hitherto been conscious of her full resemblance to the old lady, and the other to the effect that, as I had said to my sister-in-law at Christmas, "Europe," even as reaching her only through Jane's sensibilities, had really at last brought her out. She was in fact "out" in a manner of which this encounter offered to my eyes a unique example: it was the single hour, often as I had been at Brookbridge, of my meeting her elsewhere than in her mother's drawing-room. I surmise that, besides being adjusted to her more marked time of life, the garments she wore abroad, and in particular her little plain bonnet, presented points of resemblance to the close sable sheath and the quaint old headgear that, in the white house behind the elms, I had from far back associated with the eternal image in the stiff chair. Of course I immediately spoke of Jane, showing an interest and asking for news; on which she answered me with a smile, but not at all as I had expected.

"*Those* are not really the things you want to know—where she is, whom she's with, how she manages and where she's going next —oh, no!" And the admirable woman gave a laugh that was somehow both light and sad—sad, in particular, with a strange, long weariness. "What you do want to know is when she's coming back."

I shook my head very kindly, but out of a wealth of experience that, I flattered myself, was equal to Miss Becky's. "I do know it. Never."

Miss Becky at this exchanged with me a long deep look. "Never."

We had, in silence, a little luminous talk about it, in the course of which she seemed to tell me the most interesting things. "And how's your mother?" I then enquired.

She hesitated, but finally spoke with the same serenity. "My mother's all right. You see, she's not alive."

"Oh, Becky!" my sister-in-law pleadingly interjected.

But Becky only addressed herself to me. "Come and see if she is. *I* think she isn't—but Maria perhaps isn't so clear. Come, at all events, and judge and tell me."

It was a new note, and I was a little bewildered. "Ah, but I'm not a doctor!"

"No, thank God—you're not. That's why I ask you." And now she said good-bye.

I kept her hand a moment. "*You're* more alive than ever!"

"I'm very tired." She took it with the same smile, but for Becky it was much to say.

IV

"NOT ALIVE," the next day, was certainly what Mrs. Rimmle looked when, coming according to my promise, I found her, with Miss Maria, in her usual place. Though shrunken and diminished, she still occupied her high-backed chair with a visible theory of erectness, and her intensely aged face—combined with something dauntless that belonged to her very presence and that was effective even in this extremity—might have been that of some centenarian sovereign, of indistinguishable sex, brought forth to be shown to the people as a disproof of the rumour of extinction. Mummified and open-eyed she looked at me, but I had no impression that she made me out. I had come this time without my sister-in-law, who had frankly pleaded to me—which also, for a daughter of Brookbridge, was saying much—that the house had grown too painful. Poor Miss Maria excused Miss Becky on the score of her not being well—and that, it struck me, was saying most of all. The absence of the others gave the occasion a different note; but I talked with Miss Maria for five minutes and perceived that—save for her saying, of her own movement, anything about Jane—she now spoke as if her mother had lost hearing or sense, or both, alluding freely and distinctly, though indeed favourably, to her condition. "She has expected your visit and she much enjoys it," my interlocutress said, while the old woman, soundless and motionless, simply fixed me without expression. Of course there was little to keep me; but I became aware, as I rose to go, that there was more than I had supposed. On my approaching her to take leave, Mrs. Rimmle gave signs of consciousness.

"Have you heard about Jane?"

I hesitated, feeling a responsibility, and appealed for direction to Maria's face. But Maria's face was troubled, was turned altogether to her mother's. "About her life in Europe?" I then rather helplessly asked.

The old woman fronted me, on this, in a manner that made me

feel silly. "Her life?"—and her voice, with this second effort, came out stronger. "Her death, if you please."

"Her death?" I echoed, before I could stop myself, with the accent of deprecation.

Miss Maria uttered a vague sound of pain, and I felt her turn away, but the marvel of her mother's little unquenched spark still held me. "Jane's dead. We've heard," said Mrs. Rimmle. "We've heard from—where is it we've heard from?" She had quite revived—she appealed to her daughter.

The poor old girl, crimson, rallied to her duty. "From Europe."

Mrs. Rimmle made at us both a little grim inclination of the head. "From Europe." I responded, in silence, with a deflexion from every rigour, and, still holding me, she went on: "And now Rebecca's going."

She had gathered by this time such emphasis to say it that again, before I could help myself, I vibrated in reply. "To Europe —now?" It was as if for an instant she had made me believe it.

She only stared at me, however, from her wizened mask; then her eyes followed my companion. "Has she gone?"

"Not yet, mother." Maria tried to treat it as a joke, but her smile was embarrassed and dim.

"Then where is she?"

"She's lying down."

The old woman kept up her hard, queer gaze, but directing it, after a minute, to me. "She's going."

"Oh, some day!" I foolishly laughed; and on this I got to the door, where I separated from my younger hostess, who came no further. Only, as I held the door open, she said to me under cover of it and very quietly:

"It's poor mother's idea."

I saw—it was her idea. Mine was—for some time after this, even after I had returned to New York and to my usual occupations—that I should never again see Becky. I had seen her for the last time, I believed, under my sister-in-law's roof, and in the autumn it was given to me to hear from that fellow-admirer that she had succumbed at last to the situation. The day of the call I have just described had been a date in the process of her slow shrinkage—it was literally the first time she had, as they said at Brookbridge, given up. She had been ill for years, but the other state of health in the contemplation of which she had spent so much of her life had left her, till too late, no margin for meeting it. The encounter at last came simply in the form of the discovery that it *was* too late; on which, naturally, she had given up more and more. I had heard indeed, all summer, by letter, how Brookbridge had watched her do so; whereby the end found me in a manner prepared. Yet in spite of my preparation there remained with me a soreness, and when I was next—it was some six months later—on the scene of her martyrdom I replied I fear with an almost rabid negative to the question put to me in due course by my kinswoman. "Call on them? Never again!"

I went, none the less, the very next day. Everything was the same in the sunny parlour—everything that most mattered, I mean: the immemorial mummy in the high chair and the tributes, in the little frames on the walls, to the celebrity of its late husband. Only Maria Rimmle was different: if Becky, on my last seeing her, had looked as old as her mother, Maria—save that she moved about—looked older. I remember that she moved about, but I scarce remember what she said; and indeed what was there to say? When I risked a question, however, she had a reply.

"But *now* at least—?" I tried to put it to her suggestively.

At first she was vague. "'Now'?"

"Won't Miss Jane come back?"

Oh, the headshake she gave me! "Never." It positively pictured to me, for the instant, a well-preserved woman, a sort of rich, ripe *seconde jeunesse* by the Arno.

"Then that's only to make more sure of your finally joining her."

Maria Rimmle repeated her headshake. "Never."

We stood so, a moment, bleakly face to face; I could think of no attenuation that would be particularly happy. But while I tried I heard a hoarse gasp that, fortunately, relieved me—a signal strange and at first formless from the occupant of the high-backed chair. "Mother wants to speak to you," Maria then said.

So it appeared from the drop of the old woman's jaw, the expression of her mouth opened as if for the emission of sound. It was difficult to me somehow to seem to sympathise without hypocrisy, but, so far as a step nearer could do so, I invited communication. "Have you heard where Becky's gone?" the wonderful witch's white lips then extraordinarily asked.

It drew from Maria, as on my previous visits, an uncontrollable groan, and this, in turn, made me take time to consider. As I considered, however, I had an inspiration. "To Europe?"

I must have adorned it with a strange grimace, but my inspiration had been right. "To Europe," said Mrs. Rimmle.

STUDY

❦

The Notebooks of Henry James

F. O. MATTHIESSEN AND KENNETH B. MURDOCK (eds.)*

[Entry dated February 27, 1895]

I was greatly struck, the other day, with something that Lady Playfair told me of the prolongation—and the effects of it—of her aunt, old Mrs. Palfrey, of Cambridge, Mass. She is, or was, 95, or some such extraordinary age; and the little idea that struck me as a small *motif* in it was that of the consequences of this fact on the existence of her 2 or 3 poor old maid daughters, who have themselves grown old (old enough to die), while sitting there waiting, waiting endlessly for her to depart. She has never departed, and yet has always been supposed to be going to, and they have had endlessly to be ready, to be near her, at hand—never to be away. So Sarah P., whom I vaguely remember, has come to be 70. They have never been anywhere, never done anything—their lives have passed in this long, blank patience. Some small thing might perhaps be done with the situation, with the picture. One of the daughters—the eldest—might die—of old age; and the thing, all the while, have to be kept from the old woman. She wonders what has become of her, tries to find out; and then, at last, one of the others tells her—tells her So-and-So has died. The old woman stares. "What did she die of?" She died of old age. This makes the old woman realize—it finishes her. Or 2, the 2 elder, must die (of old age!) and *one* be left simply to watch—to conceal it. Only I think that 2 sisters is the right number originally—there had better not be more.

❋ ❋ ❋

[Entry dated May 7, 1898]

Les Vieux again or *The Waiters:*—Lady P.'s story of the Miss Palfreys. The last one—she remains. Or perhaps there is only *one* who waits. The mother survives her. (25 pages.) The daughter dies. The way they put it to the mother or *she* puts it. "Oh, I knew she would: she has gone to Europe!"

The Author of Beltraffic and Other Tales

HENRY JAMES*

Preface [1907–1909]

I had preserved for long years an impression of an early time, a visit, in a sedate American city . . . to an ancient lady whose talk, whose allusions and relics and spoils and mementoes and credentials . . . bore upon a triumphant sojourn in Europe, long years before, in the hey-day of the high scholarly reputation of her husband, a dim displaced superseded celebrity at the time of my own observation. They had been "much made of," he and she, at various foreign centres of polite learning, . . . and my hostess had lived ever since on the name and fame of it; a treasure of legend and anecdote laid up against the comparatively lean half-century . . . that was to follow. For myself even, after this, a good slice of such a period had elapsed; yet with my continuing to believe that fond memory would still somehow be justified of this scrap too, along with so many others. . . .

The justification I awaited, however, only came much later, on my catching some tender mention of certain admirable ladies, sisters and spinsters under the maternal roof, for whom the century was ebbing without remedy brought to their eminent misfortune . . . of not having "been to Europe." Exceptionally prepared by culture for going, they yet couldn't leave their immemorial mother, the headspring, precisely, of that grace in them, who on the occasion of each proposed start announced her approaching end— only to postpone it again after the plan was dished and the flight relinquished. So the century ebbed, and so Europe altered—for the worse—and so perhaps even a little did the sisters who sat in bondage; only so didn't at all the immemorial, the inextinguishable, the eternal mother.

The Image of Europe in Henry James

Christof Wegelin [*]

The story called "Europe" (1899) . . . deals with no Europe outside the minds of its characters, hence the quotation marks belonging to the title [in its first publication]. It dramatizes the morbid perversity of a mother's idea that the old world is a mere storehouse of "food for conversation" by contrasting it with the late fulfilment, the "rich ripe *seconde jeunesse*" one of her spinster daughters finds there.

[*] (Dallas, Southern Methodist University Press, 1958).

The Liar

[1888]

❦

I

THE TRAIN was half an hour late and the drive from the station longer than he had supposed, so that when he reached the house its inmates had dispersed to dress for dinner and he was conducted straight to his room. The curtains were drawn in this asylum, the candles were lighted, the fire was bright, and when the servant had quickly put out his clothes the comfortable little place became suggestive—seemed to promise a pleasant house, a various party, talks, acquaintances, affinities, to say nothing of very good cheer. He was too occupied with his profession to pay many country visits, but he had heard people who had more time for them speak of establishments where "they do you very well." He foresaw that the proprietors of Stayes would do him very well. In his bedroom at a country house he always looked first at the books on the shelf and the prints on the walls; he considered that these things gave a sort of measure of the culture and even of the character of his hosts. Though he had but little time to devote to them on this occasion a cursory inspection assured him that if the literature, as usual, was mainly American and humorous the art consisted neither of the water-colour studies of the children nor of 'goody' engravings. The walls were adorned with old-fashioned lithographs, principally portraits of country gentlemen with high collars and riding gloves: this suggested—and it was encouraging —that the tradition of portraiture was held in esteem. There was the customary novel of Mr. Le Fanu, for the bedside; the ideal reading in a country house for the hours after midnight. Oliver Lyon could scarcely forbear beginning it while he buttoned his shirt.

Perhaps that is why he not only found every one assembled in

FROM *A London Life* (New York, Macmillan & Co., 1889).

the hall when he went down, but perceived from the way the move to dinner was instantly made that they had been waiting for him. There was no delay, to introduce him to a lady, for he went out in a group of unmatched men, without this appendage. The men, straggling behind, sidled and edged as usual at the door of the dining-room, and the *dénouement* of this little comedy was that he came to his place last of all. This made him think that he was in a sufficiently distinguished company, for if he had been humiliated (which he was not), he could not have consoled himself with the reflection that such a fate was natural to an obscure, struggling young artist. He could no longer think of himself as very young, alas, and if his position was not so brilliant as it ought to be he could no longer justify it by calling it a struggle. He was something of a celebrity and he was apparently in a society of celebrities. This idea added to the curiosity with which he looked up and down the long table as he settled himself in his place.

It was a numerous party—five and twenty people; rather an odd occasion to have proposed to him, as he thought. He would not be surrounded by the quiet that ministers to good work; however, it had never interfered with his work to see the spectacle of human life before him in the intervals. And though he did not know it, it was never quiet at Stayes. When he was working well he found himself in that happy state—the happiest of all for an artist—in which things in general contribute to the particular idea and fall in with it, help it on and justify it, so that he feels for the hour as if nothing in the world can happen to him, even if it come in the guise of disaster or suffering, that will not be an enhancement of his subject. Moreover there was an exhilaration (he had felt it before) in the rapid change of scene—the jump, in the dusk of the afternoon, from foggy London and his familiar studio to a centre of festivity in the middle of Hertfordshire and a drama half acted, a drama of pretty women and noted men and wonderful orchids in silver jars. He observed as a not unimportant fact that one of the pretty women was beside him: a gentleman sat on his other hand. But he went into his neighbours little as yet: he was busy looking out for Sir David, whom he had never seen and about whom he naturally was curious.

Evidently, however, Sir David was not at dinner, a circumstance sufficiently explained by the other circumstance which constituted our friend's principal knowledge of him—his being ninety years of age. Oliver Lyon had looked forward with great pleasure to the chance of painting a nonagenarian, and though the old man's absence from table was something of a disappointment (it was an opportunity the less to observe him before going to work), it seemed a sign that he was rather a sacred and perhaps therefore an impressive relic. Lyon looked at his son with the greater interest —wondered whether the glazed bloom of his cheek had been transmitted from Sir David. That would be jolly to paint, in the old man —the withered ruddiness of a winter apple, especially if the eye were still alive and the white hair carried out the frosty look. Arthur Ashmore's hair had a midsummer glow, but Lyon was glad his commission had been to delineate the father rather than the son, in spite of his never having seen the one and of the other being seated there before him now in the happy expansion of liberal hospitality.

Arthur Ashmore was a fresh-coloured, thick-necked English gentleman, but he was just not a subject; he might have been a farmer and he might have been a banker: you could scarcely paint him in characters. His wife did not make up the amount; she was a large, bright, negative woman, who had the same air as her husband of being somehow tremendously new; a sort of appearance of fresh varnish (Lyon could scarcely tell whether it came from her complexion or from her clothes), so that one felt she ought to sit in a gilt frame, suggesting reference to a catalogue or a price-list. It was as if she were already rather a bad though expensive portrait, knocked off by an eminent hand, and Lyon had no wish to copy that work. The pretty woman on his right was engaged with her neighbour and the gentleman on his other side looked shrinking and scared, so that he had time to lose himself in his favourite diversion of watching face after face. This amusement gave him the greatest pleasure he knew, and he often thought it a mercy that the human mask did interest him and that it was not less vivid than it was (sometimes it ran its success in this line very close), since he was to make his living by reproducing it. Even if Arthur Ashmore would not be inspiring to paint (a certain anxiety rose in him lest if he should make a hit with her father-in-law Mrs. Arthur should take it into her head that he had now proved himself worthy to *aborder* her husband); even if he had looked a little less like a page (fine as to print and margin) without punctuation, he would still be a refreshing, iridescent surface. But the gentleman four persons off—what was he? Would he be a subject, or was his face only the legible door-plate of his identity, burnished with punctual washing and shaving—the least thing that was decent that you would know him by?

This face arrested Oliver Lyon: it struck him at first as very handsome. The gentleman might still be called young, and his features were regular: he had a plentiful, fair moustache that curled up at the ends, a brilliant, gallant, almost adventurous air, and a big shining breastpin in the middle of his shirt. He appeared a fine satisfied soul, and Lyon perceived that wherever he rested his friendly eye there fell an influence as pleasant as the September sun—as if he could make grapes and pears or even human affection ripen by looking at them. What was odd in him was a certain mixture of the correct and the extravagant: as if he were an adventurer imitating a gentleman with rare perfection or a gentleman who had taken a fancy to go about with hidden arms. He might have been a dethroned prince or the war-correspondent of a newspaper: he represented both enterprise and tradition, good manners and bad taste. Lyon at length fell into conversation with the lady beside him—they dispensed, as he had had to dispense at dinner-parties before, with an introduction—by asking who this personage might be.

'Oh, he's Colonel Capadose, don't you know?' Lyon didn't know and he asked for further information. His neighbour had a sociable manner and evidently was accustomed to quick transitions; she turned from her other interlocutor with a methodical air, as a good cook lifts the cover of the next saucepan. 'He has been a great deal in India—isn't he rather celebrated?' she inquired. Lyon confessed he had never heard of him, and she went on, 'Well, perhaps he isn't; but he says he is, and if you think it, that's just the same, isn't it?'

'If *you* think it?'

'I mean if he thinks it—that's just as good, I suppose.'

'Do you mean that he says that which is not?'

'Oh dear, no—because I never know. He is exceedingly clever and amusing—quite the cleverest person in the house, unless indeed you are more so. But that I can't tell yet, can I? I only know about the people I know; I think that's celebrity enough!'

'Enough for them?'

'Oh, I see you're clever. Enough for me! But I have heard of you, the lady went on. 'I know your pictures; I admire them. But I don't think you look like them.'

'They are mostly portraits,' Lyon said; 'and what I usually try for is not my own resemblance.'

'I see what you mean. But they have much more colour. And now you are going to do some one here?'

'I have been invited to do Sir David. I'm rather disappointed at not seeing him this evening.'

'Oh, he goes to bed at some unnatural hour—eight o'clock or something of that sort. You know he's rather an old mummy.'

'An old mummy?' Oliver Lyon repeated.

'I mean he wears half a dozen waistcoats, and that sort of thing. He's always cold.'

'I have never seen him and never seen any portrait or photograph of him,' Lyon said. 'I'm surprised at his never having had anything done—at their waiting all these years.'

'Ah, that's because he was afraid, you know; it was a kind of superstition. He was sure that if anything were done he would die directly afterwards. He has only consented to-day.'

'He's ready to die then?'

'Oh, now he's so old he doesn't care.'

'Well, I hope I shan't kill him,' said Lyon. 'It was rather unnatural in his son to send for me.'

'Oh, they have nothing to gain—everything is theirs already!' his companion rejoined, as if she took this speech quite literally. Her talkativeness was systematic—she fraternised as seriously as she might have played whist. 'They do as they like—they fill the house with people—they have *carte blanche*.'

'I see—but there's still the title.'

'Yes, but what is it?'

Our artist broke into laughter at this, whereat his companion stared. Before he had recovered himself she was scouring the plain with her other neighbour. The gentleman on his left at last risked an observation, and they had some fragmentary talk. This personage played his part with difficulty: he uttered a remark as a lady fires a pistol, looking the other way. To catch the ball Lyon had to bend his ear, and this movement led to his observing a handsome creature who was seated on the same side, beyond his interlocutor. Her profile was presented to him and at first he was only struck with its beauty; then it produced an impression still more agreeable—a sense of undimmed remembrance and intimate association. He had not recognised her on the instant only because he had so little expected to see her there; he had not seen her anywhere for so long, and no news of her ever came to him. She was often in his thoughts, but she had passed out of his life. He thought of her twice a week; that may be called often in relation to a person one has not seen for twelve years. The moment after he recognised her he felt how true it was that it was only she who could look like that: of the most charming head in the world (and this lady had it) there could never be a replica. She was leaning forward a little; she remained in profile, apparently listening to some one on the other side of her. She was listening, but she was also looking, and after a moment Lyon followed the direction of her eyes. They rested upon the gentleman who had been described to him as Colonel Capadose—rested, as it appeared to him, with a kind of habitual, visible complacency. This was not strange, for the Colonel was unmistakably formed to attract the sympathetic gaze of woman; but Lyon was slightly disappointed that she could let *him* look at her so long without giving him a glance. There was nothing between them to-day and he had no rights, but she must have known he was coming (it was of course not such a tremendous event, but she could not have been staying in the house without hearing of it), and it was not natural that that should absolutely fail to affect her.

She was looking at Colonel Capadose as if she were in love with him—a queer accident for the proudest, most reserved of women. But doubtless it was all right, if her husband liked it or didn't notice it: he had heard indefinitely, years before, that she was married, and he took for granted (as he had not heard that she had become a widow) the presence of the happy man on whom she had conferred what she had refused to *him*, the poor art-student at Munich. Colonel Capadose appeared to be aware of nothing, and this circumstance, incongruously enough, rather irritated Lyon than gratified him. Suddenly the lady turned her head, showing her full face to our hero. He was so prepared with a greeting that he instantly smiled, as a shaken jug overflows; but she gave him no response, turned away again and sank back in her chair. All that her face said in that instant was, 'You see I'm as handsome as ever.' To which he mentally subjoined, 'Yes, and as much good it does me!' He asked the young man beside him if he knew who that beautiful being was—the fifth person beyond him. The young man leaned forward, considered and then said, 'I think she's Mrs. Capadose.'

'Do you mean his wife—that fellow's?' And Lyon indicated the subject of the information given him by his other neighbour.

'Oh, is *he* Mr. Capadose?' said the young man, who appeared very vague. He admitted his vagueness and explained it by saying that there were so many people and he had come only the day before. What was definite to Lyon was that Mrs. Capadose was in love with her husband; so that he wished more than ever that he had married her.

'She's very faithful,' he found himself saying three minutes later to the lady on his right. He added that he meant Mrs. Capadose.

'Ah, you know her then?'

'I knew her once upon a time—when I was living abroad.'

'Why then were you asking me about her husband?'

'Precisely for that reason. She married after that—I didn't even know her present name.'

'How then do you know it now?'

'This gentleman has just told me—he appears to know.'

'I didn't know he knew anything,' said the lady, glancing forward.

'I don't think he knows anything but that.'

'Then you have found out for yourself that she is faithful. What do you mean by that?'

'Ah, you mustn't question me—I want to question you,' Lyon said. 'How do you all like her here?'

'You ask too much! I can only speak for myself. I think she's hard.'

'That's only because she's honest and straightforward.'

'Do you mean I like people in proportion as they deceive?'

'I think we all do, so long as we don't find them out,' Lyon said. 'And then there's something in her face—a sort of Roman type, in spite of her having such an English eye. In fact she's English down to the ground; but her complexion, her low forehead and that beautiful close little wave in her dark hair make her look like a glorified *contadina*.'

'Yes, and she always sticks pins and daggers into her head, to increase that effect. I must say I like her husband better: he is so clever.'

'Well, when I knew her there was no comparison that could

injure her. She was altogether the most delightful thing in Munich.'

'In Munich?'

'Her people lived there; they were not rich—in pursuit of economy in fact, and Munich was very cheap. Her father was the younger son of some noble house; he had married a second time and had a lot of little mouths to feed. She was the child of the first wife and she didn't like her stepmother, but she was charming to her little brothers and sisters. I once made a sketch of her as Werther's Charlotte, cutting bread and butter while they clustered all round her. All the artists in the place were in love with her but she wouldn't look at 'the likes' of us. She was too proud—I grant you that; but she wasn't stuck up nor young ladyish; she was simple and frank and kind about it. She used to remind me of Thackeray's Ethel Newcome. She told me she must marry well: it was the one thing she could do for her family. I suppose you would say that she *has* married well.'

'She told *you?*' smiled Lyon's neighbour.

'Oh, of course I proposed to her too. But she evidently thinks so herself!' he added.

When the ladies left the table the host as usual bade the gentlemen draw together, so that Lyon found himself opposite to Colonel Capadose. The conversation was mainly about the 'run,' for it had apparently been a great day in the hunting-field. Most of the gentlemen communicated their adventures and opinions, but Colonel Capadose's pleasant voice was the most audible in the chorus. It was a bright and fresh but masculine organ, just such a voice as, to Lyon's sense, such a 'fine man' ought to have had. It appeared from his remarks that he was a very straight rider, which was also very much what Lyon would have expected. Not that he swaggered, for his allusions were very quietly and casually made; but they were all too dangerous experiments and close shaves Lyon perceived after a little that the attention paid by the company to the Colonel's remarks was not in direct relation to the interest they seemed to offer; the result of which was that the speaker, who noticed that *he* at least was listening, began to treat him as his particular auditor and to fix his eyes on him as he talked. Lyon had nothing to do but to look sympathetic and assent—Colonel Capadose appeared to take so much sympathy and assent for granted. A neighbouring squire had had an accident; he had come a cropper in an awkward place—just at the finish—with consequences that looked grave. He had struck his head; he remained insensible, up to the last accounts: there had evidently been concussion of the brain. There was some exchange of views as to his recovery—how soon it would take place or whether it would take place at all; which led the Colonel to confide to our artist across the table that *he* shouldn't despair of a fellow even if he didn't come round for weeks—for weeks and weeks and weeks— for months, almost for years. He leaned forward; Lyon leaned forward to listen, and Colonel Capadose mentioned that he knew from personal experience that there was really no limit to the time one might lie unconscious without being any the worse for it. It had happened to him in Ireland, years before; he had been pitched out of a dogcart, had turned a sheer somersault and landed on his head. They thought he was dead, but he wasn't; they carried him first to the nearest cabin, where he lay for some days with the pigs, and then to an inn in a neighbouring town—it was a near thing they didn't put him under ground. He had been completely insensible—without a ray of recognition of any human thing—for three whole months; had not a glimmer of consciousness of any blessed thing. It was touch and go to that degree that they couldn't come near him, they couldn't feed him, they could scarcely look at him. Then one day he had opened his eyes—as fit as a flea!

'I give you my honour it had done me good—it rested my brain.' He appeared to intimate that with an intelligence so active as his these periods of repose were providential. Lyon thought his story very striking, but he wanted to ask him whether he had not shammed a little—not in relating it, but in keeping so quiet. He hesitated however, in time, to imply a doubt—he was so impressed with the tone in which Colonel Capadose said that it was the turn of a hair that they hadn't buried him alive. That had happened to a friend of his in India—a fellow who was supposed to have died of jungle fever—they clapped him into a coffin. He was going on to recite the further fate of this unfortunate gentleman when Mr. Ashmore made a move and every one got up to adjourn to the drawing-room. Lyon noticed that by this time no one was heeding what his new friend said to him. They came round on either side of the table and met while the gentlemen dawdled before going out.

'And do you mean that your friend was literally buried alive?' asked Lyon, in some suspense.

Colonel Capadose looked at him a moment, as if he had already lost the thread of the conversation. Then his face brightened—and when it brightened it was doubly handsome. 'Upon my soul he was chucked into the ground!'

'And was he left there?'

'He was left there till I came and hauled him out.'

'*You* came?'

'I dreamed about him—it's the most extraordinary story: I heard him calling to me in the night. I took upon myself to dig him up. You know there are people in India—a kind of beastly race, the ghouls—who violate graves. I had a sort of presentiment that they would get at him first. I rode straight, I can tell you; and, by Jove, a couple of them had just broken ground! Crack—crack, from a couple of barrels, and they showed me their heels, as you may believe. Would you credit that I took him out myself? The air brought him to and he was none the worse. He has got his pension—he came home the other day; he would do anything for me.'

'He called to you in the night?' said Lyon, much startled.

'That's the interesting point. Now *what was it?* It wasn't his ghost, because he wasn't dead. It wasn't himself, because he couldn't. It was something or other! You see India's a strange country—there's an element of the mysterious: the air is full of things you can't explain.'

They passed out of the dining-room, and Colonel Capadose, who went among the first, was separated from Lyon; but a minute later, before they reached the drawing-room, he joined him again. 'Ashmore tells me who you are. Of course I have often heard of you—I'm very glad to make your acquaintance; my wife used to know you.'

'I'm glad she remembers me. I recognised her at dinner and I was afraid she didn't.'

'Ah, I daresay she was ashamed,' said the Colonel, with indulgent humour.

'Ashamed of me?' Lyon replied, in the same key.

'Wasn't there something about a picture? Yes; you painted her portrait.'

'Many times,' said the artist; 'and she may very well have been ashamed of what I made of her.'

'Well, I wasn't, my dear sir; it was the sight of that picture,

which you were so good as to present to her, that made me first
fall in love with her.'

'Do you mean that one with the children—cutting bread and
butter?'

'Bread and butter? Bless me, no—vine leaves and a leopard
skin—a kind of Bacchante.'

'Ah, yes,' said Lyon; 'I remember. It was the first decent portrait
I painted. I should be curious to see it to-day.'

'Don't ask her to show it to you—she'll be mortified!' the Colonel
exclaimed.

'Mortified?'

'We parted with it—in the most disinterested manner,' he
laughed. 'An old friend of my wife's—her family had known him
intimately when they lived in Germany—took the most extraordinary fancy to it: The Grand Duke of Silberstadt-Schreckenstein, don't you know? He came out to Bombay while we were there
and he spotted your picture (you know he's one of the greatest
collectors in Europe), and made such eyes at it that, upon my word
—it happened to be his birthday—she told him he might have it,
to get rid of him. He was perfectly enchanted—but we miss the
picture.'

'It is very good of you,' Lyon said. 'If it's in a great collection—
a work of my incompetent youth—I am infinitely honoured.'

'Oh, he has got it in one of his castles; I don't know which—
you know he has so many. He sent us, before he left India—to
return the compliment—a magnificent old vase.'

'That was more than the thing was worth,' Lyon remarked.

Colonel Capadose gave no heed to this observation; he seemed
to be thinking of something. After a moment he said, 'If you'll come
and see us in town she'll show you the vase.' And as they passed
into the drawing-room he gave the artist a friendly propulsion. 'Go
and speak to her; there she is—she'll be delighted.'

Oliver Lyon took but a few steps into the wide saloon; he stood
there a moment looking at the bright composition of the lamplit
group of fair women, the single figures, the great setting of white
and gold, the panels of old damask, in the centre of each of which
was a single celebrated picture. There was a subdued lustre in the
scene and an air as of the shining trains of dresses tumbled over
the carpet. At the furthest end of the room sat Mrs. Capadose,
rather isolated; she was on a small sofa, with an empty place beside

her. Lyon could not flatter himself she had been keeping it for him; her failure to respond to his recognition at table contradicted that, but he felt an extreme desire to go and occupy it. Moreover he had her husband's sanction; so he crossed the room, stepping over the tails of gowns, and stood before his old friend.

'I hope you don't mean to repudiate me,' he said.

She looked up at him with an expression of unalloyed pleasure. 'I am so glad to see you. I was delighted when I heard you were coming.'

'I tried to get a smile from you at dinner—but I couldn't.'

'I didn't see—I didn't understand. Besides, I hate smirking and telegraphing. Also I'm very shy—you won't have forgotten that. Now we can communicate comfortably.' And she made a better place for him on the little sofa. He sat down and they had a talk that he enjoyed, while the reason for which he used to like her so came back to him, as well as a good deal of the very same old liking. She was still the least spoiled beauty he had ever seen, with an absence of coquetry or any insinuating art that seemed almost like an omitted faculty; there were moments when she struck her interlocutor as some fine creature from an asylum—a surprising deaf-mute or one of the operative blind. Her noble pagan head gave her privileges that she neglected, and when people were admiring her brow she was wondering whether there were a good fire in her bedroom. She was simple, kind and good; inexpressive but not inhuman or stupid. Now and again she dropped something that had a sifted, selected air—the sound of an impression at first hand. She had no imagination, but she had added up her feelings, some of her reflections, about life. Lyon talked of the old days in Munich, reminded her of incidents, pleasures and pains, asked her about her father and the others; and she told him in return that she was so impressed with his own fame, his brilliant position in the world, that she had not felt very sure he would speak to her or that his little sign at table was meant for her. This was plainly a perfectly truthful speech—she was incapable of any other—and he was affected by such humility on the part of a woman whose grand line was unique. Her father was dead; one of her brothers was in the navy and the other on a ranch in America; two of her sisters were married and the youngest was just coming out and very pretty. She didn't mention her stepmother. She asked him about his own personal history and he said that the principal thing that had happened to him was that he had never married.

'Oh, you ought to,' she answered. 'It's the best thing.'

'I like that—from you!' he returned.

'Why not from me? I am very happy.'

'That's just why I can't be. It's cruel of you to praise your state. But I have had the pleasure of making the acquaintance of your husband. We had a good bit of talk in the other room.'

'You must know him better—you must know him really well,' said Mrs. Capadose.

'I am sure that the further you go the more you find. But he makes a fine show, too.'

She rested her good gray eyes on Lyon. 'Don't you think he's handsome?'

'Handsome and clever and entertaining. You see I'm generous.'

'Yes; you must know him well,' Mrs. Capadose repeated.

'He has seen a great deal of life,' said her companion.

'Yes, we have been in so many places. You must see my little girl. She is nine years old—she's too beautiful.'

'You must bring her to my studio some day—I should like to paint her.'

'Ah, don't speak of that,' said Mrs. Capadose. 'It reminds me of something so distressing.'

'I hope you don't mean when *you* used to sit to me—though that may well have bored you.'

'It's not what you did—it's what we have done. It's a confession I must make—it's a weight on my mind! I mean about that beautiful picture you gave me—it used to be so much admired. When you come to see me in London (I count on your doing that very soon) I shall see you looking all round. I can't tell you I keep it in my own room because I love it so, for the simple reason——' And she paused a moment.

'Because you can't tell wicked lies,' said Lyon.

'No, I can't. So before you ask for it——'

'Oh, I know you parted with it—the blow has already fallen,' Lyon interrupted.

'Ah then, you have heard? I was sure you would! But do you know what we got for it? Two hundred pounds.'

'You might have got much more,' said Lyon, smiling.

'That seemed a great deal at the time. We were in want of the money—it was a good while ago, when we first married. Our means were very small then, but fortunately that has changed rather for the better. We had the chance; it really seemed a big sum, and I am afraid we jumped at it. My husband had expectations which have partly come into effect, so that now we do well enough. But meanwhile the picture went.'

'Fortunately the original remained. But do you mean that two hundred was the value of the vase?' Lyon asked.

'Of the vase?'

'The beautiful old Indian vase—the Grand Duke's offering.'

'The Grand Duke?'

'What's his name?—Silberstadt-Schreckenstein. Your husband mentioned the transaction.'

'Oh, my husband,' said Mrs. Capadose; and Lyon saw that she coloured a little.

Not to add to her embarrassment, but to clear up the ambiguity, which he perceived the next moment he had better have left alone, he went on: 'He tells me it's now in his collection.'

'In the Grand Duke's? Ah, you know its reputation? I believe it contains treasures.' She was bewildered, but she recovered herself, and Lyon made the mental reflection that for some reason which would seem good when he knew it the husband and the wife had prepared different versions of the same incident. It was true that he did not exactly see Everina Brant preparing a version; that was not her line of old, and indeed it was not in her eyes to-day. At any rate they both had the matter too much on their conscience. He changed the subject, said Mrs. Capadose must really bring the little girl. He sat with her some time longer and thought—perhaps it was only a fancy—that she was rather absent, as if she were annoyed at their having been even for a moment at cross-purposes. This did not prevent him from saying to her at the last, just as the ladies began to gather themselves together to go to bed: 'You seem much impressed, from what you say, with my renown and my prosperity, and you are so good as greatly to exaggerate them. Would you have married me if you had known that I was destined to success?'

' I did know it.'

'Well, I didn't.'

'You were too modest.'

'You didn't think so when I proposed to you.'

'Well, if I had married you I couldn't have married *him*—and he's so nice,' Mrs. Capadose said. Lyon knew she thought it—he had learned that at dinner—but it vexed him a little to hear her say it. The gentleman designated by the pronoun came up, amid the prolonged handshaking for good-night, and Mrs. Capadose remarked to her husband as she turned away, 'He wants to paint Amy.'

'Ah, she's a charming child, a most interesting little creature,' the Colonel said to Lyon. 'She does the most remarkable things.'

Mrs. Capadose stopped, in the rustling procession that followed the hostess out of the room. 'Don't tell him, please don't,' she said.

'Don't tell him what?'

'Why, what she does. Let him find out for himself.' And she passed on.

'She thinks I swagger about the child—that I bore people,' said the Colonel. 'I hope you smoke.' He appeared ten minutes later in the smoking-room, in a brilliant equipment, a suit of crimson foulard covered with little white spots. He gratified Lyon's eye, made him feel that the modern age has its splendour too and its opportunities for costume. If his wife was an antique he was a fine specimen of the period of colour: he might have passed for a Venetian of the sixteenth century. They were a remarkable couple, Lyon thought, and as he looked at the Colonel standing in bright erectness before the chimney-piece while he emitted great smoke-puffs he did not wonder that Everina could not regret she had not married *him*. All the gentlemen collected at Stayes were not smokers and some of them had gone to bed. Colonel Capadose remarked that there probably would be a smallish muster, they had had such a hard day's work. That was the worst of a hunting-house—the men were so sleepy after dinner; it was devilish stupid for the ladies, even for those who hunted themselves—for women were so extraordinary, they never showed it. But most fellows revived under the stimulating influences of the smoking-room, and some of them, in this confidence, would turn up yet. Some of the grounds of their confidence—not all of them—might have been seen in a cluster of glasses and bottles on a table near the fire, which made the great salver and its contents twinkle sociably. The others lurked as yet in various improper corners of the minds of the most loquacious. Lyon was alone with Colonel Capadose for some moments before their companions, in varied eccentricities of uni-

form, straggled in, and he perceived that this wonderful man had
but little loss of vital tissue to repair.

They talked about the house, Lyon having noticed an oddity
of construction in the smoking-room; and the Colonel explained
that it consisted of two distinct parts, one of which was of very great
antiquity. They were two complete houses in short, the old one
and the new, each of great extent and each very fine in its way.
The two formed together an enormous structure—Lyon must
make a point of going all over it. The modern portion had been
erected by the old man when he bought the property; oh yes, he
had bought it, forty years before—it hadn't been in the family:
there hadn't been any particular family for it to be in. He had had
the good taste not to spoil the original house—he had not touched
it beyond what was just necessary for joining it on. It was very
curious indeed—a most irregular, rambling, mysterious pile, where
they every now and then discovered a walled-up room or a secret
staircase. To his mind it was essentially gloomy, however; even
the modern additions, splendid as they were, failed to make it
cheerful. There was some story about a skeleton having been found
years before, during some repairs, under a stone slab of the floor
of one of the passages; but the family were rather shy of its being
talked about. The place they were in was of course in the old part,
which contained after all some of the best rooms: he had an idea
it had been the primitive kitchen, half modernised at some inter-
mediate period.

'My room is in the old part too then—I'm very glad,' Lyon said.
'It's very comfortable and contains all the latest conveniences,
but I observed the depth of the recess of the door and the evident
antiquity of the corridor and staircase—the first short one—after
I came out. That panelled corridor is admirable; it looks as if it
stretched away, in its brown dimness (the lamps didn't seem to me
to make much impression on it), for half a mile.'

'Oh, don't go to the end of it!' exclaimed the Colonel, smiling.

'Does it lead to the haunted room?' Lyon asked.

His companion looked at him a moment. 'Ah, you know about
that?'

'No, I don't speak from knowledge, only from hope. I have never
had any luck—I have never stayed in a dangerous house. The
places I go to are always as safe as Charing Cross. I want to see
—whatever there is, the regular thing. *Is* there a ghost here?'

'Of course there is—a rattling good one.'

'And have you seen him?'

'Oh, don't ask me what *I've* seen—I should tax your credulity. I don't like to talk of these things. But there are two or three as bad —that is, as good!—rooms as you'll find anywhere.'

'Do you mean in my corridor?' Lyon asked.

'I believe the worst is at the far end. But you would be ill-advised to sleep there.'

'Ill-advised?'

'Until you've finished your job. You'll get letters of importance the next morning, and you'll take the 10.20.'

'Do you mean I will invent a pretext for running away?'

'Unless you are braver than almost any one has ever been. They don't often put people to sleep there, but sometimes the house is so crowded that they have to. The same thing always happens— ill-concealed agitation at the breakfast-table and letters of the greatest importance. Of course it's a bachelor's room, and my wife and I are at the other end of the house. But we saw the comedy three days ago—the day after we got here. A young fellow had been put there—I forget his name—the house was so full; and the usual consequence followed. Letters at breakfast—an awfully queer face—an urgent call to town—so very sorry his visit was cut short. Ashmore and his wife looked at each other, and off the poor devil went.'

'Ah, that wouldn't suit me; I must paint my picture,' said Lyon. 'But do they mind your speaking of it? Some people who have a good ghost are very proud of it, you know.'

What answer Colonel Capadose was on the point of making to this inquiry our hero was not to learn, for at that moment their host had walked into the room accompanied by three or four gentlemen. Lyon was conscious that he was partly answered by the Colonel's not going on with the subject. This however on the other hand was rendered natural by the fact that one of the gentlmen appealed to him for an opinion on a point under discussion, something to do with the everlasting history of the day's run. To Lyon himself Mr. Ashmore began to talk, expressing his regret at having had so little direct conversation with him as yet. The topic that suggested itself was naturally that most closely connected with the motive of the artist's visit. Lyon remarked that it was a great disadvantage to him not to have had some preliminary acquaintance with Sir David

—in most cases he found that so important. But the present sitter was so far advanced in life that there was doubtless no time to lose. 'Oh, I can tell you all about him,' said Mr. Ashmore; and for half an hour he told him a good deal. It was very interesting as well as very eulogistic, and Lyon could see that he was a very nice old man, to have endeared himself so to a son who was evidently not a gusher. At last he got up—he said he must go to bed if he wished to be fresh for his work in the morning. To which his host replied, 'Then you must take your candle; the lights are out; I don't keep my servants up.'

In a moment Lyon had his glimmering taper in hand, and as he was leaving the room (he did not disturb the others with a good-night; they were absorbed in the lemon-squeezer and the soda-water cork) he remembered other occasions on which he had made his way to bed alone through a darkened country-house; such occasions had not been rare, for he was almost always the first to leave the smoking-room. If he had not stayed in houses conspicuously haunted he had, none the less (having the artistic temperament), sometimes found the great black halls and staircases rather 'creepy': there had been often a sinister effect, to his imagination, in the sound of his tread in the long passages or the way the winter moon peeped into tall windows on landings. It occurred to him that if houses without supernatural pretensions could look so wicked at night, the old corridors of Stayes would certainly give him a sensation. He didn't know whether the proprietors were sensitive; very often, as he had said to Colonel Capadose, people enjoyed the impeachment. What determined him to speak, with a certain sense of the risk, was the impression that the Colonel told queer stories. As he had his hand on the door he said to Arthur Ashmore, 'I hope I shan't meet any ghosts.'

'Any ghosts?'

'You ought to have some—in this fine old part.'

'We do our best, but *que voulez-vous?*' said Mr. Ashmore. 'I don't think they like the hot-water pipes.'

'They remind them too much of their own climate? But haven't you a haunted room—at the end of my passage?'

'Oh, there are stories—we try to keep them up.'

'I should like very much to sleep there,' Lyon said.

'Well, you can move there to-morrow if you like.'

'Perhaps I had better wait till I have done my work.'

'Very good; but you won't work there, you know. My father will sit to you in his own apartments.'

'Oh, it isn't that; it's the fear of running away, like that gentleman three days ago.'

'Three days ago? What gentleman?' Mr. Ashmore asked.

'The one who got urgent letters at breakfast and fled by the 10.20. Did he stand more than one night?'

'I don't know what you are talking about. There was no such gentleman—three days ago.'

'Ah, so much the better,' said Lyon, nodding good-night and departing. He took his course, as he remembered it, with his wavering candle, and, though he encountered a great many gruesome objects, safely reached the passage out of which his room opened. In the complete darkness it seemed to stretch away still further, but he followed it, for the curiosity of the thing, to the end. He passed several doors with the name of the room painted upon them, but he found nothing else. He was tempted to try the last door—to look into the room of evil fame; but he reflected that this would be indiscreet, since Colonel Capadose handled the brush—as a *raconteur*—with such freedom. There might be a ghost and there might not; but the Colonel himself, he inclined to think, was the most mystifying figure in the house.

II

LYON found Sir David Ashmore a capital subject and a very comfortable sitter into the bargain. Moreover he was a very agreeable old man, tremendously puckered but not in the least dim; and he wore exactly the furred dressing-gown that Lyon would have chosen. He was proud of his age but ashamed of his infirmities, which however he greatly exaggerated and which did not prevent him from sitting there as submissive as if portraiture in oils had been a branch of surgery. He demolished the legend of his having feared the operation would be fatal, giving an explanation which pleased our friend much better. He held that a gentleman should be painted but once in his life—that it was eager and fatuous to be hung up all over the place. That was good for women, who made a pretty wall-pattern; but the male face didn't lend itself to decorative repetition. The proper time for the likeness was at the last, when the whole man was there—you got the totality of his experience. Lyon could not reply that that period was not a real compendium—you had to allow so for leakage; for there had been no crack in Sir David's crystallisation. He spoke of his portrait as a plain map of the country, to be consulted by his children in a case of uncertainty. A proper map could be drawn up only when the country had been travelled. He gave Lyon his mornings, till luncheon, and they talked of many things, not neglecting, as a stimulus to gossip, the people in the house. Now that he did not 'go out,' as he said, he saw much less of the visitors at Stayes: people came and went whom he knew nothing about, and he liked to hear Lyon describe them. The artist sketched with a fine point and did not caricature, and it usually befell that when Sir David did not know the sons and daughters he had known the fathers and mothers. He was one of those terrible old gentlemen who are a repository of antecedents. But in the case of the Capadose family, at whom they arrived by an easy stage, his knowledge embraced two, or even three, generations. General Capadose was an old crony, and he remembered his father before him. The general was rather a smart soldier, but in private life of too speculative a turn—always sneaking into the City to put his money into some rotten thing. He married a girl who brought him something and they had half a dozen children. He scarcely knew what had become of the rest of them, except that one was in the Church and had found preferment—wasn't he Dean of Rockingham? Clement, the fellow who was at Stayes, had some military talent; he had served in the East, he had married a pretty girl. He had been at Eton with his son, and he used to come to Stayes in his holidays. Lately, coming back to England, he had turned up with his wife again; that was before he—the old man— had been put to grass. He was a taking dog, but he had a monstrous foible.

'A monstrous foible?' said Lyon.

'He's a thumping liar.'

Lyon's brush stopped short, while he repeated, for somehow the formula startled him, 'A thumping liar?'

'You are very lucky not to have found it out.'

'Well I confess I have noticed a romantic tinge——'

'Oh, it isn't always romantic. He'll lie about the time of day, about the name of his hatter. It appears there are people like that.'

'Well, they are precious scoundrels,' Lyon declared, his voice trembling a little with the thought of what Everina Brant had done with herself.

'Oh, not always,' said the old man. 'This fellow isn't in the least a scoundrel. There is no harm in him and no bad intention; he doesn't steal nor cheat nor gamble nor drink; he's very kind—he sticks to his wife, is fond of his children. He simply can't give you a straight answer.'

'Then everything he told me last night, I suppose, was mendacious: he delivered himself of a series of the stiffest statements. They stuck, when I tried to swallow them, but I never thought of so simple an explanation.'

'No doubt he was in the vein,' Sir David went on. 'It's a natural peculiarity—as you might limp or stutter or be left-handed. I believe it comes and goes, like intermittent fever. My son tells me that his friends usually understand it and don't haul him up— for the sake of his wife.'

'Oh, his wife—his wife!' Lyon murmured, painting fast.

'I daresay she's used to it.'

'Never in the world, Sir David. How can she be used to it?'

'Why, my dear sir, when a woman's fond!—And don't they mostly handle the long bow themselves? They are connoisseurs— they have a sympathy for a fellow-performer.'

Lyon was silent a moment; he had no ground for denying that Mrs. Capadose was attached to her husband. But after a little he rejoined: 'Oh, not this one! I knew her years ago—before her marriage; knew her well and admired her. She was as clear as a bell.'

'I like her very much,' Sir David said, 'but I have seen her back him up.'

Lyon considered Sir David for a moment, not in the light of a model. 'Are you very sure?'

The old man hesitated; then he answered, smiling, 'You're in love with her.'

'Very likely. God knows I used to be!'

'She must help him out—she can't expose him.'

'She can hold her tongue,' Lyon remarked.

'Well, before you probably she will.'

'That's what I'm curious to see.' And Lyon added, privately, 'Mercy on us, what he must have made of her!' He kept this reflection to himself, for he considered that he had sufficiently betrayed his state of mind with regard to Mrs. Capadose. None the less it occupied him now immensely, the question of how such a woman would arrange herself in such a predicament. He watched her with an interest deeply quickened when he mingled with the company; he had had his own troubles in life, but he had rarely been so anxious about anything as he was now to see what the loyalty of a wife and the infection of an example would have made of an absolutely truthful mind. Oh, he held it as immutably established that whatever other women might be prone to do she, of old, had been perfectly incapable of a deviation. Even if she had not been too simple to deceive she would have been too proud; and if she had not had too much conscience she would have had too little eagerness. It was the last thing she would have endured or condoned—the particular thing she would not have forgiven. Did she sit in torment while her husband turned his somersaults, or was she now too so perverse that she thought it a fine thing to be striking at the expense of one's honour? It would have taken a wondrous alchemy—working backwards, as it were—to produce this latter result. Besides these two alternatives (that she suffered tortures in silence and that she was so much in love that her husband's humiliating idiosyncrasy seemed to her only an added richness—a proof of life and talent), there was still the possibility that she had not found him out, that she took his false pieces at his own valuation. A little reflection rendered this hypothesis untenable; it was too evident that the account he gave of things must repeatedly have contradicted her own knowledge. Within an hour or two of his meeting them Lyon had seen her confronted with that perfectly gratuitous invention about the profit they had made off his early picture. Even then indeed she had not, so far as he could see, smarted, and—but for the present he could only contemplate the case.

Even if it had not been interfused, through his uneradicated tenderness for Mrs. Capadose, with an element of suspense, the question would still have presented itself to him as a very curious problem, for he had not painted portraits during so many years without becoming something of a psychologist. His inquiry was limited for the moment to the opportunity that the following three days might yield, as the Colonel and his wife were going on to another house. It fixed itself largely of course upon the Colonel too— this gentleman was such a rare anomaly. Moreover it had to go on very quickly. Lyon was too scrupulous to ask other people what they thought of the business—he was too afraid of exposing the woman he once had loved. It was probable also that light would come to him from the talk of the rest of the company: the Colonel's queer habit, both as it affected his own situation and as it affected his wife, would be a familiar theme in any house in which he was in the habit of staying. Lyon had not observed in the circles in which he visited any marked abstention from comment on the singularities of their members. It interfered with his progress that the Colonel hunted all day, while he plied his brushes and chatted with Sir David; but a Sunday intervened and that partly made it up. Mrs. Capadose fortunately did not hunt, and when his work was over she was not inaccessible. He took a couple of longish walks with her (she was fond of that), and beguiled her at tea into a friendly nook in the hall. Regard her as he might he could not make out to himself that she was consumed by a hidden shame; the sense of being married to a man whose word had no worth was not, in her spirit, so far as he could guess, the canker within the rose. Her mind appeared to have nothing on it but its own placid frankness, and when he looked into her eyes (deeply, as he occasionally permitted himself to do), they had no uncomfortable consciousness. He talked to her again and still again of the dear old days—reminded her of things that he had not (before this reunion) the least idea that he remembered. Then he spoke to her of her husband, praised his appearance, his talent for conversation, professed to have felt a quick friendship for him and asked (with an inward audacity at which he trembled a little) what manner of man he was. 'What manner?' said Mrs. Capadose. 'Dear me, how can one describe one's husband? I like him very much.'

'Ah, you have told me that already!' Lyon exclaimed, with exaggerated ruefulness.

'Then why do you ask me again?' She added in a moment, as if she were so happy that she could afford to take pity on him, 'He is everything that's good and kind. He's a soldier—and a gentleman —and a dear! He hasn't a fault. And he has great ability.'

'Yes; he strikes one as having great ability. But of course I can't think him a dear.'

'I don't care what you think him!' said Mrs. Capadose, looking, it seemed to him, as she smiled, handsomer than he had ever seen her. She was either deeply cynical or still more deeply impenetrable, and he had little prospect of winning from her the intimation that he longed for—some hint that it had come over her that after all she had better have married a man who was not a by-word for the most contemptible, the least heroic, of vices. Had she not seen—had she not felt—the smile go round when her husband executed some especially characteristic conversational caper? How could a woman of her quality endure that day after day, year after year, except by her quality's altering? But he would believe in the alteration only when he should have heard *her* lie. He was fascinated by his problem and yet half exasperated, and he asked himself all kinds of questions. Did she not lie, after all, when she let his falsehoods pass without a protest? Was not her life a perpetual complicity, and did she not aid and abet him by the simple fact that she was not disgusted with him? Then again perhaps she *was* disgusted and it was the mere desperation of her pride that had given her an inscrutable mask. Perhaps she protested in private, passionately; perhaps every night, in their own apartments, after the day's hideous performance, she made him the most scorching scene. But if such scenes were of no avail and he took no more trouble to cure himself, how could she regard him, and after so many years of marriage too, with the perfectly artless complacency that Lyon had surprised in her in the course of the first day's dinner? If our friend had not been in love with her he could have taken the diverting view of the Colonel's delinquencies; but as it was they turned to the tragical in his mind, even while he had a sense that his solicitude might also have been laughed at.

The observation of these three days showed him that if Capadose was an abundant he was not a malignant liar and that his fine faculty exercised itself mainly on subjects of small direct importance. 'He is the liar platonic,' he said to himself; 'he is disinterested, he doesn't operate with a hope of gain or with a desire to injure. It is art for art and he is prompted by the love of beauty. He has an inner vision of what might have been, of what ought to be, and he helps on the good cause by the simple substitution of a *nuance*. He paints, as it were, and so do I!' His manifestations had a considerable variety, but a family likeness ran through them, which consisted mainly of their singular futility. It was this that made them offensive; they encumbered the field of conversation, took up valuable space, converted it into a sort of brilliant sun-shot fog. For a fib told under pressure a convenient place can usually be found, as for a person who presents himself with an author's order at the first night of a play. But the supererogatory lie is the gentleman without a voucher or a ticket who accommodates himself with a stool in the passage.

In one particular Lyon acquitted his successful rival; it had puzzled him that irrepressible as he was he had not got into a mess in the service. But he perceived that he respected the service—that august institution was sacred from his depredations. Moreover though there was a great deal of swagger in his talk it was, oddly enough, rarely swagger about his military exploits. He had a passion for the chase, he had followed it in far countries and some of his finest flowers were reminiscences of lonely danger and escape. The more solitary the scene the bigger of course the flower. A new acquaintance, with the Colonel, always received the tribute of a bouquet: that generalisation Lyon very promptly made. And this extraordinary man had inconsistencies and unexpected lapses—lapses into flat veracity. Lyon recognised what Sir David had told him, that his aberrations came in fits or periods—that he would sometimes keep the truce of God for a month at a time. The muse breathed upon him at her pleasure; she often left him alone. He would neglect the finest openings and then set sail in the teeth of the breeze. As a general thing he affirmed the false rather than denied the true; yet this proportion was sometimes strikingly reversed. Very often he joined in the laugh against himself—he admitted that he was trying it on and that a good many of his anecdotes had an experimental character. Still he never completely retracted nor retreated—he dived and came up in another place. Lyon divined that he was capable at intervals of defending his position with violence, but only when it was a very bad one. Then he might easily be dangerous—then he would hit out and become calumnious. Such occasions would test his wife's equanimity—Lyon would have liked to see her there. In the smoking-room and elsewhere the company, so far as it was composed of his familiars, had an hilarious protest always at hand; but among the men who had known him long his rich tone was an old story, so old that they had ceased to talk about it, and Lyon did not care, as I have said, to elicit the judgement of those who might have shared his own surprise.

The oddest thing of all was that neither surprise nor familiarity prevented the Colonel's being liked; his largest drafts on a sceptical attention passed for an overflow of life and gaiety—almost of

good looks. He was fond of portraying his bravery and used a
very big brush, and yet he was unmistakably brave. He was a
capital rider and shot, in spite of his fund of anecdote illustrating
these accomplishments: in short he was very nearly as clever and
his career had been very nearly as wonderful as he pretended.
His best quality however remained that indiscriminate sociability
which took interest and credulity for granted and about which he
bragged least. It made him cheap, it made him even in a manner
vulgar; but it was so contagious that his listener was more or less
on his side as against the probabilities. It was a private reflection of
Oliver Lyon's that he not only lied but made one feel one's self
a bit of a liar, even (or especially) if one contradicted him. In the
evening, at dinner and afterwards, our friend watched his wife's
face to see if some faint shade or spasm never passed over it. But
she showed nothing, and the wonder was that when he spoke she
almost always listened. That was her pride: she wished not to be
even suspected of not facing the music. Lyon had none the less an
importunate vision of a veiled figure coming the next day in the
dusk to certain places to repair the Colonel's ravages, as the relatives of kleptomaniacs punctually call at the shops that have suffered from their pilferings.

'I must apologise, of course it wasn't true, I hope no harm is
done, it is only his incorrigible——' Oh, to hear that woman's voice
in that deep abasement! Lyon had no nefarious plan, no conscious
wish to practise upon her shame or her loyalty; but he did say to
himself that he should like to bring her round to feel that there
would have been more dignity in a union with a certain other person. He even dreamed of the hour when, with a burning face, she
would ask *him* not to take it up. Then he should be almost consoled—he would be magnanimous.

Lyon finished his picture and took his departure, after having
worked in a glow of interest which made him believe in his success, until he found he had pleased every one, especially Mr. and
Mrs. Ashmore, when he began to be sceptical. The party at any
rate changed: Colonel and Mrs. Capadose went their way. He was
able to say to himself however that his separation from the lady
was not so much an end as a beginning, and he called on her soon
after his return to town. She had told him the hours she was at
home—she seemed to like him. If she liked him why had she not
married him or at any rate why was she not sorry she had not? If

she was sorry she concealed it too well. Lyon's curiosity on this point may strike the reader as fatuous, but something must be allowed to a disappointed man. He did not ask much after all; not that she should love him to-day or that she should allow him to tell her that he loved her, but only that she should give him some sign she was sorry. Instead of this, for the present, she contented herself with exhibiting her little daughter to him. The child was beautiful and had the prettiest eyes of innocence he had ever seen: which did not prevent him from wondering whether she told horrid fibs. This idea gave him much entertainment—the picture of the anxiety with which her mother would watch as she grew older for the symptoms of heredity. That was a nice occupation for Everina Brant! Did she lie to the child herself, about her father—was that necessary, when she pressed her daughter to her bosom, to cover up his tracks? Did he control himself before the little girl—so that she might not hear him say things she knew to be other than he said? Lyon doubted this: his genius would be too strong for him, and the only safety for the child would be in her being too stupid to analyse. One couldn't judge yet—she was too young. If she should grow up clever she would be sure to tread in his steps—a delightful improvement in her mother's situation! Her little face was not shifty, but neither was her father's big one: so that proved nothing.

Lyon reminded his friends more than once of their promise that Amy should sit to him, and it was only a question of his leisure. The desire grew in him to paint the Colonel also—an operation from which he promised himself a rich private satisfaction. He would draw him out, he would set him up in that totality about which he had talked with Sir David, and none but the initiated would know. They, however, would rank the picture high, and it would be indeed six rows deep—a masterpiece of subtle characterisation, of legitimate treachery. He had dreamed for years of producing something which should bear the stamp of the psychologist as well as of the painter, and here at last was his subject. It was a pity it was not better, but that was not *his* fault. It was his impression that already no one drew the Colonel out more than he, and he did it not only by instinct but on a plan. There were moments when he was almost frightened at the success of his plan—the poor gentleman went so terribly far. He would pull up some day, look at Lyon between the eyes—guess he was being played upon—which would lead to his wife's guessing it also. Not that Lyon cared much for that however, so long as she failed to suppose (as she must) that *she* was a part of his joke. He formed such a habit now of going to see her of a Sunday afternoon that he was angry when she went out of town. This occurred often, as the couple were great visitors and the Colonel was always looking for sport, which he liked best when it could be had at other people's expense. Lyon would have supposed that this sort of life was particularly little to her taste, for he had an idea that it was in country-houses that her husband came out strongest. To let him go off without her, not to see him expose himself—that ought properly to have been a relief and a luxury to her. She told Lyon in fact that she preferred staying at home; but she neglected to say it was because in other people's houses she was on the rack: the reason she gave was that she liked so to be with the child. It was not perhaps criminal to draw such a bow, but it was vulgar: poor Lyon was delighted when he arrived at that formula. Certainly some day too he would cross the line—he would become a noxious animal. Yes, in the meantime he was vulgar, in spite of his talents, his fine person, his impunity. Twice, by exception, toward the end of the winter, when he left town for a few days' hunting, his wife remained at home. Lyon had not yet reached the point of asking himself whether the desire not to miss two of his visits had something to do with her immobility. That inquiry would perhaps have been more in place later, when he began to paint the child and she always came with her. But it was not in her to give the wrong name, to pretend, and Lyon could see that she had the maternal passion, in spite of the bad blood in the little girl's veins.

She came inveterately, though Lyon multiplied the sittings: Amy was never entrusted to the governess or the maid. He had knocked off poor old Sir David in ten days, but the portrait of the simple-faced child bade fair to stretch over into the following year. He asked for sitting after sitting, and it would have struck any one who might have witnessed the affair that he was wearing the little girl out. He knew better however and Mrs. Capadose also knew: they were present together at the long intermissions he gave her, when she left her pose and roamed about the great studio, amusing herself with its curiosities, playing with the old draperies and costumes, having unlimited leave to handle. Then her mother and Mr. Lyon sat and talked; he laid aside his brushes and leaned back in his chair; he always gave her tea. What Mrs. Capadose did not know was the way that during these weeks he neglected other orders: women have no faculty of imagination with regard to a man's work beyond a vague idea that it doesn't matter. In fact Lyon put off everything and made several celebrities wait. There were half-hours of silence, when he plied his brushes, during which he was mainly conscious that Everina was sitting there. She easily fell into that if he did not insist on talking, and she was not embarrassed nor bored by it. Sometimes she took up a book—there were plenty of them about; sometimes, a little way off, in her chair, she watched his progress (though without in the least advising or correcting), as if she cared for every stroke that represented her daughter. These strokes were occasionally a little wild; he was thinking so much more of his heart than of his hand. He was not more embarrassed than she was, but he was agitated: it was as if in the sittings (for the child, too, was beautifully quiet) something was growing between them or had already grown—a tacit confidence, an inexpressible secret. He felt it that way; but after all he could not be sure that she did. What he wanted her to do for him was very little; it was not even to confess that she was unhappy. He would be superabundantly gratified if she should simply let him know, even by a silent sign, that she recognised that with him her life would have been finer. Sometimes he guessed —his presumption went so far—that he might see this sign in her contentedly sitting there.

III

At last he broached the question of painting the Colonel: it was now very late in the season—there would be little time before the general dispersal. He said they must make the most of it; the great thing was to begin; then in the autumn, with the resumption of their London life, they could go forward. Mrs. Capadose objected to this that she really could not consent to accept another present of such value. Lyon had given her the portrait of herself of old, and he had seen what they had had the indelicacy to do with it. Now he had offered her this beautiful memorial of the child— beautiful it would evidently be when it was finished, if he could ever satisfy himself; a precious possession which they would cherish for ever. But his generosity must stop there—they couldn't be so

tremendously 'beholden' to him. They couldn't order the picture
—of course he would understand that, without her explaining: it
was a luxury beyond their reach, for they knew the great prices he
received. Besides, what had they ever done—what above all had
she ever done, that he should overload them with benefits? No, he
was too dreadfully good; it was really impossible that Clement
should sit. Lyon listened to her without protest, without interruption, while he bent forward at his work, and at last he said:
'Well, if you won't take it why not let him sit for me for my own
pleasure and profit? Let it be a favour, a service I ask of him. It
will do me a lot of good to paint him and the picture will remain
in my hands.'

'How will it do you a lot of good?' Mrs. Capadose asked.

'Why, he's such a rare model—such an interesting subject. He
has such an expressive face. It will teach me no end of things.'

'Expressive of what?' said Mrs. Capadose.

'Why, of his nature.'

'And do you want to paint his nature?'

'Of course I do. That's what a great portrait gives you, and I
shall make the Colonel's a great one. It will put me up high. So you
see my request is eminently interested.'

'How can you be higher than you are?'

'Oh, I'm insatiable! Do consent,' said Lyon.

'Well, his nature is very noble,' Mrs. Capadose remarked.

'Ah, trust me, I shall bring it out!' Lyon exclaimed, feeling a little
ashamed of himself.

Mrs. Capadose said before she went away that her husband
would probably comply with his invitation, but she added, 'Nothing would induce me to let you pry into *me* that way!'

'Oh, you,' Lyon laughed—'I could do you in the dark!'

The Colonel shortly afterwards placed his leisure at the painter's
disposal and by the end of July had paid him several visits. Lyon
was disappointed neither in the quality of his sitter nor in the degree to which he himself rose to the occasion; he felt really confident
that he should produce a fine thing. He was in the humour; he was
charmed with his *motif* and deeply interested in his problem. The
only point that troubled him was the idea that when he should
send his picture to the Academy he should not be able to give the
title, for the catalogue, simply as 'The Liar.' However, it little
mattered, for he had now determined that this character should

be perceptible even to the meanest intelligence—as overtopping as it had become to his own sense in the living man. As he saw nothing else in the Colonel to-day, so he gave himself up to the joy of painting nothing else. How he did it he could not have told you, but it seemed to him that the mystery of how to do it was revealed to him afresh every time he sat down to his work. It was in the eyes and it was in the mouth, it was in every line of the face and every fact of the attitude, in the indentation of the chin, in the way the hair was planted, the moustache was twisted, the smile came and went, the breath rose and fell. It was in the way he looked out at a bamboozled world in short—the way he would look out for ever. There were half a dozen portraits in Europe that Lyon rated as supreme; he regarded them as immortal, for they were as perfectly preserved as they were consummately painted. It was to this small exemplary group that he aspired to annex the canvas on which he was now engaged. One of the productions that helped to compose it was the magnificent Moroni of the National Gallery —the young tailor, in the white jacket, at his board with his shears. The Colonel was not a tailor, nor was Moroni's model, unlike many tailors, a liar; but as regards the masterly clearness with which the individual should be rendered his work would be on the same line as that. He had to a degree in which he had rarely had it before the satisfaction of feeling life grow and grow under his brush. The Colonel, as it turned out, liked to sit and he liked to talk while he was sitting: which was very fortunate, as his talk largely constituted Lyon's inspiration. Lyon put into practice that idea of drawing him out which he had been nursing for so many weeks: he could not possibly have been in a better relation to him for the purpose. He encouraged, beguiled, excited him, manifested an unfathomable credulity, and his only interruptions were when the Colonel did not respond to it. He had his intermissions, his hours of sterility, and then Lyon felt that the picture also languished. The higher his companion soared, the more gyrations he executed, in the blue, the better he painted; he couldn't make his flights long enough. He lashed him on when he flagged; his apprehension became great at moments that the Colonel would discover his game. But he never did, apparently; he basked and expanded in the fine steady light of the painter's attention. In this way the picture grew very fast; it was astonishing what a short business it was, compared with the little girl's. By the fifth of August it was pretty well finished:

that was the date of the last sitting the Colonel was for the present able to give, as he was leaving town the next day with his wife. Lyon was amply content—he saw his way so clear: he should be able to do at his convenience what remained, with or without his friend's attendance. At any rate, as there was no hurry, he would let the thing stand over till his own return to London, in November, when he would come back to it with a fresh eye. On the Colonel's asking him if his wife might come and see it the next day, if she should find a minute—this was so greatly her desire—Lyon begged as a special favour that she would wait: he was so far from satisfied as yet. This was the repetition of a proposal Mrs. Capadose had made on the occasion of his last visit to her, and he had then asked for a delay—declared that he was by no means content. He was really delighted, and he was again a little ashamed of himself.

By the fifth of August the weather was very warm, and on that day, while the Colonel sat straight and gossiped, Lyon opened for the sake of ventilation a little subsidiary door which led directly from his studio into the garden and sometimes served as an entrance and an exit for models and for visitors of the humbler sort, and as a passage for canvases, frames, packing-boxes and other professional gear. The main entrance was through the house and his own apartments, and this approach had the charming effect of admitting you first to a high gallery, from which a crooked picturesque staircase enabled you to descend to the wide, decorated, encumbered room. The view of this room, beneath them, with all its artistic ingenuities and the objects of value that Lyon had collected, never failed to elicit exclamations of delight from persons stepping into the gallery. The way from the garden was plainer and at once more practicable and more private. Lyon's domain, in St. John's Wood, was not vast, but when the door stood open of a summer's day it offered a glimpse of flowers and trees, you smelt something sweet and you heard the birds. On this particular morning the side-door had been found convenient by an unannounced visitor, a youngish woman who stood in the room before the Colonel perceived her and whom he perceived before she was noticed by his friend. She was very quiet, and she looked from one of the men to the other. 'Oh, dear, here's another!' Lyon exclaimed, as soon as his eyes rested on her. She belonged, in fact, to a somewhat importunate class—the model in search of employment, and she explained that she had ventured to come straight in, that way, because very often when she went to call upon gentlemen the servants played her tricks, turned her off and wouldn't take in her name.

'But how did you get into the garden?' Lyon asked.

'The gate was open, sir—the servants' gate. The butcher's cart was there.'

'The butcher ought to have closed it,' said Lyon.

'Then you don't require me, sir?' the lady continued.

Lyon went on with his painting; he had given her a sharp look at first, but now his eyes lighted on her no more. The Colonel, however, examined her with interest. She was a person of whom you could scarcely say whether being young she looked old or old she looked young; she had at any rate evidently rounded several of the corners of life and had a face that was rosy but that somehow failed to suggest freshness. Nevertheless she was pretty and even looked as if at one time she might have sat for the complexion. She wore a hat with many feathers, a dress with many bugles, long black gloves, encircled with silver bracelets, and very bad shoes. There was something about her that was not exactly of the governess out of place nor completely of the actress seeking an engagement, but that savoured of an interrupted profession or even of a blighted career. She was rather soiled and tarnished, and after she had been in the room a few moments the air, or at any rate the nostril, became acquainted with a certain alcoholic waft. She was unpractised in the *h*, and when Lyon at last thanked her and said he didn't want her—he was doing nothing for which she could be useful—she replied with rather a wounded manner, 'Well, you know you *'ave*'ad me!'

'I don't remember you,' Lyon answered.

'Well, I daresay the people that saw your pictures do! I haven't much time, but I thought I would look in.'

'I am much obliged to you.'

'If ever you should require me, if you just send me a post-card——'

'I never send postcards,' said Lyon.

'Oh well, I should value a private letter! Anything to Miss Geraldine, Mortimer Terrace Mews, Notting 'ill——'

'Very good; I'll remember,' said Lyon.

Miss Geraldine lingered. 'I thought I'd just stop, on the chance.'

'I'm afraid I can't hold out hopes, I'm so busy with portraits,' Lyon continued.

'Yes; I see you are. I wish I was in the gentleman's place.'

'I'm afraid in that case it wouldn't look like me,' said the Colonel, laughing.

'Oh, of course it couldn't compare—it wouldn't be so 'andsome! But I do hate them portraits!' Miss Geraldine declared. 'It's so much bread out of our mouths.'

'Well, there are many who can't paint them,' Lyon suggested, comfortingly.

'Oh, I've sat to the very first—and only to the first! There's many that couldn't do anything without me.'

'I'm glad you're in such demand.' Lyon was beginning to be bored and he added that he wouldn't detain her—he would send for her in case of need.

'Very well; remember it's the Mews—more's the pity! You don't sit so well as *us!*' Miss Geraldine pursued, looking at the Colonel. 'If *you* should require me, sir——'

'You put him out; you embarrass him,' said Lyon.

'Embarrass him, oh gracious!' the visitor cried, with a laugh which diffused a fragrance. 'Perhaps *you* send postcards, eh?' she went on to the Colonel; and then she retreated with a wavering step. She passed out into the garden as she had come.

'How very dreadful—she's drunk!' said Lyon. He was painting hard, but he looked up, checking himself: Miss Geraldine, in the open doorway, had thrust back her head.

'Yes, I do hate it—that sort of thing!' she cried with an explosion of mirth which confirmed Lyon's declaration. And then she disappeared.

'What sort of thing—what does she mean?' the Colonel asked.

'Oh, my painting you, when I might be painting her.'

'And have you ever painted her?'

'Never in the world; I have never seen her. She is quite mistaken.'

The Colonel was silent a moment; then he remarked, 'She was very pretty—ten years ago.'

'I daresay, but she's quite ruined. For me the least drop too much spoils them; I shouldn't care for her at all.'

'My dear fellow, she's not a model,' said the Colonel, laughing.

'To-day, no doubt, she's not worthy of the name; but she has been one.'

'*Jamais de la vie!* That's all a pretext.'

'A pretext?' Lyon pricked up his ears—he began to wonder what was coming now.

'She didn't want you—she wanted me.'

'I noticed she paid you some attention. What does she want of you?'

'Oh, to do me an ill turn. She hates me—lots of women do. She's watching me—she follows me.'

Lyon leaned back in his chair—he didn't believe a word of this. He was all the more delighted with it and with the Colonel's bright, candid manner. The story had bloomed, fragrant, on the spot. 'My dear Colonel!' he murmured, with friendly interest and commiseration.

'I was annoyed when she came in—but I wasn't startled,' his sitter continued.

'You concealed it very well, if you were.'

'Ah, when one has been through what I have! To-day however I confess I was half prepared. I have seen her hanging about—she knows my movements. She was near my house this morning—she must have followed me.'

'But who is she then—with such a *toupet?*'

'Yes, she has that,' said the Colonel; 'but as you observe she was primed. Still, there was a cheek, as they say, in her coming in. Oh, she's a bad one! She isn't a model and she never was; no doubt she has known some of those women and picked up their form. She had hold of a friend of mine ten years ago—a stupid young gander who might have been left to be plucked but whom I was obliged to take an interest in for family reasons. It's a long story—I had really forgotten all about it. She's thirty-seven if she's a day. I cut in and made him get rid of her—I sent her about her business. She knew it was me she had to thank. She has never forgiven me—I think she's off her head. Her name isn't Geraldine at all and I doubt very much if that's her address.'

'Ah, what is her name?' Lyon asked, most attentive. The details always began to multiply, to abound, when once his companion was well launched—they flowed forth in battalions.

'It's Pearson—Harriet Pearson; but she used to call herself Grenadine—wasn't that a rum appellation? Grenadine—Geraldine —the jump was easy.' Lyon was charmed with the promptitude of this response, and his interlocutor went on: 'I hadn't thought of her for years—I had quite lost sight of her. I don't know what her idea is, but practically she's harmless. As I came in I thought I saw her a little way up the road. She must have found out I come here and have arrived before me. I daresay—or rather I'm sure—she is waiting for me there now.'

'Hadn't you better have protection?' Lyon asked, laughing.

'The best protection is five shillings—I'm willing to go that length. Unless indeed she has a bottle of vitriol. But they only throw vitriol on the men who have deceived them, and I never deceived her—I told her the first time I saw her that it wouldn't do. Oh, if she's there we'll walk a little way together and talk it over and, as I say, I'll go as far as five shillings.'

'Well,' said Lyon, 'I'll contribute another five.' He felt that this was little to pay for his entertainment.

That entertainment was interrupted however for the time by the Colonel's departure. Lyon hoped for a letter recounting the fictive sequel; but apparently his brilliant sitter did not operate with the pen. At any rate he left town without writing; they had taken a rendezvous for three months later. Oliver Lyon always passed the holidays in the same way; during the first weeks he paid a visit to his elder brother, the happy possesser, in the south of England, of a rambling old house with formal gardens, in which he delighted, and then he went abroad—usually to Italy or Spain. This year he carried out his custom after taking a last look at his all but finished work and feeling as nearly pleased with it as he ever felt with the translation of the idea by the hand—always, as it seemed to him, a pitiful compromise. One yellow afternoon, in the country, as he was smoking his pipe on one of the old terraces he was seized with the desire to see it again and do two or three things more to it: he had thought of it so often while he lounged there. The impulse was too strong to be dismissed, and though he expected to return to town in the course of another week he was unable to face the delay. To look at the picture for five minutes would be enough—it would clear up certain questions which hummed in his brain, so that the next morning, to give himself this luxury, he took the train for London. He sent no word in advance; he would lunch at his club and probably return into Sussex by the 5.45.

In St. John's Wood the tide of human life flows at no time very fast, and in the first days of September Lyon found unmitigated emptiness in the straight sunny roads where the little plastered garden-walls, with their incommunicative doors, looked slightly Oriental. There was definite stillness in his own house, to which he admitted himself by his pass-key, having a theory that it was well sometimes to take servants unprepared. The good woman who was mainly in charge and who cumulated the functions of cook and housekeeper was, however, quickly summoned by his step, and (he cultivated frankness of intercourse with his domestics) received him without the confusion of surprise. He told her that she needn't mind the place being not quite straight, he had only come up for a few hours—he should be busy in the studio. To this she replied that he was just in time to see a lady and a gentleman who were there at the moment—they had arrived five minutes before. She had told them he was away from home but they said it was all right; they only wanted to look at a picture and would be very careful of everything. 'I hope it is all right, sir,' the housekeeper concluded. 'The gentleman says he's a sitter and he gave me his name—rather an odd name; I think it's military. The lady's a very fine lady, sir; at any rate there they are.'

'Oh, it's all right,' Lyon said, the identity of his vistors being clear. The good woman couldn't know, for she usually had little to do with the comings and goings; his man, who showed people in and out, had accompanied him to the country. He was a good deal surprised at Mrs. Capadose's having come to see her husband's portrait when she knew that the artist himself wished her to forbear; but it was a familiar truth to him that she was a woman of a high spirit. Besides, perhaps the lady was not Mrs. Capadose; the Colonel might have brought some inquisitive friend, a person who wanted a portrait of *her* husband. What were they doing in town, at any rate, at that moment? Lyon made his way to the studio with a certain curiosity; he wondered vaguely what his friends were 'up to.' He pushed aside the curtain that hung in the door of communication—the door opening upon the gallery which it had been found convenient to construct at the time the studio was added to the house. When I say he pushed it aside I should amend my phrase; he laid his hand upon it, but at that moment he was arrested by a very singular sound. It came from the floor of the room beneath him and it startled him extremely, consisting apparently as it did of a passionate wail—a sort of smothered shriek—accompanied by a violent burst of tears. Oliver Lyon listened intently a moment, and then he passed out upon the balcony, which was

covered with an old thick Moorish rug. His step was noiseless,
though he had not endeavoured to make it so, and after that first
instant he found himself profiting irresistibly by the accident of
his not having attracted the attention of the two persons in the
studio, who were some twenty feet below him. In truth they were
so deeply and so strangely engaged that their unconsciousness of
observation was explained. The scene that took place before Lyon's
eyes was one of the most extraordinary they had ever rested upon.
Delicacy and the failure to comprehend kept him at first from
interrupting it—for what he saw was a woman who had thrown
herself in a flood of tears on her companion's bosom—and these
influences were succeeded after a minute (the minutes were very
few and very short) by a definite motive which presently had the
force to make him step back behind the curtain. I may add that it
also had the force to make him avail himself for further contemplation of a crevice formed by his gathering together the two
halves of the *portière*. He was perfectly aware of what he was
about—he was for the moment an eavesdropper, a spy; but he was
also aware that a very odd business, in which his confidence had
been trifled with, was going forward, and that if in a measure it
didn't concern him, in a measure it very definitely did. His observation, his reflections, accomplished themselves in a flash.

His visitors were in the middle of the room; Mrs. Capadose clung
to her husband, weeping, sobbing as if her heart would break. Her
distress was horrible to Oliver Lyon but his astonishment was
greater than his horror when he heard the Colonel respond to it by
the words, vehemently uttered, 'Damn him, damn him, damn him!'
What in the world had happened? why was she sobbing and whom
was he damning? What had happened, Lyon saw the next instant,
was that the Colonel had finally rummaged out his unfinished
portrait (he knew the corner where the artist usually placed it,
out of the way, with its face to the wall) and had set it up before
his wife on an empty easel. She had looked at it a few moments
and then—apparently—what she saw in it had produced an ex
plosion of dismay and resentment. She was too busy sobbing and
the Colonel was too busy holding her and reiterating his objurga
tion, to look round or look up. The scene was so unexpected to
Lyon that he could not take it, on the spot, as a proof of the
triumph of his hand—of a tremendous hit: he could only wonde

what on earth was the matter. The idea of the triumph came a
little later. Yet he could see the portrait from where he stood; he
was startled with its look of life—he had not thought it so masterly.
Mrs. Capadose flung herself away from her husband—she dropped
into the nearest chair, buried her face in her arms, leaning on a
table. Her weeping suddenly ceased to be audible, but she
shuddered there as if she were overwhelmed with anguish and
shame. Her husband remained a moment staring at the picture;
then he went to her, bent over her, took hold of her again, soothed
her. 'What is it, darling, what the devil is it?' he demanded.

Lyon heard her answer. 'It's cruel—oh, it's too cruel!'

'Damn him—damn him—damn him!' the Colonel repeated.

'It's all there—it's all there!' Mrs. Capadose went on.

'Hang it, what's all there?'

'Everything there oughtn't to be—everything he has seen—it's
too dreadful!'

'Everything he has seen? Why, ain't I a good-looking fellow?
He has made me rather handsome.'

Mrs. Capadose had sprung up again; she had darted another
glance at the painted betrayal. 'Handsome? Hideous, hideous! Not
that—never, never!'

'Not *what*, in heaven's name?' the Colonel almost shouted. Lyon
could see his flushed, bewildered face.

'What he has made of you—what you know! *He* knows—he has
seen. Every one will know—every one will see. Fancy that thing
in the Academy!'

'You're going wild, darling; but if you hate it so it needn't go.'

'Oh, he'll send it—it's so good! Come away—come away!' Mrs.
Capadose wailed, seizing her husband.

'It's so good?' the poor man cried.

'Come away—come away,' she only repeated, and she turned
toward the staircase that ascended to the gallery.

'Not that way—not through the house, in the state you're in,'
Lyon heard the Colonel object. 'This way—we can pass,' he added;
and he drew his wife to the small door that opened into the garden.
It was bolted, but he pushed the bolt and opened the door. She
passed out quickly, but he stood there looking back into the room.
'Wait for me a moment!' he cried out to her; and with an excited
stride he re-entered the studio. He came up to the picture again,

and again he stood looking at it. 'Damn him—damn him—damn him!' he broke out once more. It was not clear to Lyon whether this malediction had for its object the original or the painter of the portrait. The Colonel turned away and moved rapidly about the room, as if he were looking for something; Lyon was unable for the instant to guess his intention. Then the artist said to himself, below his breath, 'He's going to do it a harm!' His first impulse was to rush down and stop him; but he paused, with the sound of Everina Brant's sobs still in his ears. The Colonel found what he was looking for—found it among some odds and ends on a small table and rushed back with it to the easel. At one and the same moment Lyon perceived that the object he had seized was a small Eastern dagger and that he had plunged it into the canvas. He seemed animated by a sudden fury, for with extreme vigour of hand he dragged the instrument down (Lyon knew it to have no very fine edge) making a long, abominable gash. Then he plucked it out and dashed it again several times into the face of the likeness, exactly as if he were stabbing a human victim: it had the oddest effect—that of a sort of figurative suicide. In a few seconds more the Colonel had tossed the dagger away—he looked at it as he did so, as if he expected it to reek with blood—and hurried out of the place, closing the door after him.

The strangest part of all was—as will doubtless appear—that Oliver Lyon made no movement to save his picture. But he did not feel as if he were losing it or cared not if he were, so much more did he feel that he was gaining a certitude. His old friend *was* ashamed of her husband, and he had made her so, and he had scored a great success, even though the picture had been reduced to rags. The revelation excited him so—as indeed the whole scene did—that when he came down the steps after the Colonel had gone he trembled with his happy agitation; he was dizzy and had to sit down a moment. The portrait had a dozen jagged wounds—the Colonel literally had hacked it to death. Lyon left it where it was, never touched it, scarcely looked at it; he only walked up and down his studio, still excited, for an hour. At the end of this time his good woman came to recommend that he should have some luncheon; there was a passage under the staircase from the offices

'Ah, the lady and gentleman have gone, sir? I didn't hear them.

'Yes; they went by the garden.'

But she had stopped, staring at the picture on the easel. 'Gracious, how you *'ave* served it, sir!'

Lyon imitated the Colonel. 'Yes, I cut it up—in a fit of disgust.'

'Mercy, after all your trouble! Because they weren't pleased, sir?'

'Yes; they weren't pleased.'

'Well, they must be very grand! Blessed if I would!'

'Have it chopped up; it will do to light fires,' Lyon said.

He returned to the country by the 3.30 and a few days later passed over to France. During the two months that he was absent from England he expected something—he could hardly have said what; a manifestation of some sort on the Colonel's part. Wouldn't he write, wouldn't he explain, wouldn't he take for granted Lyon had discovered the way he had, as the cook said, served him and deem it only decent to take pity in some fashion or other on his mystification? Would he plead guilty or would he repudiate suspicion? The latter course would be difficult and make a considerable draft upon his genius, in view of the certain testimony of Lyon's housekeeper, who had admitted the visitors and would establish the connection between their presence and the violence wrought. Would the Colonel proffer some apology or some amends, or would any word from him be only a further expression of that destructive petulance which our friend had seen his wife so suddenly and so potently communicate to him? He would have either to declare that he had not touched the picture or to admit that he had, and in either case he would have to tell a fine story. Lyon was impatient for the story and, as no letter came, disappointed that it was not produced. His impatience however was much greater in respect to Mrs. Capadose's version, if version there was to be; for certainly that would be the real test, would show how far she would go for her husband, on the one side, or for him, Oliver Lyon, on the other. He could scarcely wait to see what line she would take; whether she would simply adopt the Colonel's, whatever it might be. He wanted to draw her out without waiting, to get an idea in advance. He wrote to her, to this end, from Venice, in the tone of their established friendship, asking for news, narrating his wanderings, hoping they should soon meet in town and not saying a word about the picture. Day followed day, after the time, and he received no answer; upon which he reflected that she couldn't trust herself to write—was still too much under the influence of the emotion produced by his 'betrayal.' Her husband

has espoused that emotion and she had espoused the action he had
taken in consequence of it, and it was a complete rupture and
everything was at an end. Lyon considered this prospect rather
ruefully, at the same time that he thought it deplorable that such
charming people should have put themselves so grossly in the
wrong. He was at last cheered, though little further enlightened,
by the arrival of a letter, brief but breathing good-humour and
hinting neither at a grievance nor at a bad conscience. The most
interesting part of it to Lyon was the postscript, which consisted
of these words: 'I have a confession to make to you. We were in
town for a couple of days, the 1st of September, and I took the
occasion to defy your authority—it was very bad of me but I
couldn't help it. I made Clement take me to your studio—I wanted
so dreadfully to see what you had done with him, your wishes to
the contrary notwithstanding. We made your servants let us in and
I took a good look at the picture. It is really wonderful!' 'Wonderful' was non-committal, but at least with this letter there was no
rupture.

The third day after Lyon's return to London was a Sunday, so
that he could go and ask Mrs. Capadose for luncheon. She had
given him in the spring a general invitation to do so and he had
availed himself of it several times. These had been the occasions
(before he sat to him) when he saw the Colonel most familiarly.
Directly after the meal his host disappeared (he went out, as he
said, to call on *his* women) and the second half-hour was the best,
even when there were other people. Now, in the first days of
December, Lyon had the luck to find the pair alone, without
even Amy, who appeared but little in public. They were in the
drawing-room, waiting for the repast to be announced, and as soon
as he came in the Colonel broke out, 'My dear fellow, I'm delighted
to see you! I'm so keen to begin again.'

'Oh, do go on, it's so beautiful,' Mrs. Capadose said, as she gave
him her hand.

Lyon looked from one to the other; he didn't know what he
had expected, but he had not expected this. 'Ah, then, you think
I've got something?'

'You've got everything,' said Mrs. Capadose, smiling from her
golden-brown eyes.

'She wrote you of our little crime?' her husband asked. 'She dragged me there—I had to go.' Lyon wondered for a moment whether he meant by their little crime the assault on the canvas; but the Colonel's next words didn't confirm this interpretation. 'You know I like to sit—it gives such a chance to my *bavardise*. And just now I have time.'

'You must remember I had almost finished,' Lyon remarked.

'So you had. More's the pity. I should like you to begin again.'

'My dear fellow, I shall have to begin again!' said Oliver Lyon with a laugh, looking at Mrs. Capadose. She did not meet his eyes— she had got up to ring for luncheon. 'The picture has been smashed,' Lyon continued.

'Smashed? Ah, what did you do that for?' Mrs. Capadose asked, standing there before him in all her clear, rich beauty. Now that she looked at him she was impenetrable.

'I didn't—I found it so—with a dozen holes punched in it!'

'I say!' cried the Colonel.

Lyon turned his eyes to him, smiling. 'I hope *you* didn't do it?'

'Is it ruined?' the Colonel inquired. He was as brightly true as his wife and he looked simply as if Lyon's question could not be serious. 'For the love of sitting to you? My dear fellow, if I had thought of it I would!'

'Nor you either?' the painter demanded of Mrs. Capadose.

Before she had time to reply her husband had seized her arm, as if a highly suggestive idea had come to him. 'I say, my dear, that woman—that woman!'

'That woman?' Mrs. Capadose repeated; and Lyon too wondered what woman he meant.

'Don't you remember when we came out, she was at the door— or a little way from it? I spoke to you of her—I told you about her. Geraldine—Grenadine—the one who burst in that day,' he explained to Lyon. 'We saw her hanging about—I called Everina's attention to her.'

'Do you mean she got at my picture?'

'Ah yes, I remember,' said Mrs. Capadose, with a sigh.

'She burst in again—she had learned the way—she was waiting for her chance,' the Colonel continued. 'Ah, the little brute!'

Lyon looked down; he felt himself colouring. This was what he had been waiting for—the day the Colonel should wantonly sacrifice some innocent person. And could his wife be a party to that final atrocity? Lyon had reminded himself repeatedly during the previous weeks that when the Colonel perpetrated his misdeed she had already quitted the room; but he had argued none the less—it was a virtual certainty—that he had on rejoining her immediately made his achievement plain to her. He was in the flush of performance; and even if he had not mentioned what he had done she would have guessed it. He did not for an instant believe that poor Miss Geraldine had been hovering about his door, nor had the account given by the Colonel the summer before of his relations with this lady deceived him in the slightest degree. Lyon had never seen her before the day she planted herself in his studio; but he knew her and classified her as if he had made her. He was acquainted with the London female model in all her varieties—in every phase of her development and every step of her decay. When he entered his house that September morning just after the arrival of his two friends there had been no symptoms whatever, up and down the road, of Miss Geraldine's reappearance. That fact had been fixed in his mind by his recollecting the vacancy of the prospect when his cook told him that a lady and a gentleman were in his studio: he had wondered there was not a carriage nor a cab at his door. Then he had reflected that they would have come by the underground railway; he was close to the Marlborough Road station and he knew the Colonel, coming to his sittings, more than once had availed himself of that convenience. 'How in the world did she get in?' He addressed the question to his companions indifferently.

'Let us go down to luncheon,' said Mrs. Capadose, passing out of the room.

'We went by the garden—without troubling your servant—I wanted to show my wife.' Lyon followed his hostess with her husband and the Colonel stopped him at the top of the stairs. 'My dear fellow, I *can't* have been guilty of the folly of not fastening the door?'

'I am sure I don't know, Colonel,' Lyon said as they went down. 'It was a very determined hand—a perfect wild-cat.'

'Well, she *is* a wild-cat—confound her! That's why I wanted to get him away from her.'

'But I don't understand her motive.'

'She's off her head—and she hates me; that was her motive.'

'But she doesn't hate me, my dear fellow!' Lyon said, laughing.

'She hated the picture—don't you remember she said so? The more portraits there are the less employment for such as her.'

'Yes; but if she is not really the model she pretends to be, how can that hurt her?' Lyon asked.

The inquiry baffled the Colonel an instant—but only an instant. 'Ah, she was in a vicious muddle! As I say, she's off her head.'

They went into the dining-room, where Mrs. Capadose was taking her place. 'It's too bad, it's too horrid!' she said. 'You see the fates are against you. Providence won't let you be so disinterested— painting masterpieces for nothing.'

'Did *you* see the woman?' Lyon demanded, with something like a sternness that he could not mitigate.

Mrs. Capadose appeared not to perceive it or not to heed it if she did. 'There was a person, not far from your door, whom Clement called my attention to. He told me something about her but we were going the other way.'

'And do you think she did it?'

'How can I tell? If she did she was mad, poor wretch.'

'I should like very much to get hold of her,' said Lyon. This was a false statement, for he had no desire for any further conversation with Miss Geraldine. He had exposed his friends to himself, but he had no desire to expose them to any one else, least of all to themselves.

'Oh, depend upon it she will never show again. You're safe!' the Colonel exclaimed.

'But I remember her address—Mortimer Terrace Mews, Notting Hill.'

'Oh, that's pure humbug; there isn't any such place.'

'Lord, what a deceiver!' said Lyon.

'Is there any one else you suspect?' the Colonel went on.

'Not a creature.'

'And what do your servants say?'

'They say it wasn't *them*, and I reply that I never said it was. That's about the substance of our conferences.'

'And when did they discover the havoc?'

'They never discovered it at all. I noticed it first—when I came back.'

'Well, she could easily have stepped in,' said the Colonel. 'Don't you remember how she turned up that day, like the clown in the ring?'

'Yes, yes; she could have done the job in three seconds, except that the picture wasn't out.'

'My dear fellow, don't curse me!—but of course I dragged it out.'

'You didn't put it back?' Lyon asked tragically.

'Ah, Clement, Clement, didn't I tell you to?' Mrs. Capadose exclaimed in a tone of exquisite reproach.

The Colonel groaned, dramatically; he covered his face with his hands. His wife's words were for Lyon the finishing touch; they made his whole vision crumble—his theory that she had secretly kept herself true. Even to her old lover she wouldn't be so! He was sick; he couldn't eat; he knew that he looked very strange. He murmured something about it being useless to cry over spilled milk—he tried to turn the conversation to other things. But it was a horrid effort and he wondered whether they felt it as much as he. He wondered all sorts of things: whether they guessed he disbelieved them (that he had seen them of course they would never guess); whether they had arranged their story in advance or it was only an inspiration of the moment; whether she had resisted, protested, when the Colonel proposed it to her, and then had been borne down by him; whether in short she didn't loathe herself as she sat there. The cruelty, the cowardice of fastening their unholy act upon the wretched woman struck him as monstrous— no less monstrous indeed than the levity that could make them run the risk of her giving them, in her righteous indignation, the lie. Of course that risk could only exculpate her and not inculpate them—the probabilities protected them so perfectly; and what the Colonel counted on (what he would have counted upon the day he delivered himself, after first seeing her, at the studio, if he had thought about the matter then at all and not spoken from the pure spontaneity of his genius) was simply that Miss Geraldine had really vanished for ever into her native unknown. Lyon wanted so much to quit the subject that when after a little Mrs. Capadose said to him, 'But can nothing be done, can't the picture be repaired? You know they do such wonders in that way now,' he only replied, 'I don't know, I don't care, it's all over, *n'en parlons plus!*' Her hypocrisy revolted him. And yet, by way of plucking off the last veil of her shame, he broke out to her again, shortly afterward, 'And you *did* like it, really?' To which she returned, looking him straight in his face, without a blush, a pallor, an evasion, 'Oh, I loved it!' Truly her husband had trained her well. After that Lyon said no more and his companions forbore temporarily to insist, like people of tact and sympathy aware that the odious accident had made him sore.

When they quitted the table the Colonel went away without coming upstairs; but Lyon returned to the drawing-room with his hostess, remarking to her however on the way that he could remain but a moment. He spent that moment—it prolonged itself a little—standing with her before the chimney-piece. She neither sat down nor asked him to; her manner denoted that she intended to go out. Yes, her husband had trained her well; yet Lyon dreamed for a moment that now he was alone with her she would perhaps break down, retract, apologise, confide, say to him, 'My dear old friend, forgive this hideous comedy—you understand!' And then how he would have loved her and pitied her, guarded her, helped her always! If she were not ready to do something of that sort why had she treated him as if he were a dear old friend; why had she let him for months suppose certain things—or almost; why had she come to his studio day after day to sit near him on the pretext of her child's portrait, as if she liked to think what might have been? Why had she come so near a tacit confession, in a word, if she was not willing to go an inch further? And she was not willing—she was not; he could see that as he lingered there. She moved about the room a little, rearranging two or three objects on the tables, but she did nothing more. Suddenly he said to her: 'Which way was she going, when you came out?'

'She—the woman we saw?'

'Yes, your husband's strange friend. It's a clew worth following.' He had no desire to frighten her; he only wanted to communicate the impulse which would make her say, 'Ah, spare me—and spare *him!* There was no such person.'

Instead of this Mrs. Capadose replied, 'She was going away from us—she crossed the road. We were coming towards the station.'

'And did she appear to recognise the Colonel—did she look round?'

'Yes; she looked round, but I didn't notice much. A hansom came along and we got into it. It was not till then that Clement told me

who she was: I remember he said that she was there for no good.
I suppose we ought to have gone back.'

'Yes; you would have saved the picture.'

For a moment she said nothing; then she smiled. 'For you, I am
very sorry. But you must remember that I possess the original!'

At this Lyon turned away. 'Well, I must go,' he said; and he left
her without any other farewell and made his way out of the house.
As he went slowly up the street the sense came back to him of
that first glimpse of her he had had at Stayes—the way he had seen
her gaze across the table at her husband. Lyon stopped at the
corner, looking vaguely up and down. He would never go back—he
couldn't. She was still in love with the Colonel—he had trained
her too well.

STUDY

❦

The Notebooks of Henry James

F. O. MATTHIESSEN AND KENNETH B. MURDOCK (eds.) *

[Entry dated June 19, 1884]

One might write a tale (very short) about a woman married to a
man of the most amiable character who is a tremendous, though
harmless, liar. She is very intelligent, a fine, quiet, high, pure
nature, and she has to sit by and hear him romance—mainly out
of vanity, the desire to be interesting, and a peculiar irresistible
impulse. He is good, kind, personally very attractive, very handsome, etc.: it is almost his only fault though of course he is increasingly very *light*. What she suffers—what she goes through—
generally she tries to rectify, to remove any bad effect by toning
down a little, etc. But there comes a day when he tells a very big
lie which she has—for reasons to be related—to adopt, to reinforce.

* FROM *The Notebooks of Henry James,* edited by F. O. Matthiessen and
Kenneth B. Murdock. Copyright, 1947, by Oxford University Press Inc. Reprinted by permission.

To save him from exposure, in a word, she has to lie herself. The struggle, etc.; she lies—but after that she hates him (*Numa Roumestan*).

*   *   *

[The change in the ending of "The Liar" as James actually wrote it] increases the effectiveness of the story by making it almost a case of the "possession" of a pure spirit by an impure one, and by saving it from the relative banality of a presentation simply of a wife loyal to her husband under unpleasant circumstances.

The Aspern Papers and Other Tales

HENRY JAMES[*]
Preface [1907–1909]

[I] come back, for "The Liar," . . . to holding my personal experience . . . immediately accountable. For by what else . . . but by fatal design had I been placed at dinner one autumn evening of old London days face to face with a gentleman, met for the first time, though favourably known to me by name and fame, in whom I recognised the most unbridled colloquial romancer the "joy of life" had ever found occasion to envy? Under what other conceivable coercion had I been invited to reckon, through the evening, with the type, with the character, with the countenance, of this magnificent master's wife, who, veracious, serene and charming, yet not once meeting straight the eyes of one of us, did her duty by each, and by her husband most of all, without so much as . . . turning a hair? It was long ago, but I have never, to this hour, forgotten the evening itself. . . . I made but a fifth person, the other couple our host and hostess; between whom and one of the company, while we listened to the woven wonders of a summer holiday, the exploits of a salamander, among Mediterranean isles, were exchanged, dimly and discreetly, ever so guardedly, but all expressively, imperceptible lingering looks. It was exquisite, it *could* but become, inevitably, some "short story" or other, which it clearly pre-fitted as the hand the glove.

The Art of Modern Fiction

Ray B. West, Jr. and Robert Wooster Stallman[*]

Lyon is ignorant of the doom and disillusionment he is heading
for, the ironic consequences of his whole scheming.

The whole meaning of "The Liar" emerges from Lyon's defeat,
not from the humiliation and defeat of the Capadoses. . . . The
Capadoses get their due. But so does Lyon. And Lyon deserves
the punishment meted out to him, not only as a kind of poetic
justice for his machinations against the Capadoses, but, more
significantly, because he has committed an offense against society,
or, as it were, against the gods of society. His stripping of the social
mask, we are made to feel, constitutes a breach of the mores, a
betrayal of the social codes whose mechanism must be preserved
even though it produces hypocrisies and grinds out falsities instead of truths. *Irony thus inheres in the very theme of the story.
And it inheres too in the author's world view or outlook on life.*
The ironic will that mocks the deluded hero imparts the voice of
Henry James dictating the law of the golden mean. . . .

Life . . . is a masking. At *that*, the Capadoses are artists—she
in her way and he in his. Mrs. Capadose . . . has no illusions
about her husband's character. Nor has the Colonel himself. . . .
The "painted betrayal" exposes not one liar but two. For Mrs.
Capadose's portrait is, so to speak, superimposed upon that of her
husband.

But this disclosure of their corruption is, ironically, wholly at
Lyon's expense. It has cost him the loss of his ideal. Seeing her
now, finally, for what she is, "Her hypocrisy revolted him." It is
his moral being, not hers, that suffers the disillusioning shock. Her
life, no less than her husband's, is a lie—with the difference that
her life wears "an inscrutable mask." But, after all, duplicity patterns the life of everyone engaged in the social game. In society,
if not in all human relationships, the wearing of the mask is a
necessity, and hence there is for the Capadoses this social—and
indeed this moral—justification for not declaring their crime. The
precept was declared by Lyon himself when he observed to his
dinner companion that we like people in proportion as they de-

[*] (New York, Holt, Rinehart & Winston, Inc., 1949.) By permission.

ceive, so long as we don't find them out. It is ironic that Lyon, holding this cynical view of the world, should contrive, at the risk of his finding out, the unmasking of the woman he loves.

"*Appearance and Reality in Henry James*"

MARIUS BEWLEY*

[It is easy to read "The Liar"] without its occurring to anyone that the essential question is: Who is the liar? [This] ambiguity is . . . intricately embedded in the narrative. . . .

[Lyon allows his gift of the daughter's portrait] to form the prelude towards his asking, as a special favour, that Colonel Capadose should also sit for his portrait—the object merely being that Lyon, as he tells them, wishes to render the Colonel's interesting face as a subject pre-eminently suitable to his art. James puts it in these terms:

> The desire grew in him to paint the Colonel also—an operation from which he promised himself a rich private satisfaction. He would draw him out, he would set him in that totality about which he had talked with Sir David, and none but the initiated would know. They, however, would rank the picture high, and it would be indeed six rows deep—a masterpiece of subtle characterization, of legitimate treachery.

The Colonel, out of amiability, consents to sit, and as the portrait grows under Lyon's hand, the "legitimate treachery" of Lyon's original intention also grows:

> The only point that troubled him was the idea that when he should send his picture to the Academy he should not be able to give the title, for the catalogue, simply as "The Liar." However, it little mattered, for he had now determined that his character should be perceptible even to the meanest intelligence—as overtopping as it had become to his own sense of the living man.

Two things are worth noting here. First: that reference to the quality of the future audience is significant. It supplies a clue to what is happening in Lyon's consciousness. He no longer looks for

* FROM *Scrutiny*, XVII (Summer, 1950) and *The Complex Fate* (London, Chatto & Windus, Ltd., 1952). By permission.

fineness of appreciation, but has grown eager for the most vulgar public applause, whereas a few pages earlier he had wished to appeal only to the initiated few. Now, to secure this applause, he is willing to betray his friendship with Mrs. Capadose, and simulate a friendship with the husband that is entirely a lie. Second: his static conception of Colonel Capadose as a liar has blotted out any finer sense of the Colonel as a human being. It has become completely "overtopping . . . to his own sense of the living man." Oliver Lyon is on the point of committing that crime which for both Hawthorne and James was the worst possible: of violating the integrity of another man's personality, of seeking to take possession of it through false images and conventional laws.

But Lyon's treachery is deeper yet. He hopes, by exposing the husband to public scorn, to enter into an emotional union with the wife—a kind of adulterous liaison of the spirit in which the two lovers of earlier years will find a deeper communion than ever yet in the sense of the wife's revulsion from the vulgarity of her lying husband. Having earlier failed to marry her, Lyon's triumph will be the final one. . . . But in actual fact things do not work out as Lyon wishes. . . . [When] Colonel Capadose denies the act of vandalism his wife supports her husband in the lie—supports him wholeheartedly, beautifully, competently. She is thus presented to the reader through Lyon's eyes as a contaminated nature, and a shudder is invited. But in actual fact it is only Mrs. Capadose who has known how to discriminate between appearance and reality in this story, who knows that it is not her husband but Lyon who is the liar.

The Real Thing

[1892]

❧

I

WHEN THE PORTER'S WIFE (she used to answer the house-bell), announced "A gentleman—with a lady, sir," I had, as I often had in those days, for the wish was father to the thought, an immediate vision of sitters. Sitters my visitors in this case proved to be; but not in the sense I should have preferred. However, there was nothing at first to indicate that they might not have come for a portrait. The gentleman, a man of fifty, very high and very straight, with a moustache slightly grizzled and a dark grey walking-coat admirably fitted, both of which I noted professionally—I don't mean as a barber or yet as a tailor—would have struck me as a celebrity if celebrities often were striking. It was a truth of which I had for some time been conscious that a figure with a good deal of frontage was, as one might say, almost never a public institution. A glance at the lady helped to remind me of this paradoxical law: she also looked too distinguished to be a "personality." Moreover one would scarcely come across two variations together.

Neither of the pair spoke immediately—they only prolonged the preliminary gaze which suggested that each wished to give the other a chance. They were visibly shy; they stood there letting me take them in—which, as I afterwards perceived, was the most practical thing they could have done. In this way their embarrassment served their cause. I had seen people painfully reluctant to mention that they desired anything so gross as to be represented on canvas, but the scruples of my new friends appeared almost insurmountable. Yet the gentleman might have said "I should like a portrait of my wife," and the lady might have said "I should like a portrait of my husband." Perhaps they were not husband and wife—this naturally would make the matter more delicate. Per-

FROM *The Real Thing* (New York, Macmillan & Co., 1893).

haps they wished to be done together—in which case they ought to have brought a third person to break the news.

"We come from Mr. Rivet," the lady said at last, with a dim smile which had the effect of a moist sponge passed over a "sunk" piece of painting, as well as of a vague allusion to vanished beauty. She was as tall and straight, in her degree, as her companion, and with ten years less to carry. She looked as sad as a woman could look whose face was not charged with expression; that is her tinted oval mask showed friction as an exposed surface shows it. The hand of time had played over her freely, but only to simplify. She was slim and stiff, and so well-dressed, in dark blue cloth, with lappets and pockets and buttons, that it was clear she employed the same tailor as her husband. The couple had an indefinable air of prosperous thrift—they evidently got a good deal of luxury for their money. If I was to be one of their luxuries it would behoove me to consider my terms.

"Ah, Claude Rivet recommended me?" I inquired; and I added that it was very kind of him, though I could reflect that, as he only painted landscape, this was not a sacrifice.

The lady looked very hard at the gentleman, and the gentleman looked round the room. Then staring at the floor a moment and stroking his moustache, he rested his pleasant eyes on me with the remark: "He said you were the right one."

"I try to be, when people want to sit."

"Yes, we should like to," said the lady anxiously.

"Do you mean together?"

My visitors exchanged a glance. "If you could do anything with *me,* I suppose it would be double," the gentleman stammered.

"Oh yes, there's naturally a higher charge for two figures than for one."

"We should like to make it pay," the husband confessed.

"That's very good of you," I returned, appreciating so unwonted a sympathy—for I supposed he meant pay the artist.

A sense of strangeness seemed to dawn on the lady. "We mean for the illustrations—Mr. Rivet said you might put one in."

"Put one in—an illustration?" I was equally confused.

"Sketch her off, you know," said the gentleman, colouring.

It was only then that I understood the service Claude Rivet had rendered me; he had told them that I worked in black-and-white, for magazines, for storybooks, for sketches of contemporary life, and consequently had frequent employment for models. These things were true, but it was not less true (I may confess it now—whether because the aspiration was to lead to everything or to nothing I leave the reader to guess), that I couldn't get the honours, to say nothing of the emoluments, of a great painter of portraits out of my head. My "illustrations" were my pot-boilers; I looked to a different branch of art (far and away the most interesting it had always seemed to me) to perpetuate my fame. There was no shame in looking to it also to make my fortune; but that fortune was by so much further from being made from the moment my visitors wished to be "done" for nothing. I was disappointed; for in the pictorial sense I had immediately *seen* them. I had seized their type—I had already settled what I would do with it. Something that wouldn't absolutely have pleased them, I afterwards reflected.

"Ah you're—you're—a—?" I began as soon as I had mastered my surprise. I couldn't bring out the dingy word "models": it seemed to fit the case so little.

"We haven't had much practice," said the lady.

"We've got to *do* something, and we've thought that an artist in your line might perhaps make something of us," her husband threw off. He further mentioned that they didn't know many artists and that they had gone first, on the off-chance (he painted views of course, but sometimes put in figures—perhaps I remembered), to Mr. Rivet, whom they had met a few years before at a place in Norfolk where he was sketching.

"We used to sketch a little ourselves," the lady hinted.

"It's very awkward, but we absolutely *must* do something," her husband went on.

"Of course, we're not so *very* young," she admitted, with a wan smile.

With the remark that I might as well know something more about them, the husband had handed me a card extracted from a neat new pocket-book (their appurtenances were all of the freshest) and inscribed with the words "Major Monarch." Impressive as these words were they didn't carry my knowledge much further; but my visitor presently added: "I've left the army, and we've had the misfortune to lose our money. In fact our means are dreadfully small."

"It's an awful bore," said Mrs. Monarch.

They evidently wished to be discreet—to take care not to swagger because they were gentlefolks. I perceived they would have been willing to recognise this as something of a drawback, at the same time that I guessed at an underlying sense—their consolation in adversity—that they *had* their points. They certainly had; but these advantages struck me as preponderantly social; such for instance as would help to make a drawing-room look well. However, a drawing-room was always, or ought to be, a picture.

In consequence of his wife's allusion to their age Major Monarch observed: "Naturally, it's more for the figure that we thought of going in. We can still hold ourselves up." On the instant I saw that the figure was indeed their strong point. His "naturally" didn't sound vain, but it lighted up the question. "*She* has got the best," he continued, nodding at his wife, with a pleasant after-dinner absence of circumlocution. I could only reply, as if we were in fact sitting over our wine, that this didn't prevent his own from being very good; which led him in turn to rejoin: "We thought that if you ever have to do people like us, we might be something like it. *She* particularly—for a lady in a book, you know."

I was so amused by them that, to get more of it, I did my best to take their point of view; and though it was an embarrassment to find myself appraising physically, as if they were animals on hire or useful blacks, a pair whom I should have expected to meet only in one of the relations in which criticism is tacit, I looked at Mrs. Monarch judicially enough to be able to exclaim, after a moment, with conviction: "Oh yes, a lady in a book!" She was singularly like a bad illustration.

"We'll stand up, if you like," said the Major; and he raised himself before me with a really grand air.

I could take his measure at a glance—he was six feet two and a perfect gentleman. It would have paid any club in process of formation and in want of a stamp to engage him at a salary to stand in the principal window. What struck me immediately was that in coming to me they had rather missed their vocation; they could surely have been turned to better account for advertising purposes. I couldn't of course see the thing in detail, but I could see them make someone's fortune—I don't mean their own. There was something in them for a waistcoat-maker, an hotel-keeper or a soap-vendor. I could imagine "We always use it" pinned on their bosoms with the greatest effect; I had a vision of the promptitude with which they would launch a table d'hôte.

Mrs. Monarch sat still, not from pride but from shyness, and presently her husband said to her: "Get up, my dear, and show how smart you are." She obeyed, but she had no need to get up to show it. She walked to the end of the studio, and then she came back blushing, her fluttered eyes on her husband. I was reminded of an incident I had accidentally had a glimpse of in Paris—being with a friend there, a dramatist about to produce a play—when an actress came to him to ask to be entrusted with a part. She went through her paces before him, walked up and down as Mrs. Monarch was doing. Mrs. Monarch did it quite as well, but I abstained from applauding. It was very odd to see such people apply for such poor pay. She looked as if she had ten thousand a year. Her husband had used the word that described her: she was, in the London current jargon, essentially and typically "smart." Her figure was, in the same order of ideas, conspicuously and irreproachably "good." For a woman of her age her waist was surprisingly small; her elbow moreover had the orthodox crook. She held her head at the conventional angle; but why did she come to *me?* She ought to have tried on jackets at a big shop. I feared my visitors were not only destitute, but "artistic"—which would be a great complication. When she sat down again I thanked her, observing that what a draughtsman most valued in his model was the faculty of keeping quiet.

"Oh, *she* can keep quiet," said Major Monarch. Then he added, jocosely: "I've always kept her quiet."

"I'm not a nasty fidget, am I?" Mrs. Monarch appealed to her husband.

He addressed his answer to me. "Perhaps it isn't out of place to mention—because we ought to be quite business-like, oughtn't we?—that when I married her she was known as the Beautiful Statue."

"Oh dear!" said Mrs. Monarch, ruefully.

"Of course I should want a certain amount of expression," I rejoined.

"Of *course!*" they both exclaimed.

"And then I suppose you know that you'll get awfully tired."

"Oh we *never* get tired!" they eagerly cried.

"Have you had any kind of practice?"

They hesitated—they looked at each other. "We've been photo-graphed, *immensely*," said Mrs. Monarch.

"She means the fellows have asked us," added the Major.

"I see—because you're so good-looking."

"I don't know what they thought, but they were always after us."

"We always got our photographs for nothing," smiled Mrs. Monarch.

"We might have brought some, my dear," her husband remarked.

"I'm not sure we have any left. We've given quantities away," she explained to me.

"With our autographs and that sort of thing," said the Major.

"Are they to be got in the shops?" I enquired, as a harmless pleasantry.

"Oh yes, *hers*—they used to be."

"Not now," said Mrs. Monarch, with her eyes on the floor.

II

I COULD fancy the "sort of thing" they put on the presentation-copies of their photographs, and I was sure they wrote a beautiful hand. It was odd how quickly I was sure of everything that concerned them. If they were now so poor as to have to earn shillings and pence, they never had had much of a margin. Their good looks had been their capital, and they had good-humouredly made the most of the career that this resource marked out for them. It was in their faces, the blankness, the deep intellectual repose of the twenty years of country-house visiting which had given them pleasant intonations. I could see the sunny drawing-rooms, sprinkled with periodicals she didn't read, in which Mrs. Monarch had continuously sat; I could see the wet shrubberies in which she had walked, equipped to admiration for either exercise. I could see the rich covers the Major had helped to shoot and the wonderful garments in which, late at night, he repaired to the smoking-room to talk about them. I could imagine their leggings and waterproofs, their knowing tweeds and rugs, their rolls of sticks and cases of tackle and neat umbrellas; and I could evoke the exact appearance of their servants and the compact variety of their luggage on the platforms of country stations.

They gave small tips, but they were liked; they didn't do anything themselves, but they were welcome. They looked so well everywhere; they gratified the general relish for stature, complexion and "form." They knew it without fatuity or vulgarity, and they respected themselves in consequence. They were not superficial; they were thorough and kept themselves up—it had been their line. People with such a taste for activity had to have some line. I could feel how even in a dull house, they could have been counted upon for cheerfulness. At present something had happened —it didn't matter what, their little income had grown less, it had grown least—and they had to do something for pocket-money. Their friends liked them, but didn't like to support them. There was something about them that represented credit—their clothes, their manners, their type; but if credit is a large empty pocket in which an occasional chink reverberates, the chink at least must be audible. What they wanted of me was to help to make it so. Fortunately they had no children—I soon divined that. They would also perhaps wish our relations to be kept secret: this was why it was "for the figure"—the reproduction of the face would betray them.

I liked them—they were so simple; and I had no objection to them if they would suit. But, somehow, with all their perfections I didn't easily believe in them. After all they were amateurs, and the ruling passion of my life was the detestation of the amateur. Combined with this was another perversity—an innate preference for the represented subject over the real one: the defect of the real one was so apt to be a lack of representation. I like things that appeared; then one was sure. Whether they *were* or not was a subordinate and almost always a profitless question. There were other considerations, the first of which was that I already had two or three people in use, notably a young person with big feet, in alpaca, from Kilburn, who for a couple of years had come to me regularly for my illustrations and with whom I was still—perhaps ignobly—satisfied. I frankly explained to my visitors how the case stood; but they had taken more precautions than I supposed. They had reasoned out their opportunity, for Claude Rivet had told them of the projected *édition de luxe* of one of the writers of our day—the rarest of the novelists—who, long neglected by the multitudinous vulgar and dearly prized by the attentive (need I mention Philip Vincent?) had had the happy fortune of seeing, late in life, the dawn and then the full light of a higher criticism—an estimate in which, on the part of the public, there was something really of expiation. The edition in question, planned by a publisher of taste, was practically an act of high reparation; the wood-cuts with which it was to be enriched were the homage of English art to one of the most independent representatives of English letters. Major and Mrs. Monarch confessed to me they had hoped I might be able to work *them* into my share of the enterprise. They knew I was to do the first of the books, "Rutland Ramsay," but I had to make clear to them that my participation in the rest of the affair— this first book was to be a test—was to depend on the satisfaction I should give. If this should be limited my employers would drop me without a scruple. It was therefore a crisis for me, and naturally I was making special preparations, looking about for new people, if they should be necessary, and securing the best types. I admitted however that I should like to settle down to two or three good models who would do for everything.

"Should we have often to—a—put on special clothes?" Mrs. Monarch timidly demanded.

"Dear, yes—that's half the business."

"And should we be expected to supply our own costumes?"

"Oh, no; I've got a lot of things. A painter's models put on— or put off—anything he likes."

"And do you mean—a—the same?"

"The same?"

Mrs. Monarch looked at her husband again.

"Oh, she was just wondering," he explained, "if the costumes are in *general* use." I had to confess that they were, and I mentioned further that some of them (I had a lot of genuine, greasy last-century things), had served their time, a hundred years ago, on living, world-stained men and women. "We'll put on anything that *fits*," said the Major.

"Oh, I arrange that—they fit in the pictures."

"I'm afraid I should do better for the modern books. I would come as you like," said Mrs. Monarch.

"She has got a lot of clothes at home: they might do for contemporary life," her husband continued.

"Oh, I can fancy scenes in which you'd be quite natural." And indeed I could see the slipshod rearrangements of stale properties —the stories I tried to produce pictures for without the exasperation of reading them—whose sandy tracts the good lady might help to people. But I had to return to the fact for this sort of work—the daily mechanical grind—I was already equipped: the people I was working with were fully adequate.

"We only thought we might be more like *some* characters," said Mrs. Monarch mildly, getting up.

Her husband also rose; he stood looking at me with a dim wistfulness that was touching in so fine a man. "Wouldn't it be rather a pull sometimes to have—a—to have—?" He hung fire; he wanted me to help him by phrasing what he meant. But I couldn't—I didn't know. So he brought it out, awkwardly: "The *real* thing; a gentleman, you know, or a lady." I was quite ready to give a general assent—I admitted that there was a great deal in that. This encouraged Major Monarch to say, following up his appeal with an unacted gulp: "It's awfully hard—we've tried everything." The gulp was communicative; it proved too much for his wife. Before I knew it Mrs. Monarch had dropped again upon a divan and burst into tears. Her husband sat down beside her, holding one of her hands; whereupon she quickly dried her eyes with the other, while I felt embarrassed as she looked up at me. "There isn't a confounded job I haven't applied for—waited for—prayed for. You can fancy we'd be pretty bad first. Secretaryships and that sort of thing? You might as well ask for a peerage. I'd be *any-thing*—I'm strong; a messenger or a coalheaver. I'd put on a gold-laced cap and open carriage-doors in front of the haberdasher's; I'd hang about a station, to carry portmanteaux; I'd be a postman. But they won't *look* at you; there are thousands, as good as yourself, already on the ground. *Gentlemen,* poor beggars, who have drunk their wine, who have kept their hunters!"

I was as reassuring as I knew how to be, and my visitors were presently on their feet again while, for the experiment, we agreed on an hour. We were discussing it when the door opened and Miss Churm came in with a wet umbrella. Miss Churm had to take the omnibus to Maida Vale and then walk half a mile. She looked a trifle blowsy and slightly splashed. I scarcely ever saw her come in without thinking afresh how odd it was that, being so little in herself, she should yet be so much in others. She was a meagre little Miss Churm, but she was an ample heroine of romance. She was only a freckled cockney, but she could represent everything, from a fine lady to a shepherdess; she had the faculty, as she might have had a fine voice or long hair. She couldn't spell, and she loved beer, but she had two or three "points," and practice, and a knack, and mother-wit, and a whimsical sensibility, and a love of the theatre, and seven sisters, and not an ounce of respect, especially for the *h*. The first thing my visitors saw was that her umbrella was wet, and in their spotless perfection they visibly winced at it. The rain had come on since their arrival.

"I'm all in a soak; there *was* a mess of people in the 'bus. I wish you lived near a stytion," said Miss Churm. I requested her to get ready as quickly as possible, and she passed into the room in which she always changed her dress. But before going out she asked me what she was to get into this time.

"It's the Russian princess, don't you know?" I answered; "the one with the 'golden eyes,' in black velvet, for the long thing in the *Cheapside*."

"Golden eyes? I *say!*" cried Miss Churm, while my companions watched her with intensity as she withdrew. She always arranged herself, when she was late, before I could turn around; and I kept my visitors a little on purpose, so that they might get an idea, from seeing her, what would be expected of themselves. I mentioned that she was quite my notion of an excellent model—she was really very clever.

"Do you think she looks like a Russian princess?" Major Monarch asked with lurking alarm.

"When I make her, yes."

"Oh if you have to *make* her—!" he reasoned, acutely.

"That's the most you can ask. There are so many that are not makeable."

"Well now, *here's* a lady"—and with a persuasive smile he passed his arm into his wife's—"who's already made!"

"Oh, I'm not a Russian princess," Mrs. Monarch protested, a little coldly. I could see that she had known some and didn't like them. There, immediately, was a complication of a kind I never had to fear with Miss Churm.

This young lady came back in black velvet—the gown was rather rusty and very low on her lean shoulders—and with a Japanese fan in her red hands. I reminded her that in the scene I was doing she had to look over some one's head. "I forgot whose it is; but it doesn't matter. Just look over a head."

"I'd rather look over a stove," said Miss Churm; and she took her station near the fire. She fell into position, settled herself into a tall attitude, gave a certain backward inclination to her head and a certain forward droop to her fan, and looked, at least to my prejudiced sense, distinguished and charming, foreign and dangerous. We left her looking so, while I went downstairs with Major and Mrs. Monarch.

"I think I could come about as near it as that," said Mrs. Monarch.

"Oh, you think she's shabby, but you must allow for the alchemy of art."

However, they went off with an evident increase of comfort, founded on their demonstrable advantage in being the real thing. I could fancy them shuddering over Miss Churm. She was very droll about them when I went back, for I told her what they wanted.

"Well, if *she* can sit I'll tyke to book-keeping," said my model.

"She's very ladylike," I replied, as an innocent form of aggravation.

"So much the worse for *you*. That means she can't turn round."

"She'll do for the fashionable novels."

"Oh yes, she'll *do* for them!" my model humorously declared. "Ain't they bad enough without her?" I had often sociably denounced them to Miss Churm.

III

It was for the elucidation of a mystery in one of these works that I first tried Mrs. Monarch. Her husband came with her, to be useful if necessary—it was sufficiently clear that as a general thing he would prefer to come with her. At first I wondered if this were for "propriety's" sake—if he were going to be jealous and meddling. The idea was too tiresome, and if it had been confirmed it would speedily have brought our acquaintance to a close. But I soon saw there was nothing in it and that if he accompanied Mrs. Monarch it was (in addition to the chance of being wanted), simply because he had nothing else to do. When she was away from him his occupation was gone—she never *had* been away from him. I judged, rightly, that in their awkward situation their close union was their main comfort and that this union had no weak spot. It was a real marriage, an encouragement to the hesitating, a nut for pessimists to crack. Their address was humble (I remember afterwards thinking it had been the only thing about them that was really professional), and I could fancy the lamentable lodgings in which the Major would have been left alone. He could bear them with his wife—he couldn't bear them without her.

He had too much tact to try and make himself agreeable when he couldn't be useful; so he simply sat and waited, when I was too absorbed in my work to talk. But I liked to make him talk—it made my work, when it didn't interrupt it, less sordid, less special. To listen to him was to combine the excitement of going out with the economy of staying at home. There was only one hindrance: that I seemed not to know any of the people he and his wife had known. I think he wondered extremely, during the term of our intercourse, whom the deuce I *did* know. He hadn't a stray sixpence of an idea to fumble for, so we didn't spin it very fine—we confined ourselves to questions of leather and even of liquor (saddlers and breeches-makers and how to get good claret cheap), and matters like "good trains" and the habits of small game. His lore on these last subjects was astonishing—he managed to interweave the station-master with the ornithologist. When he couldn't talk about greater things he could talk cheerfully about smaller, and since I couldn't accompany him into reminiscences of the fashionable world he could lower the conversation without a visible effort to my level.

So earnest a desire to please was touching in a man who could so easily have knocked one down. He looked after the fire and had an opinion on the draught of the stove without my asking him, and I could see that he thought many of my arrangements not half clever enough. I remember telling him that if I were only rich I'd offer him a salary to come and teach me how to live. Sometimes he gave a random sigh of which the essence was: "Give me even such a bare old barrack as *this,* and I'd do something with it!" When I wanted to use him he came alone; which was an illustration of the superior courage of women. His wife could bear her solitary second floor, and she was in general more discreet; showing by various small reserves that she was alive to the propriety of keeping our relations markedly professional—not letting them slide into sociability. She wished it to remain clear that she and the Major were employed, not cultivated, and if she approved of me as a superior, who could be kept in his place, she never thought me quite good enough for an equal.

She sat with great intensity, giving the whole of her mind to it, and was capable of remaining for an hour almost as motionless as if she were before a photographer's lens. I could see she had been photographed often, but somehow the very habit that made her good for that purpose unfitted her for mine. At first I was extremely pleased with her ladylike air, and it was a satisfaction, on coming to follow her lines, to see how good they were and how far they could lead the pencil. But after a few times I began to find her too insurmountably stiff; do what I would with it my drawing looked like a photograph or a copy of a photograph. Her figure had no variety of expression—she herself had no sense of variety. You may say that this was my business and was only a question of placing her. I placed her in every conceivable position but she managed to obliterate their differences. She was always a lady certainly, and into the bargain was always the same lady. She was the real thing, but always the same thing. There were moments when I was oppressed by the serenity of her confidence that she *was* the real thing. All her dealings with me and all her husband's were an implication that this was lucky for *me*. Meanwhile I found myself trying to invent types that approached her own, instead of making her own transform itself—in the clever way that was not impossible, for instance, to poor Miss Churm. Arrange as I would and take the precautions I would, she always, in my pictures, came out too tall—landing me in the dilemma of having represented a fascinating woman as seven feet high, which, out of respect perhaps to my own very much scantier inches, was far from my idea of such a personage.

The case was worse with the Major—nothing I could do would keep *him* down, so that he became useful only for the representation of brawny giants. I adored variety and range, I cherished human accidents, the illustrative note; I wanted to characterise closely, and the thing in the world I most hated was the danger of being ridden by a type. I had quarrelled with some of my friends about it; I had parted company with them for maintaining that one *had* to be, and that if the type was beautiful (witness Raphael and Leonardo), the servitude was only a gain. I was neither Leonardo nor Raphael; I might only be a presumptuous young modern searcher, but I held that everything was to be sacrificed sooner than character. When they averred that the haunting type in question could easily *be* character, I retorted, perhaps superficially, "Whose?" It couldn't be everybody's—it might end in being nobody's.

After I had drawn Mrs. Monarch a dozen times I perceived more clearly than before that the value of such a model as Miss Churm resided precisely in the fact that she had no positive stamp, combined of course with the other fact that what she did have was a curious and inexplicable talent for imitation. Her usual appearance was like a curtain which she could draw up at request for a capital performance. This performance was simply suggestive; but it was a word to the wise—it was vivid and pretty. Sometimes, even, I thought it, though she was plain herself, too insipidly pretty; I made it a reproach to her that the figures drawn from her were monotonously (*bêtement,* as we used to say) graceful. Nothing made her more angry; it was so much her pride to feel she could sit for characters that had nothing in common with each other. She would accuse me at such moments of taking away her "reputytion."

It suffered a certain shrinkage, this queer quantity, from the repeated visits of my new friends. Miss Churm was greatly in demand, never in want of employment, so I had no scruple in putting her off occasionally, to try them more at my ease. It was certainly amusing at first to do the real thing—it was amusing to do Major Monarch's trousers. They *were* the real thing, even if he did come out colossal. It was amusing to do his wife's back hair (it was so mathematically neat), and the particular "smart" tension of her tight stays. She lent herself especially to positions in which the face was somewhat averted or blurred; she abounded in ladylike back views and *profils perdus.* When she stood erect she took naturally one of the attitudes in which court-painters represent queens and princesses; so that I found myself wondering whether, to draw out this accomplishment, I couldn't get the editor of the *Cheapside* to publish a really royal romance, "A Tale of Buckingham Palace." Sometimes, however, the real thing and the make-believe came into contact; by which I mean that Miss Churm keeping an appointment or coming to make one on days when I had much work in hand, encountered her invidious rivals. The encounter was not on their part, for they noticed her no more than if she had been the housemaid; not from intentional loftiness, bu

simply because as yet, professionally, they didn't know how to
fraternise, as I could guess they would have liked—or at least
that the Major would. They couldn't talk about the omnibus—
they always walked; and they didn't know what else to try—she
wasn't interested in good trains or cheap claret. Besides, they must
have felt—in the air—that she was amused at them, secretly
derisive of their ever knowing how. She wasn't a person to conceal
her skepticism if she had had a chance to show it. On the other hand
Mrs. Monarch didn't think her tidy; for why else did she take
pains to say to me (it was going out of the way, for Mrs. Monarch),
that she didn't like dirty women?

One day when my young lady happened to be present with my
other sitters (she even dropped in, when it was convenient, for a
chat), I asked her to be so good as to lend a hand in getting tea—
a service with which she was familiar and which was one of a
class that, living as I did in a small way, with slender domestic
resources, I often appealed to my models to render. They liked
to lay hands on my property, to break the sitting, and sometimes
the china—I made them feel Bohemian. The next time I saw Miss
Churm after this incident she surprised me greatly by making
a scene about it—she accused me of having wished to humiliate
her. She hadn't resented the outrage at the time, but had seemed
obliging and amused, enjoying the comedy of asking Mrs. Monarch, who sat vague and silent, whether she would have cream
and sugar, and putting an exaggerated simper into the question.
She had tried intonations—as if she too wished to pass for the real
thing; till I was afraid my other visitors would take offence.

Oh, they were determined not to do this, and their touching
patience was the measure of their great need. They would sit by
the hour, uncomplaining, till I was ready to use them; they would
come back on the chance of being wanted and would walk away
cheerfully if they were not. I used to go to the door with them to
see in what magnificent order they retreated. I tried to find other
employment for them—I introduced them to several artists. But
they didn't "take," for reasons I could appreciate, and I became
conscious, rather anxiously, that after such disappointments they
fell back upon me with a heavier weight. They did me the honour
to think that it was I who was most *their* form. They were not picturesque enough for the painters, and in those days there were not
so many serious workers in black-and-white. Besides, they had

an eye to the great job I had mentioned to them—they had secretly set their hearts on supplying the right essence for my pictorial vindication of our fine novelist. They knew that for this undertaking I should want no costume-effects, none of the frippery of past ages—that it was a case in which everything would be contemporary and satirical and presumably genteel. If I could work them into it their future would be assured, for the labour would of course be long and the occupation steady.

One day Mrs. Monarch came without her husband—she explained his absence by his having had to go to the City. While she sat there in her usual anxious stiffness, there came at the door a knock which I immediately recognised as the subdued appeal of a model out of work. It was followed by the entrance of a young man whom I easily perceived to be a foreigner and who proved in fact an Italian acquainted with no English word but my name, which he uttered in a way that made it seem to include all others. I had not then visited his country, nor was I proficient in his tongue; but as he was not so meanly constituted—what Italian is?—as to depend only on that member for expression he conveyed to me, in familiar but graceful mimicry, that he was in search of exactly the employment in which the lady before me was engaged. I was not struck with him at first, and while I continued to draw I emitted rough sounds of discouragement or dismissal. He stood his ground however—not importunately, but with a dumb, dog-like fidelity in his eyes which amounted to innocent impudence, the manner of a devoted servant (he might have been in the house for years), unjustly suspected. Suddenly I saw that this very attitude and expression made a picture; whereupon I told him to sit down and wait till I should be free. There was another picture in the way he obeyed me, and I observed as I worked that there were others still in the way he looked wonderingly, with his head thrown back, about the high studio. He might have been crossing himself in Saint Peter's. Before I finished I said to myself "The fellow's a bankrupt orange-monger, but he's a treasure."

When Mrs. Monarch withdrew he passed across the room like a flash to open the door for her, standing there with the rapt, pure gaze of the young Dante spellbound by the young Beatrice. As never insisted, in such situations, on the blankness of the British domestic, I reflected that he had the making of a servant (and needed one, but couldn't pay him to be only that), as well as of model; in short I made up my mind to adopt my bright adventurer if he would agree to officiate in the double capacity. He jumped at my offer, and in the event my rashness (for I had known nothing about him), was not brought home to me. He proved a sympathetic though a desultory ministrant, and had in a wonderful degree the *sentiment de la pose*. It was uncultivated, instinctive, a part of the happy instinct which had guided him to my door and helped him to spell out my name on the card nailed to it. He had had no other introduction to me than a guess, from the shape of my high north window, seen outside, that my place was a studio and that as a studio it would contain an artist. He had wandered to England in search of fortune, like other itinerants, and had embarked, with a partner and a small green hand-cart, on the sale of penny ices. The ices had melted away and the partner had dissolved in their train. My young man wore tight yellow trousers with reddish stripes and his name was Oronte. He was sallow but fair, and when I put him into some old clothes of my own he looked like an Englishman. He was as good as Miss Churm, who could look, when required, like an Italian.

IV

I THOUGHT Mrs. Monarch's face slightly convulsed when, on her coming back with her husband, she found Oronte installed. It was strange to have to recognise in a scrap of a lazzarone a competitor to her magnificent Major. It was she who scented danger first, for the Major was anecdotically unconscious. But Oronte gave us tea, with a hundred eager confusions (he had never seen such a queer process), and I think she thought better of me for having at last an "establishment." They saw a couple of drawings that I had made of the establishment, and Mrs. Monarch hinted that it never would have struck her that he had sat for them. "Now the drawings you make from *us*, they look exactly like us," she reminded me, smiling in triumph; and I recognised that this was indeed just their defect. When I drew the Monarchs I couldn't somehow get away from them—get into the character I wanted to represent; and I had not the least desire my model should be discoverable in my picture. Miss Churm never was, and Mrs. Monarch thought I hid her, very properly, because she was vulgar;

whereas if she was lost it was only as the dead who go to heaven are lost—in the gain of an angel the more.

By this time I had got a certain start with "Rutland Ramsay," the first novel in the great projected series; that is I had produced a dozen drawings, several with the help of the Major and his wife, and I had sent them in for approval. My understanding with the publishers, as I have already hinted, had been that I was to be left to do my work, in this particular case, as I liked, with the whole book committed to me; but my connexion with the rest of the series was only contingent. There were moments when, frankly, it *was* a comfort to have the real thing under one's hand; for there were characters in "Rutland Ramsay" that were very much like it. There were people presumably as straight as the Major and women of as good a fashion as Mrs. Monarch. There was a great deal of country-house life—treated, it is true, in a fine, fanciful, ironical, generalised way—and there was a considerable implication of knickerbockers and kilts. There were certain things I had to settle at the outset; such things for instance as the exact appearance of the hero, the particular bloom of the heroine. The author of course gave me a lead, but there was a margin for interpretation. I took the Monarchs into my confidence. I told them frankly what I was about, I mentioned my embarrassments and alternatives. "Oh, take *him!*" Mrs. Monarch murmured sweetly looking at her husband; and "What could you want better than my wife?" the Major enquired, with the comfortable candour that now prevailed between us.

I was not obliged to answer these remarks—I was only obliged to place my sitters. I was not easy in mind, and I postponed, a little timidly perhaps, the solution of the question. The book was a large canvas, the other figures were numerous, and I worked off at first some of the episodes in which the hero and the heroine were no concerned. When once I had set *them* up I should have to stick to them—I couldn't make my young man seven feet high in one place and five feet nine in another. I inclined on the whole to the latter measurement, though the Major more than once reminded me that *he* looked about as young as any one. It was indeed quite possible to arrange him, for the figure, so that it would have been difficult to detect his age. After the spontaneous Oronte had been with me a month, and after I had given him to understand several different times that his native exuberance would presently com stitute an insurmountable barrier to our further intercourse, I waked to a sense of his heroic capacity. He was only five feet seven, but the remaining inches were latent. I tried him almost secretly at first, for I was really rather afraid of the judgement my other models would pass on such a choice. If they regarded Miss Churm as little better than a snare, what would they think of the representation by a person so little the real thing as an Italian street-vendor of a protagonist formed by a public school?

If I went a little in fear of them it was not because they bullied me, because they had got an oppressive foothold, but because in their really pathetic decorum and mysteriously permanent newness they counted on me so intensely. I was therefore very glad when Jack Hawley came home: he was always of such good counsel. He painted badly himself, but there was no one like him for putting his finger on the place. He had been absent from England for a year; he had been somewhere—I don't remember where—to get a fresh eye. I was in a good deal of dread of any such organ, but we were old friends; he had been away for months and a sense of emptiness was creeping into my life. I hadn't dodged a missile for a year.

He came back with a fresh eye, but with the same old black velvet blouse, and the first evening he spent in my studio we smoked cigarettes till the small hours. He had done no work himself, he had only got the eye; so the field was clear for the production of my little things. He wanted to see what I had done for the *Cheapside*, but he was disappointed in the exhibition. That at least seemed the meaning of two or three comprehensive groans which, as he lounged on my big divan, on a folded leg, looking at my latest drawings, issued from his lips with the smoke of the cigarette.

"What's the matter with you?" I asked.

"What's the matter with *you?*"

"Nothing save that I'm mystified."

"You are indeed. You're quite off the hinge. What's the meaning of this new fad?" And he tossed me, with visible irreverence, a drawing in which I happened to have depicted both my majestic models. I asked if he didn't think it good, and he replied that it struck him as execrable, given the sort of thing I had always represented myself to him as wishing to arrive at; but I let that pass —I was so anxious to see exactly what he meant. The two figures

in the picture looked colossal, but I supposed this was *not* what
he meant, inasmuch as, for aught he knew to the contrary, I might
have been trying for that. I maintained that I was working exactly in the same way as when he last had done me the honour
to commend me. "Well, there's a big hole somewhere," he answered; "wait a bit and I'll discover it." I depended upon him to
do so: where else was the fresh eye? But he produced at last nothing more luminous than "I don't know—I don't like your types."
This was lame for a critic who had never consented to discuss
with me anything but the question of execution, the direction of
strokes and the mystery of values.

"In the drawings you've been looking at I think my types are
very handsome."

"Oh, they won't do!"

"I've had a couple of new models."

"I see you have. *They* won't do."

"Are you very sure of that?"

"Absolutely—they're stupid."

"You mean *I* am—for I ought to get round that."

"You *can't*—with such people. Who are they?"

I told him, as far as was necessary, and he declared, heartlessly
"Ce sont des gens qu'il faut mettre à la porte."

"You've never seen them; they're awfully good," I compassion-
ately objected.

"Not seen them? Why, all this recent work of yours drops to
pieces with them. It's all I want to see of them."

"No one else has said anything against it—the *Cheapside* people
are pleased."

"Every one else is an ass, and the *Cheapside* people the biggest
asses of all. Come, don't pretend at this time of day to have
pretty illusions about the public, especially about publishers and
editors. It's not for *such* animals you work—it's for those who
know, *coloro che sanno;* so keep straight for *me* if you can't keep
straight for yourself. There's a certain sort of thing you've tried
for from the first—and a very good thing it is. But this twaddle
isn't *in* it." When I talked with Hawley later about "Rutland Ramsay" and its possible successors he declared that I must get back into
my boat again or I should go to the bottom. His voice in short was
the voice of warning.

I noted the warning, but I didn't turn my friends out of doors.

They bored me a good deal; but the very fact that they bored me admonished me not to sacrifice them—if there was anything to be done with them—simply to irritation. As I look back at this phase they seem to me to have pervaded my life not a little. I have a vision of them as most of the time in my studio, seated against the wall on an old velvet bench to be out of the way, and looking like a pair of patient courtiers in a royal ante-chamber. I'm convinced that during the coldest weeks of the winter they held their ground because it saved them fire. Their newness was losing its gloss, and it was impossible not to feel that they were objects of charity. Whenever Miss Churm arrived they went away, and after I was fairly launched in "Rutland Ramsay" Miss Churm arrived pretty often. They managed to express to me tacitly that they supposed I wanted her for the low life of the book, and I let them suppose it, since they had attempted to study the work—it was lying about the studio—without discovering that it dealt only with the highest circles. They had dipped into the most brilliant of our novelists without deciphering many passages. I still took an hour from them, now and again, in spite of Jack Hawley's warning: it would be time enough to dismiss them, if dismissal should be necessary, when the rigour of the season was over. Hawley had made their acquaintance—he had met them at my fireside —and thought them a ridiculous pair. Learning that he was a painter they tried to approach him, to show him too that they were the real thing; but he looked at them, across the big room, as if they were miles away: they were a compendium of everything he most objected to in the social system of his country. Such people as that, all convention and patent-leather, with ejaculations that stopped conversation, had no business in a studio. A studio was a place to learn to see, and how could you see through a pair of feather-beds?

The main inconvenience I suffered at their hands was that at first I was shy of letting them discover how my artful little servant had begun to sit to me for "Rutland Ramsay." They knew I had been odd enough (they were prepared by this time to allow oddity to artists), to pick a foreign vagabond out of the streets when I might have had a person with whiskers and credentials; but it was some time before they learned how high I rated his accomplishments. They found him in an attitude more than once, but they never doubted I was doing him as an organ-grinder. There were several things they never guessed, and one of them was that for a striking scene in the novel, in which a footman briefly figured, it occurred to me to make use of Major Monarch as the menial. I kept putting this off, I didn't like to ask him to don the livery—besides the difficulty of finding a livery to fit him. At last, one day late in the winter, when I was at work on the despised Oronte (he caught one's idea in an instant), and was in the glow of feeling that I was going very straight, they came in, the Major and his wife, with their society laugh about nothing (there was less and less to laugh at), like country-callers—they always reminded me of that—who have walked across the park after church and are presently persuaded to stay to luncheon. Luncheon was over, but they could stay to tea—I knew they wanted it. The fit was on me, however, and I couldn't let my ardour cool and my work wait, with the fading daylight, while my model prepared it. So I asked Mrs. Monarch if she would mind laying it out—a request which for an instant brought all the blood to her face. Her eyes were on her husband's for a second, and some mute telegraphy passed between them. Their folly was over the next instant; his cheerful shrewdness put an end to it. So far from pitying their wounded pride, I must add, I was moved to give it as complete a lesson as I could. They bustled about together and got out the cups and saucers and made the kettle boil. I know they felt as if they were waiting on my servant, and when the tea was prepared I said: "He'll have a cup, please—he's tired." Mrs. Monarch brought him one where he stood, and he took it from her as if he had been a gentleman at a party squeezing a crush-hat with an elbow.

Then it came over me that she had made a great effort for me—made it with a kind of nobleness—and that I owed her a compensation. Each time I saw her after this I wondered what the compensation could be. I couldn't go on doing the wrong thing to oblige them. Oh, it *was* the wrong thing, the stamp of the work for which they sat—Hawley was not the only person to say it now. I sent in a large number of the drawings I had made for "Rutland Ramsay," and I received a warning that was more to the point than Hawley's. The artistic adviser of the house for which I was working was of opinion that many of my illustrations were not what had been looked for. Most of these illustrations were the subjects in which the Monarchs had figured. Without going into the question of what *had* been looked for, I saw at this rate I shouldn't get the other books to do. I hurled myself in despair upon Miss Churm—I put her through all her paces. I not only adopted Oronte publicly as my hero, but one morning when the Major looked in to see if I didn't require him to finish a figure for the *Cheapside* for which he had begun to sit the week before, I told him that I had changed my mind—I would do the drawing from my man. At this my visitor turned pale and stood looking at me. "Is *he* your idea of an English gentleman?" he asked.

I was disappointed, I was nervous, I wanted to get on with my work; so I replied with irritation: "Oh, my dear Major—I can't be ruined for *you!*"

He stood another moment; then, without a word, he quitted the studio. I drew a long breath when he was gone, for I said to myself that I shouldn't see him again. I had not told him definitely that I was in danger of having my work rejected, but I was vexed at his not having felt the catastrophe in the air, read with me the moral of our fruitless collaboration, the lesson that in the deceptive atmosphere of art even the highest respectability may fail of being plastic.

I didn't owe my friends money, but I did see them again. They reappeared together three days later, and under the circumstances, there was something tragic in the fact. It was a proof to me that they could find nothing else in life to do. They had threshed the matter out in a dismal conference—they had digested the bad news that they were not in for the series. If they were not useful to me even for the *Cheapside* their function seemed difficult to determine, and I could only judge at first that they had come, forgivingly, decorously, to take a last leave. This made me rejoice in secret that I had little leisure for a scene; for I had placed both my other models in position together and I was pegging away at a drawing from which I hoped to derive glory. It had been suggested by the passage in which Rutland Ramsay, drawing up a chair to Artemisia's piano-stool, says extraordinary things to her while she ostensibly fingers out a difficult piece of music. I had done Miss Churm at the piano before—it was an attitude in which she knew how to take on an absolutely poetic grace. I wished the two figures to "compose" together, intensely, and my little Italian had entered perfectly into my conception. The pair were vividly before me, the piano had been pulled out; it was a charming picture of blended youth and murmured love, which I had only to catch and keep. My visitors stood and looked at it, and I was friendly to them over my shoulder.

They made no response, but I was used to silent company and went on with my work, only a little disconcerted (even though exhilarated by the sense that *this* was at least the ideal thing), at not having got rid of them after all. Presently I heard Mrs. Monarch's sweet voice beside or rather above me: "I wish her hair was a little better done." I looked up and she was staring with a strange fixedness at Miss Churm, whose back was turned to her. "Do you mind my just touching it?" she went on—a question which made me spring up for an instant as with the instinctive fear that she might do the young lady a harm. But she quieted me with a glance I shall never forget—I confess I should like to have been able to paint *that*—and went for a moment to my model. She spoke to her softly, laying a hand upon her shoulder and bending over her; and as the girl, understanding, gratefully assented, she disposed her rough curls, with a few quick passes, in such a way as to make Miss Churm's head twice as charming. It was one of the most heroic personal services I've ever seen rendered. Then Mrs. Monarch turned away with a low sigh and, looking about her as if for something to do, stooped to the floor with a noble humility and picked up a dirty rag that had dropped out of my paint-box.

The Major meanwhile had also been looking for something to do, and, wandering to the other end of the studio, saw before him my breakfast-things neglected, unremoved. "I say, can't I be useful *here?*" he called out to me with an irrepressible quaver. I assented with a laugh that I fear was awkward, and for the next ten minutes, while I worked, I heard the light clatter of china and the tinkle of spoons and glass. Mrs. Monarch assisted her husband—they washed up my crockery, they put it away. They wandered off into my little scullery, and I afterwards found that they had cleaned my knives and that my slender stock of plate had an unprecedented surface. When it came over me, the latent eloquence of what they were doing, I confess that my drawing was blurred for a moment—the picture swam. They had accepted their failure, but they couldn't accept their fate. They had bowed their heads in bewilderment to the perverse and cruel law in virtue of which the real thing could be so much less precious than the unreal; but they didn't want to starve. If my servants were my models, my models might be my servants. They would reverse the parts— the others would sit for the ladies and gentlemen and *they* would do the work. They would still be in the studio—it was an intense dumb appeal to me not to turn them out. "Take us on," they wanted to say—"we'll do *anything*."

When all this hung before me, the *afflatus* vanished—my pencil dropped from my hand. My sitting was spoiled and I got rid of my sitters, who were also evidently rather mystified and awestruck. Then, alone with the Major and his wife, I had a most uncomfortable moment. He put their prayer into a single sentence: "I say, you know—just let *us* do for you, can't you?" I couldn't—it was dreadful to see them emptying my slops; but I pretended I could, to oblige them, for about a week. Then I gave them a sum of money to go away, and I never saw them again. I obtained the remaining books, but my friend Hawley repeats that Major and Mrs. Monarch did me a permanent harm, got me into a second-rate trick. If it be true I'm content to have paid the price—for the memory.

STUDY

❧⚜❧

The Notebooks of Henry James

F. O. MATTHIESSEN AND KENNETH B. MURDOCK (eds.)*

[Entry dated February 22, 1891]

I began yesterday the little story that was suggested to me some time ago by an incident related to me by George du Maurier. . . . I was struck with the pathos, the oddity and typicalness of the situation—the little tragedy of good-looking gentlefolk, who had been

all their life stupid and well-dressed, living, on a fixed income, at
country-houses, watering places and clubs, like so many others of
their class in England, and were now utterly unable to *do* anything,
had no cleverness, no art nor craft to make use of as a *gagne-pain*—
could only *show* themselves, clumsily, for the fine, clean, well-
groomed animals that they were, only hope to make a little money
by—in this manner—just simply *being*. . . . I must . . . be very clear
as to what is in [this idea] and what I wish to get out of it. I tried
a beginning yesterday, but I instantly became conscious that I must
straighten out the little idea. It must be an idea—it can't be a "story"
in the vulgar sense of the word. It must be a picture; it must illustrate something. God knows that's enough—if the thing *does*
illustrate. . . . One must put a little action—not a stupid, mechanical, arbitrary action, but something that is of the real essence of
the subject. I thought of representing the husband as jealous of the
wife when she begins to sit. But this is vulgar and obvious. . . .
What I wish to represent is the baffled, ineffectual, incompetent
character of their attempt, and how it illustrates once again
the everlasting English amateurishness—the way superficial, un-
trained, unprofessional effort goes to the wall when confronted
with trained, competitive, intelligent, *qualified* art—in whatever
line it may be a question of it. . . . Let my contrast and complication here come from the opposition—to my melancholy Major and
his wife—of a couple of little vulgar professional people *who know,*
with the consequent bewilderment . . . —their failure to understand how such people can be better than *they*—their failure,
disappointment, disappearance—going forth into the vague again.
. . . They have no pictorial sense. They are only clean and stiff
and stupid. The others are dirty, even—the melancholy Major and
his wife remark on it, wondering. The artist . . . is willing to give
them a trial [but] *he* himself is on trial. . . . He can't afford . . .
to make many mistakes. . . . I shall get every grain of "action"
that the space admits of if I make something, for the artist, hang
in the balance—depend on the way he does this particular work.
It's when he finds that he shall lose his great opportunity if he
keeps on with them, that he has to tell the gentlemanly couple,
that, frankly, they won't serve his turn—and make them wander
forth into the cold world again. . . . Picture the immanence, in
the [Monarchs], of the idle, provided-for, country-house habit—
the blankness of their *manière d'être*.

Daisy Miller and Other Tales

HENRY JAMES*

Preface [1907–1909]

[My] much-loved friend George du Maurier had spoken to me of a call from a strange and striking couple desirous to propose themselves as artist's models for his weekly "social" illustrations to *Punch,* and the acceptance of whose services would have entailed the dismissal of an undistinguished but highly expert pair, also husband and wife, who had come to him from far back on the irregular day and whom, thanks to a happy . . . appearance of "type" on the part of each, he had reproduced, to the best effect, in a thousand drawing-room attitudes and combinations. Exceedingly modest members of society, they earned their bread by looking and, with the aid of supplied toggery, dressing, greater favourites of fortune to the life; or, otherwise expressed, by skillfully feigning a virtue not in the least native to them. Here meanwhile were their so handsome proposed, so anxious, so almost haggard competitors, originally, by every sign, of the best condition and estate, but overtaken by reverses even while conforming impeccably to the standard of superficial "smartness" and pleading with well-bred ease and the right light tone, not to say with feverish gaiety, that (as in the interest of art itself) *they* at least shouldn't have to "make believe." The question thus thrown up by the two friendly critics of the rather lurid little passage was of whether their not having to make believe *would* in fact serve them, and above all serve their interpreter as well as the borrowed graces of the comparatively sordid professionals who had had, for dear life, to *know how* (which was to have learnt how) to do something. The question, I recall, struck me as exquisite, and out of a momentary fond consideration of it "The Real Thing" sprang at a bound.

"The Two Henry Jameses"

QUENTIN ANDERSON†

In this little parable James dramatizes the relationship between morality and style explicitly stated by Gabriel Nash [in *The Tragic*

* Copyright, 1908, 1909, Charles Scribner's Sons; renewal copyright, 1936, 1937, Henry James. Reprinted from *The Art of the Novel*, by Henry James, with the permission of Charles Scribner's Sons.

† FROM *Scrutiny*, XIV (September, 1947) and *The Complex Fate* (London, Chatto & Windus, Ltd., 1952). By permission.

Muse]. That so simple a story should be so widely misread is surprising. Yet James must have anticipated the misreading. He knew, that is, that his contemporaries were infatuated with the figure of the artist, and thought art a moral end in itself. He considered such a view of the artist an impiety and a horror, but he nonetheless threw the sops of apparent conformity to an audience which hungrily and blindly snatched them up. . . . [James] may be said to offer us an opportunity for salutary though vicarious moral transgression. We make much of the fate of the artist *as such* in *The Real Thing*. The author apparently expected us to discover our error by experiencing its consequences. We have been slow to do so. In this story the two sets of models are inversions of one another. Major and Mrs. Monarch are, in [a religous sense], "dead." Frozen into the forms prescribed by caste, completely generic and completely incapable of moral spontaneity, they are also, and by the same token, fixed, intractable pictorial "values." The man who collects fixed aesthetic values of this is a sinner just as the capitalist or the sexually acquisitive male is a sinner. The artist of the story sins [until he dismisses the Monarchs] not simply against art but against himself. To prize Major and Mrs. Monarch is to prize an image of one's own self-righteousness. The cockney girl and the young Italian who comprise the opposed set of models represent the "ideal thing" because they are morally spontaneous. They may be used to illustrate dramatic situations because they are capable of love for others *unlike themselves*.

" 'The Real Thing': A Parable for Writers of Fiction"

Gorham Munson*

[What] attracted James to his anecdote was the chance it gave for clarifying what might be called the "medium-test" for characters. . . .

[The] couple applying for work as models for the romances of society which he illustrated look exactly the part they play in real life, whereas the pictorial thing they *suggest* is something else, undefined except as a treatment they wouldn't like . . . and yet,

* From *The University of Kansas City Review*, XVI (Summer, 1950) and *The Writer's Workshop Companion*, by Gorham Munson (New York, Thomas Nelson & Sons; Copyright, 1951, by Gorham Munson). By permission.

despite his misgivings, he takes them on. That is, he does what the novelist, usually the immature novelist, does when he tries to put a real person into a book. . . .

[If we were to trace in detail] the "figure in the carpet" as a writer of fiction intently scanning the texture of James's story would make it out, [the] "figure" would convey something like this. There is for each art-medium a special suitability of characters. In the art of the motion picture this is discovered by a screen-test. In the medium of prose fiction, short or long, there is a fiction-test, and most real people can't pass it. Real people as a rule supply hints only for fictive people, just as Major Monarch supplies a hint for the footman he isn't and Oronte supplies hints for the gentleman he isn't. The copying of life-models for fiction is bad business; it's hard to scale them down, it's hard to avoid a sit-still photographic quality, it's hard to make them magnetic. The upshot is that you have to cast your characters especially for the short story, novelette or novel. Your invented characters must be ideal for the parts they have to play in the fictions you are inventing.

That is the parabolic substance of James's story. That I am not reading too much into Henry James's intention can, I think, be ascertained by anyone who will consult the prefaces to *The Wings of the Dove* and *The Ambassadors*. . . . In one James describes the casting of Milly Theale, over whom the sword of a fatal sickness visibly hangs by a thread but who has so many advantages apart from the disadvantage of precarious health. In the other he casts Strether, a man of mature character and of strong but not predominant imagination. James was so meticulous in describing his own fiction-tests for characters that it is impossible to think he did not have in mind the fiction writer's problems as well as the problems of the illustrative artist when he composed "The Real Thing."

The Short Story

Sean O'Faolain*

["Plot?"] There is none. . . . The story does contain, however, . . . all those elements which the word plot suggests, such as con-

* From *The Short Story*, by Sean O'Faolain, published, 1951, by The Devin-Adair Co., New York; Copyright, 1951, by Devin-Adair.

trivance, situation, suspense, invention, action; or all except, perhaps (and this is the one thing editors and public most insist on),
climax. Climax in, at any rate, the conventional sense has to be
sacrificed to that deeper verisimilitude which is the conscience of
the modern writer. In *The Real Thing* what climax there is suffices;
indeed it is searing to find Oronte and Miss Churm posing successfully as a gentleman and a lady while Major Monarch and his wife
wash up the tea things. . . .

[For my purposes, I have severely pruned James's version of the
story. My prunings] are legitimate on such counts as that what I
would excise has told us only what we might presume; or that he
has indulged in passing personal comment irrelevent to the kernel
of the tale, or in illustrations, or elaborations which savour of self-
indulgence, or even of sheer laziness. Thus, when he says that his
two characters "were visibly shy" we might be expected to gather
this for ourselves; or when he says "after all they were amateurs"
this is something too obvious to need statement; and the largest
pruning would remove a whole character and incident, the conversation with Hawley, a cumbersome piece of machinery which
bursts apart the shape of the story, simply because James could
not be bothered to convey the point which Hawley makes in a
more subtle and economised way. . . . [In *The Real Thing*] James
omitted only one thing. He placed it in the artist's studio from the
beginning to end, and saw it through the artist's eyes. This com-
pactness pleases. He focused his camera clearly on Major and Mrs.
Monarch and this clarity is satisfying. The passage of time is not
obtrusive though it is felt sufficiently to suggest a certain degree
of sprawl. The reader will observe that there is virtually no
characterisation—Major and Mrs. Monarch are little more than
social types, nicely defined, though her kindness is evident [*e.g.*
her rearrangement of the model's hair, . . . a nice and useful touch
of character]; and the loyal affection of husband and wife is also
touching. This is quite enough characterisation for the realist convention. . . . Situation is, as usual, necessary to fill in these light
outlines, and the story is based on one of the happiest of situations.
We have, therefore, almost everything requisite. All that is needed
is that construction should be added or merged with situation to
give dramatic compression and eloquent form. This is the one thing
missing. Henry James either would not or did not know how to
construct his shorter tales into a satisfying form.

It must be said, however, that his stories have a special verte-brate quality of their own which, if not exactly form, is at any rate anatomy: he moulded the flesh about an *intellectual* idea. Perhaps he merely hung it on his idea? Here his idea is that "the real thing," *e.g.* a real gentleman, may be such a conventional reality that it loses all the plastic quality of life. He may even be proposing that the lower orders, as represented by the Cockney and the Italian ice-cream vendor, have more plasticity because more reality? It will rest with each reader to measure the interest of this proposition which James chases hither and over like a retriever, though I am not sure that he does not also tend to chew the game. But though one may happen to have a strong personal liking for stories with an intelligent point to them the fact remains that point is not form. Henry James's stories dangle from his point like tapestry trailing from a hook.

"*A Note on Henry James's 'The Real Thing'*"
SEYMOUR LAINOFF[*]

In his depiction of the Monarchs, James attacks not simply a theory of literal imitation in the arts, but an important variation of that theory, the late Renaissance and eighteenth-century theory of type or norm, the *beau idéal*. This variation finds its most famous ex-position in English in Reynolds' *Discourses*. The Monarchs are not merely specimens of humanity; they represent types or norms of a superior humanity, in the eighteenth-century fashion. We can deduce as much from their names, from the fact that the artist cannot help exaggerating their heights in his portraits and blurring the woman's features, from the fact that Mrs. Monarch was called, in an earlier day, the Beautiful Statue. . . .

The Monarchs, evidently, have symbolic reference; they incar-nate both social and . . . aesthetic values. In their social incarna-tions or selves, they represent aristocratic anachronisms, belonging as they do to an earlier age and lacking present-day function. The story implies that eighteenth-century insistence on the *beau idéal*, or aristocratic normality, was an outgrowth of upper-class attitudes. . . . Now that these social conventions are outworn, the theory of

[*] FROM *Modern Language Notes*, LXXI (March, 1956).

the *beau idéal* is no longer serviceable; it no longer has relation to social reality.

What theory of art and social reality does the story substitute instead? The artist of the story seeks a more expressive and imaginative realism than that suggested by the Monarchs. Anomalously, he discovers the sources of such a realism in Miss Churm and Oronte . . . , who can adopt aristocratic poses even better than those who are *the real thing*. His realism can therefore be defined as giving the *shape of reality* . . . or the air of reality to that which may not be real.

This nominalistic theory seems the result of the fact that the older system of manners (represented by the Monarchs)—no longer applicable, even absurd, in contemporary life—has not been replaced by an identifiable corresponding social code (Miss Churm and Oronte represent this amorphousness). The artist in this story . . . seems to be caught in a paradox: to draw manners and morals from models in a society in which standards of manners and morals seem to have disappeared.

"The Real Thing"

WALTER F. WRIGHT*

The contrast between the lack of skill as models on the part of the Monarchs and the skill on that of the others is obvious from their first juxtaposition. Were this the ultimate substance of the story, it could stop right there. Or rather, if we wished to argue, we could demand that James prove to us that—like Du Maurier's professional models, of whom he had told James—Miss Churm and Oronte could really achieve the artistic appearance claimed for them. James offers no such proof. He asks us to accept their competence as something not needing proof. It is not what is to be demonstrated, but precisely what is taken for granted.

What then is the story about? Rather early in the narration the artist says that Mrs. Monarch *is* the real thing, but he adds, with annoyance, that she is "always the same thing." The title cannot apply to her as model, for if it did the story would be at its proper end when the point was made. On the other hand, the title cannot

* FROM *Research Studies of the State College of Washington,* XXV (March, 1957).

refer to Miss Churm and Oronte, for they are certainly *not* the real thing. They can achieve the appearance only when posed by the artist and told what they represent. The value of the title is that it deepens in meaning as the story progresses. At the end, when Miss Churm and Oronte have been laid aside, the artist is concerned solely with the Monarchs. It is, after all, they who are the real thing, but they mean a great deal more to the artist now than they meant before. Like Coleridge's wedding guest, he is a much wiser man than at the beginning.

In "The Ancient Mariner" we are told that the listener has almost imperative motivation to leave, yet he is held by the fascination. The device is commonplace in literature. The temptation of James's artist to desert the Monarchs is his need to advance in his artistic career. Naturally he is annoyed by the incompetence of his two models, and yet he "cannot choose but hear." What is the tale he learns?

When one has ample wealth to entertain ladies and gentlemen as well as to be their guests, when one does not need to work for a living, it is not difficult, so far as material things are concerned, to conduct oneself in a gentlemanly or ladylike manner. There is no struggle, no story. But to make oneself welcome in homes when one gives small tips, when one is always guest and never host, is a greater matter. This the Monarchs have done. To offer oneself for employment, to discuss one's mate as a potential model, in competition with uneducated professionals, is a far greater matter in Victorian England. To submit to fate by arranging the professional's hair and emptying the slops is the supreme test. James asked himself, What is the real thing which we call lady and gentleman? To find out he stripped the man and wife of all the external supports which so easily prop people up. He threw them absolutely on their own resources and tested them well beyond a point that might have broken their spirits. Yet they did not collapse. Even when they were, in a sense, "selling" each other's physical charms they were most considerate in their language. They had only each other and each meant everything to the other. Several remarks show the Major's loneliness when away from his wife and her reliance upon him in their great adversity. Never is there a hint of dissension between them; all is deference and self-forgetful concern for the other. In short, their love has been tried by the kind of misfortune that often degrades and it has never been shaken.

Their resignation to life has about it the very highest social value. Though the artist feels compassionate, they impose their troubles upon him as little as possible. They have to admit their poverty, but they will not be beggars either for money or sympathy. To call them dead is to miss the intensity with which they live. Indeed, it is their sensitivity that makes their pathos so compelling. They have been accepted as guests in wealthy homes because they have a self-discipline that has made them unobtrusive, even interesting. They have moved in cultivated realms by choice, appreciative of what they found there. And when fortune's wheel spins they adjust; not lightly, for the shock is tremendous, but without hysteria. They never cease to be the real thing. And James pronounces a benediction upon them at the end. The artist cannot in propriety boast of his own new wisdom; he can go only so far as gentlemanly good taste permits. But his admiration is unmistakable. He repeats his artist friend's verdict that his art has suffered "a permanent harm." But he concludes, "If it be true"—and the *if* is significant—"I'm content to have paid the price—for the memory." And, of course, it is not true. The narrator could go on painting Miss Churm forever and learn from her nothing that would deepen his art. From the Major and his lady he has learned all. He does not say that he is content to pay a price for a *lesson;* in fact, he could not be, for he could have had the lesson for very little. He expressly states that he paid for the "memory."

For James and his artist narrator are much more than illustrators; they are portrait painters *in words.* They are not interested in the trappings that give verisimilitude to illustrations; they are interested in life itself as an art. Stuart Pratt Sherman and others have accused James of being obsessed with art to the neglect of moral character. The misreading of "The Real Thing" would support such a view. But in *The Portrait of a Lady* James condemned mere esthetes; in the portrait of Chad in *The Ambassadors* he deplored lack of character, however elegant Chad might be. He was interested always in man's attempt to create an orderly, disciplined life for himself. Indeed, his own personal life was very carefully ordered. In "The Real Thing" the creative art of the author consists in the portrayal of the art of living. In this art the Major and his wife are true gentleman and lady.

In the preface to "The Spoils of Poynton" James later wrote, "Life being all inclusion and confusion, and art being all discrimination and selection, the latter, in search of the hard latent *value* with which alone it is concerned, sniffs round the mass as instinctively and unerringly as a dog suspicious of some buried bone." The mass is in life itself. Art does not exist apart from it; it finds within it the "latent value." The Major and Mrs. Monarch are not actual persons whom James found in life itself. That is, they are not at all Du Maurier's would-be painter's models. About these James knew only that they were a lady and gentleman in search of work but unsuited for modeling. James's Major and his partner are not actual painter's models; they are the completed *literary* portraits. There was in the Du Maurier anecdote a hint of a latent value. Art merely excluded from it what was irrelevant and created a frame in which to study the essential.

In other words, art was for James not hostile to life, or even indifferent. It was simply the best part of it.

The Pupil

[1891]

❧

I

THE POOR YOUNG MAN hesitated and procrastinated: it cost him
such an effort to broach the subject of terms, to speak of money
to a person who spoke only of feelings and, as it were, of the aris-
tocracy. Yet he was unwilling to take leave, treating his engagement
as settled, without some more conventional glance in that direction than he could find an opening for in the manner of the large,
affable lady who sat there drawing a pair of soiled *gants de Suède*
through a fat, jewelled hand and, at once pressing and gliding, repeated over and over everything but the thing he would have liked
to hear. He would have liked to hear the figure of his salary; but
just as he was nervously about to sound that note the little boy
came back—the little boy Mrs. Moreen had sent out of the room to
fetch her fan. He came back without the fan, only with the casual
observation that he couldn't find it. As he dropped this cynical
confession he looked straight and hard at the candidate for the
honour of taking his education in hand. This personage reflected,
somewhat grimly, that the first thing he should have to teach his
little charge would be to appear to address himself to his mother
when he spoke to her—especially not to make her such an improper
answer as that.

When Mrs. Moreen bethought herself of this pretext for getting
rid of their companion, Pemberton supposed it was precisely to
approach the delicate subject of his remuneration. But it had been
only to say some things about her son which it was better that a boy
of eleven shouldn't catch. They were extravagantly to his advantage, save when she lowered her voice to sigh, tapping her left
side familiarly: "And all overclouded by *this*, you know—all at the
mercy of a weakness—!" Pemberton gathered that the weakness

FROM *The Lesson of the Master* (New York, Macmillan & Co., 1892).

was in the region of the heart. He had known the poor child was not robust: this was the basis on which he had been invited to treat, through an English lady, an Oxford acquaintance, then at Nice, who happened to know both his needs and those of the amiable American family looking out for something really superior in the way of a resident tutor.

The young man's impression of his prospective pupil, who had first come into the room, as if to see for himself, as soon as Pemberton was admitted, was not quite the soft solicitation the visitor had taken for granted. Morgan Moreen was, somehow, sickly without being delicate, and that he looked intelligent (it is true Pemberton wouldn't have enjoyed his being stupid), only added to the suggestion that, as with his big mouth and big ears he really couldn't be called pretty, he might be unpleasant. Pemberton was modest—he was even timid; and the chance that his small scholar might prove cleverer than himself had quite figured, to his nervousness, among the dangers of an untried experiment. He reflected, however, that these were risks one had to run when one accepted a position, as it was called, in a private family; when as yet one's University honours had, pecuniarily speaking, remained barren. At any rate, when Mrs. Moreen got up as if to intimate that, since it was understood he would enter upon his duties within the week she would let him off now, he succeeded, in spite of the presence of the child, in squeezing out a phrase about the rate of payment. It was not the fault of the conscious smile which seemed a reference to the lady's expensive identity, if the allusion did not sound rather vulgar. This was exactly because she became still more gracious to reply: "Oh! I can assure you that all that will be quite regular."

Pemberton only wondered, while he took up his hat, what "all that" was to amount to—people had such different ideas. Mrs. Moreen's words, however, seemed to commit the family to a pledge definite enough to elicit from the child a strange little comment, in the shape of the mocking, foreign ejaculation, "Oh, là-là!"

Pemberton, in some confusion, glanced at him as he walked slowly to the window with his back turned, his hands in his pockets and the air in his elderly shoulders of a boy who didn't play. The young man wondered if he could teach him to play, though his mother had said it would never do and that this was why school was impossible. Mrs. Moreen exhibited no discomfiture; she only continued blandly: "Mr. Moreen will be delighted to meet your wishes. As I told you, he has been called to London for a week. As soon as he comes back you shall have it out with him."

This was so frank and friendly that the young man could only reply, laughing as his hostess laughed: "Oh! I don't imagine we shall have much of a battle."

"They'll give you anything you like," the boy remarked unexpectedly, returning from the window. "We don't mind what anything costs—we live awfully well."

"My darling, you're too quaint!" his mother exclaimed, putting out to caress him a practiced but ineffectual hand. He slipped out of it, but looked with intelligent, innocent eyes at Pemberton, who had already had time to notice that from one moment to the other his small satiric face seemed to change its time of life. At this moment it was infantine; yet it appeared also to be under the influence of curious intuitions and knowledges. Pemberton rather disliked precocity, and he was disappointed to find gleams of it in a disciple not yet in his teens. Nevertheless he divined on the spot that Morgan wouldn't prove a bore. He would prove on the contrary a kind of excitement. This idea held the young man, in spite of a certain repulsion.

"You pompous little person! We're not extravagant!" Mrs. Moreen gayly protested, making another unsuccessful attempt to draw the boy to her side. "You must know what to expect," she went on to Pemberton.

"The less you expect the better!" her companion interposed. "But we *are* people of fashion."

"Only so far as *you* make us so!" Mrs. Moreen mocked, tenderly. "Well, then, on Friday—don't tell me you're superstitious—and mind you don't fail us. Then you'll see us all. I'm so sorry the girls are out. I guess you'll like the girls. And, you know, I've another son, quite different from this one."

"He tries to imitate me," said Morgan to Pemberton.

"He tries? Why, he's twenty years old!" cried Mrs. Moreen.

"You're very witty," Pemberton remarked to the child—a proposition that his mother echoed with enthusiasm, declaring that Morgan's sallies were the delight of the house. The boy paid no heed to this; he only inquired abruptly of the visitor, who was surprised afterwards that he hadn't struck him as offensively forward: "Do you *want* very much to come?"

"Can you doubt it, after such a description of what I shall hear?"

Pemberton replied. Yet he didn't want to come at all; he was coming because he had to go somewhere, thanks to the collapse of his fortune at the end of a year abroad, spent on the system of putting his tiny patrimony into a single full wave of experience. He had had his full wave, but he couldn't pay his hotel bill. Moreover, he had caught in the boy's eyes the glimpse of a far-off appeal.

"Well, I'll do the best I can for you," said Morgan; with which he turned away again. He passed out of one of the long windows; Pemberton saw him go and lean on the parapet of the terrace. He remained there while the young man took leave of his mother, who, on Pemberton's looking as if he expected a farewell from him, interposed with: "Leave him, leave him; he's so strange!" Pemberton suspected she was afraid of something he might say. "He's a genius —you'll love him," she added. "He's much the most interesting person in the family." And before he could invent some civility to oppose to this, she wound up with: "But we're all good, you know!"

"He's a genius—you'll love him!" were words that recurred to Pemberton before the Friday, suggesting, among other things, that geniuses were not invariably lovable. However, it was all the better if there was an element that would make tutorship absorbing: he had perhaps taken too much for granted that it would be dreary. As he left the villa after his interview, he looked up at the balcony and saw the child leaning over it. "We shall have great larks!" he called up.

Morgan hesitated a moment; then he answered, laughing: "By the time you come back I shall have thought of something witty!"

This made Pemberton say to himself: "After all he's rather nice."

II

ON THE FRIDAY he saw them all, as Mrs. Moreen had promised, for her husband had come back and the girls and the other son were at home. Mr. Moreen had a white moustache, a confiding manner and, in his buttonhole, the ribbon of a foreign order—bestowed, as Pemberton eventually learned, for services. For what services he never clearly ascertained: this was a point—one of a large number—that Mr. Moreen's manner never confided. What it emphatically did confide was that he was a man of the world. Ulick, the firstborn, was in visible training for the same profession—under the disadvantage as yet, however, of a buttonhole only feebly floral and a moustache with no pretensions to type. The girls had hair and figures and manners and small fat feet, but had never been out alone. As for Mrs. Moreen, Pemberton saw on a nearer view that her elegance was intermittent and her parts didn't always match. Her husband, as she had promised, met with enthusiasm Pemberton's ideas in regard to a salary. The young man had endeavoured to make them modest, and Mr. Moreen confided to him that *he* found them positively meagre. He further assured him that he aspired to be intimate with his children, to be their best friend, and that he was always looking out for them. That was what he went off for, to London and other places—to look out; and this vigilance was the theory of life, as well as the real occupation, of the whole family. They all looked out, for they were very frank on the subject of its being necessary. They desired it to be understood that they were earnest people, and also that their fortune, though quite adequate for earnest people, required the most careful administration. Mr. Moreen, as the parent bird, sought sustenance for the nest. Ulick found sustenance mainly at the club, where Pemberton guessed that it was usually served on green cloth. The girls used to do up their hair and their frocks themselves, and our young man felt appealed to to be glad, in regard to Morgan's education, that, though it must naturally be of the best, it didn't cost too much. After a little he *was* glad, forgetting at times his own needs in the interest inspired by the child's nature and education and the pleasure of making easy terms for him.

During the first weeks of their acquaintance Morgan had been as puzzling as a page in an unknown language—altogether different from the obvious little Anglo-Saxons who had misrepresented childhood to Pemberton. Indeed the whole mystic volume in which the boy had been bound demanded some practice in translation. To-day, after a considerable interval, there is something phantasmagoric, like a prismatic reflection or a serial novel, in Pemberton's memory of the queerness of the Moreens. If it were not for a few tangible tokens—a lock of Morgan's hair, cut by his own hand, and the half-dozen letters he got from him when they were separated—the whole episode and the figures peopling it would seem too inconsequent for anything but dreamland. The queerest thing about them was their success (as it appeared to him for a while at the time), for he had never seen a family so brilliantly equipped for failure. Wasn't it success to have kept him so hatefully

long? Wasn't it success to have drawn him in that first morning at
déjeuner, the Friday he came—it was enough to *make* one superstitious—so that he utterly committed himself, and this not by
calculation or a *mot d' ordre*, but by a happy instinct which made
them, like a band of gipsies, work so neatly together? They amused
him as much as if they had really been a band of gipsies. He was
still young and had not seen much of the world—his English years
had been intensely usual; therefore the reversed conventions of the
Moreens (for they had their standards), struck him as topsyturvy.
He had encountered nothing like them at Oxford; still less had any
such note been struck to his younger American ear during the four
years at Yale in which he had richly supposed himself to be react-
ing against Puritanism. The reaction of the Moreens, at any rate,
went ever so much further. He had thought himself very clever
that first day in hitting them all off in his mind with the term "cosmopolite." Later, it seemed feeble and colourless enough—confessedly, helplessly provisional.

However, when he first applied it to them he had a degree of
joy—for an instructor he was still empirical—as if from the apprehension that to live with them would really be to see life. Their
sociable strangeness was an intimation of that—their chatter of
tongues, their gaiety and good humour, their infinite dawdling
(they were always getting themselves up, but it took forever, and
Pemberton had once found Mr. Moreen shaving in the drawing-
room), their French, their Italian and, in the spiced fluency, their
cold, tough slices of American. They lived on macaroni and coffee
(they had these articles prepared in perfection), but they knew
recipes for a hundred other dishes. They overflowed with music
and song, were always humming and catching each other up, and
had a kind of professional acquaintance with continental cities.
They talked of "good places" as if they had been strolling players.
They had at Nice a villa, a carriage, a piano and a banjo, and they
went to official parties. They were a perfect calendar of the "days"
of their friends, which Pemberton knew them, when they were in-
disposed, to get out of bed to go to, and which made the week
larger than life when Mrs. Moreen talked of them with Paula and
Amy. Their romantic initiations gave their new inmate at first an
almost dazzling sense of culture. Mrs. Moreen had translated something, at some former period—an author whom it made Pemberton
feel *borné* never to have heard of. They could imitate Venetian

and sing Neapolitan, and when they wanted to say something very particular they communicated with each other in an ingenious dialect of their own—a sort of spoken cipher, which Pemberton at first took for Volapuk, but which he learned to understand as he would not have understood Volapuk.

"It's the family language—Ultramoreen," Morgan explained to him drolly enough; but the boy rarely condescended to use it himself, though he attempted colloquial Latin as if he had been a little prelate.

Among all the "days" with which Mrs. Moreen's memory was taxed she managed to squeeze in one of her own, which her friends sometimes forgot. But the house derived a frequented air from the number of fine people who were freely named there and from several mysterious men with foreign titles and English clothes whom Morgan called the princes and who, on sofas with the girls, talked French very loud, as if to show they were saying nothing improper. Pemberton wondered how the princes could ever propose in that tone and so publicly: he took for granted cynically that this was what was desired of them. Then he acknowledged that even for the chance of such an advantage Mrs. Moreen would never allow Paula and Amy to receive alone. These young ladies were not at all timid, but it was just the safeguards that made them so graceful. It was a houseful of Bohemians who wanted tremendously to be Philistines.

In one respect, however, certainly, they achieved no rigour—they were wonderfully amiable and ecstatic about Morgan. It was a genuine tenderness, an artless admiration, equally strong in each. They even praised his beauty, which was small, and were rather afraid of him, as if they recognised that he was of a finer clay. They called him a little angel and a little prodigy and pitied his want of health effusively. Pemberton feared at first that their extravagance would make him hate the boy, but before this happened he had become extravagant himself. Later, when he had grown rather to hate the others, it was a bribe to patience for him that they were at any rate nice about Morgan, going on tiptoe if they fancied he was showing symptoms, and even giving up somebody's "day" to procure him a pleasure. But mixed with this was the oddest wish to make him independent, as if they felt that they were not good enough for him. They passed him over to Pemberton very much as if they wished to force a constructive adoption on the obliging bachelor and shirk altogether a responsibility. They were delighted when they perceived that Morgan liked his preceptor, and could think of no higher praise for the young man. It was strange how they contrived to reconcile the appearance, and indeed the essential fact, of adoring the child with their eagerness to wash their hands of him. Did they want to get rid of him before he should find them out? Pemberton was finding them out month by month. At any rate, the boy's relations turned their backs with exaggerated delicacy, as if to escape the charge of interfering. Seeing in time how little he had in common with them (it was by *them* he first observed it—they proclaimed it with complete humility), his preceptor was moved to speculate on the mysteries of transmission, the far jumps of heredity. Where his detachment from most of the things they represented had come from was more than an observer could say—it certainly had burrowed under two or three generations.

As for Pemberton's own estimate of his pupil, it was a good while before he got the point of view, so little had he been prepared for it by the smug young barbarians to whom the tradition of tutorship, as hitherto revealed to him, had been adjusted. Morgan was scrappy and surprising, deficient in many properties supposed common to the *genus* and abounding in others that were the portion only of the supernaturally clever. One day Pemberton made a great stride: it cleared up the question to perceive that Morgan *was* supernaturally clever and that, though the formula was temporarily meagre, this would be the only assumption on which one could successfully deal with him. He had the general quality of a child for whom life had not been simplified by school, a kind of home-bred sensibility which might have been bad for himself but was charming for others, and a whole range of refinement and perception—little musical vibrations as taking as picked-up airs—begotten by wandering about Europe at the tail of his migratory tribe. This might not have been an education to recommend in advance, but its results with Morgan were as palpable as a fine texture. At the same time he had in his composition a sharp spice of stoicism, doubtless the fruit of having had to begin early to bear pain, which produced the impression of pluck and made it of less consequence that he might have been thought at school rather a polyglot little beast. Pemberton indeed quickly found himself rejoicing that school was out of the question: in any million of boys it was prob-

ably good for all but one, and Morgan was that millionth. It would
have made him comparative and superior—it might have made him
priggish. Pemberton would try to be school himself—a bigger
seminary than five hundred grazing donkeys; so that, winning no
prizes, the boy would remain unconscious and irresponsible and
amusing—amusing, because, though life was already intense in
his childish nature, freshness still made there a strong draught
for jokes. It turned out that even in the still air of Morgan's various
disabilities jokes flourished greatly. He was a pale, lean, acute,
undeveloped little cosmopolite, who liked intellectual gym-
nastics and who, also, as regards the behaviour of mankind, had
noticed more things than you might suppose, but who nevertheless
had his proper playroom of superstitions, where he smashed a
dozen toys a day.

III

AT NICE once, towards evening, as the pair sat resting in the open
air after a walk, looking over the sea at the pink western lights,
Morgan said suddenly to his companion: "Do you like it—you
know, being with us all in this intimate way?"

"My dear fellow, why should I stay if I didn't?"

"How do I know you will stay? I'm almost sure you won't, very
long."

"I hope you don't mean to dismiss me," said Pemberton.

Morgan considered a moment, looking at the sunset. "I think
if I did right I ought to."

"Well, I know I'm supposed to instruct you in virtue; but in that
case don't do right."

"You're very young—fortunately," Morgan went on, turning to
him again.

"Oh yes, compared with you!"

"Therefore, it won't matter so much if you do lose a lot of time."

"That's the way to look at it," said Pemberton accommodatingly.

They were silent a minute; after which the boy asked: "Do
you like my father and mother very much?"

"Dear me, yes. They're charming people."

Morgan received this with another silence; then, unexpectedly,
familiarly, but at the same time affectionately, he remarked: "You're
a jolly old humbug!"

For a particular reason the words made Pemberton change colour. The boy noticed in an instant that he had turned red, whereupon he turned red himself and the pupil and the master exchanged a longish glance in which there was a consciousness of many more things than are usually touched upon, even tacitly, in such a relation. It produced for Pemberton an embarrassment; it raised, in a shadowy form, a question (this was the first glimpse of it), which was destined to play as singular and, as he imagined, owing to the altogether peculiar conditions, an unprecedented part in his intercourse with his little companion. Later, when he found himself talking with this small boy in a way in which few small boys could ever have been talked with, he thought of that clumsy moment on the bench at Nice as the dawn of an understanding that had broadened. What had added to the clumsiness then was that he thought it his duty to declare to Morgan that he might abuse him (Pemberton) as much as he liked, but must never abuse his parents. To this Morgan had the easy reply that he hadn't dreamed of abusing them; which appeared to be true: it put Pemberton in the wrong.

"Then why am I a humbug for saying I think them charming?" the young man asked, conscious of a certain rashness.

"Well—they're not *your* parents."

"They love you better than anything in the world—never forget that," said Pemberton.

"Is that why you like them so much?"

"They're very kind to me," Pemberton replied, evasively.

"You *are* a humbug!" laughed Morgan, passing an arm into his tutor's. He leaned against him, looking off at the sea again and swinging his long, thin legs.

"Don't kick my shins," said Pemberton, while he reflected: "Hang it, I can't complain of them to the child!"

"There's another reason, too," Morgan went on, keeping his legs still.

"Another reason for what?"

"Besides their not being your parents."

"I don't understand you," said Pemberton.

"Well, you will before long. All right!"

Pemberton did understand, fully, before long; but he made a fight even with himself before he confessed it. He thought it the oddest thing to have a struggle with the child about. He wondered he didn't detest the child for launching him in such a struggle. But by the time it began the resource of detesting the child was closed to him. Morgan was a special case, but to know him was to accept him on his own odd terms. Pemberton had spent his aversion to special cases before arriving at knowledge. When at last he did arrive he felt that he was in an extreme predicament. Against every interest he had attached himself. They would have to meet things together. Before they went home that evening, at Nice, the boy had said, clinging to his arm:

"Well, at any rate you'll hang on to the last."

"To the last?"

"Till you're fairly beaten."

"*You* ought to be fairly beaten!" cried the young man, drawing him closer.

IV

A YEAR after Pemberton had come to live with them Mr. and Mrs. Moreen suddenly gave up the villa at Nice. Pemberton had got used to suddenness, having seen it practiced on a considerable scale during two jerky little tours—one in Switzerland the first summer, and the other late in the winter, when they all ran down to Florence and then, at the end of ten days, liking it much less than they had intended, straggled back in mysterious depression. They had returned to Nice "for ever," as they said; but this didn't prevent them from squeezing, one rainy, muggy May night, into a second-class railway-carriage—you could never tell by which class they would travel—where Pemberton helped them to stow away a wonderful collection of bundles and bags. The explanation of this manœuvre was that they had determined to spend the summer "in some bracing place"; but in Paris they dropped into a small furnished apartment—a fourth floor in a third-rate avenue, where there was a smell on the staircase and the *portier* was hateful—and passed the next four months in blank indigence.

The better part of this baffled sojourn was for the preceptor and his pupil, who, visiting the Invalides and Notre Dame, the Conciergerie and all the museums, took a hundred remunerative rambles. They learned to know their Paris, which was useful, for they came back another year for a longer stay, the general character of which in Pemberton's memory to-day mixes pitiably and confusedly with that of the first. He sees Morgan's shabby knickerbockers—the everlasting pair that didn't match his blouse and that as he grew longer could only grow faded. He remembers the particular holes in his three or four pair of coloured stockings.

Morgan was dear to his mother, but he never was better dressed than was absolutely necessary—partly, no doubt, by his own fault, for he was as indifferent to his appearance as a German philosopher. "My dear fellow, you *are* coming to pieces," Pemberton would say to him in sceptical remonstrance; to which the child would reply, looking at him serenely up and down: "My dear fellow, so are you! I don't want to cast you in the shade." Pemberton could have no rejoinder for this—the assertion so closely represented the fact. If however the deficiencies of his own wardrobe were a chapter by themselves he didn't like his little charge to look too poor. Later he used to say: "Well, if we are poor, why, after all, shouldn't we look it?" and he consoled himself with thinking there was something rather elderly and gentlemanly in Morgan's seediness—it differed from the untidiness of the urchin who plays and spoils his things. He could trace perfectly the degrees by which, in proportion as her little son confined himself to his tutor for society, Mrs. Moreen shrewdly forbore to renew his garments. She did nothing that didn't show, neglected him because he escaped notice, and then, as he illustrated this clever policy, discouraged at home his public appearances. Her position was logical enough—those members of her family who did show had to be showy.

During this period and several others Pemberton was quite aware of how he and his comrade might strike people; wandering languidly through the Jardin des Plantes as if they had nowhere to go, sitting, on the winter days, in the galleries of the Louvre, so splendidly ironical to the homeless, as if for the advantage of the *calorifère*. They joked about it sometimes: it was the sort of joke that was perfectly within the boy's compass. They figured themselves as part of the vast, vague, hand-to-mouth multitude of the enormous city and pretended they were proud of their position in it—it showed them such a lot of life and made them conscious of a sort of democratic brotherhood. If Pemberton could not feel a sympathy in destitution with his small companion (for after all Morgan's fond parents would never have let him really suffer), the boy would at least feel it with him, so it came to the same thing. He used sometimes to wonder what people would think they were

—fancy they were looked askance at, as if it might be a suspected case of kidnapping. Morgan wouldn't be taken for a young patrician with a preceptor—he wasn't smart enough; though he might pass for his companion's sickly little brother. Now and then he had a five-franc piece, and except once, when they bought a couple of lovely neckties, one of which he made Pemberton accept, they laid it out scientifically in old books. It was a great day, always spent on the quays, rummaging among the dusty boxes that garnish the parapets. These were occasions that helped them to live, for their books ran low very soon after the beginning of their acquaintance. Pemberton had a good many in England, but he was obliged to write to a friend and ask him kindly to get some fellow to give him something for them.

If the bracing climate was untasted that summer the young man had an idea that at the moment they were about to make a push the cup had been dashed from their lips by a movement of his own. It had been his first blow-out, as he called it, with his patrons; his first successful attempt (though there was little other success about it), to bring them to a consideration of his impossible position. As the ostensible eve of a costly journey the moment struck him as a good one to put in a signal protest—to present an ultimatum. Ridiculous as it sounded he had never yet been able to compass an uninterrupted private interview with the elder pair or with either of them singly. They were always flanked by their elder children, and poor Pemberton usually had his own little charge at his side. He was conscious of its being a house in which the surface of one's delicacy got rather smudged; nevertheless he had kept the bloom of his scruple against announcing to Mr. and Mrs. Moreen with publicity that he couldn't go on longer without a little money. He was still simple enough to suppose Ulick and Paula and Amy might not know that since his arrival he had only had a hundred and forty francs; and he was magnanimous enough to wish not to compromise their parents in their eyes. Mr. Moreen now listened to him, as he listened to every one and to everything, like a man of the world, and seemed to appeal to him—though not of course too grossly—to try and be a little more of one himself. Pemberton recognised the importance of the character from the advantage it gave Mr. Moreen. He was not even confused, whereas poor Pemberton was more so than there was any reason for. Neither was he surprised—at least any more than a gentleman had to be who freely confessed himself a little shocked, though not, strictly, at Pemberton.

"We must go into this, mustn't we, dear?" he said to his wife. He assured his young friend that the matter should have his very best attention; and he melted into space as elusively as if, at the door, he were taking an inevitable but deprecatory precedence. When, the next moment, Pemberton found himself alone with Mrs. Moreen it was to hear her say: "I see, I see," stroking the roundness of her chin and looking as if she were only hesitating between a dozen easy remedies. If they didn't make their push Mr. Moreen could at least disappear for several days. During his absence his wife took up the subject again spontaneously, but her contribution to it was merely that she had thought all the while they were getting on so beautifully. Pemberton's reply to this revelation was that unless they immediately handed him a substantial sum he would leave them for ever. He knew she would wonder how he would get away, and for a moment expected her to inquire. She didn't, for which he was almost grateful to her, so little was he in a position to tell.

"You won't, you know you won't—you're too interested," she said. "You *are* interested, you know you are, you dear, kind man!" She laughed, with almost condemnatory archness, as if it were a reproach (but she wouldn't insist), while she flirted a soiled pockethandkerchief at him.

Pemberton's mind was fully made up to quit the house the following week. This would give him time to get an answer to a letter he had despatched to England. If he did nothing of the sort —that is, if he stayed another year and then went away only for three months—it was not merely because before the answer to his letter came (most unsatisfactory when it did arrive), Mr. Moreen generously presented him—again with all the precautions of a man of the world—three hundred francs. He was exasperated to find that Mrs. Moreen was right, that he couldn't bear to leave the child. This stood out clearer for the very reason that, the night of his desperate appeal to his patrons, he had seen fully for the first time where he was. Wasn't it another proof of the success with which those patrons practiced their arts that they had managed to avert for so long the illuminating flash? It descended upon Pemberton with a luridness which perhaps would have struck a spectator as comically excessive, after he had returned to his little servile room, which looked into a close court where a bare, dirty opposite wall took, with the sound of shrill clatter, the reflection of lighted back-windows. He had simply given himself away to a band of adventurers. The idea, the word itself, had a sort of romantic horror for him—he had always lived on such safe lines. Later it assumed a more interesting, almost a soothing, sense: it pointed a moral, and Pemberton could enjoy a moral. The Moreens were adventurers not merely because they didn't pay their debts, because they lived on society, but because their whole view of life, dim and confused and instinctive, like that of clever colour-blind animals, was speculative and rapacious and mean. Oh! they were "respectable," and that only made them more *immondes*. The young man's analysis of them put it at last very simply—they were adventurers because they were abject snobs. That was the completest account of them—it was the law of their being. Even when this truth became vivid to their ingenious inmate he remained unconscious of how much his mind had been prepared for it by the extraordinary little boy who had now become such a complication in his life. Much less could he then calculate on the information he was still to owe to the extraordinary little boy.

V

But it was during the ensuing time that the real problem came up—the problem of how far it was excusable to discuss the turpitude of parents with a child of twelve, of thirteen, of fourteen. Absolutely inexcusable and quite impossible it of course at first appeared; and indeed the question didn't press for a while after Pemberton had received his three hundred francs. They produced a sort of lull, a relief from the sharpest pressure. Pemberton frugally amended his wardrobe and even had a few francs in his pocket. He thought the Moreens looked at him as if he were almost too smart, as if they ought to take care not to spoil him. If Mr. Moreen hadn't been such a man of the world he would perhaps have said something to him about his neckties. But Mr. Moreen was always enough of a man of the world to let things pass—he had certainly shown that. It was singular how Pemberton guessed that Morgan, though saying nothing about it, knew something had happened. But three hundred francs, especially when one owed money, couldn't last for ever; and when they were gone—the boy knew

when they were gone—Morgan did say something. The party had
returned to Nice at the beginning of the winter, but not to the
charming villa. They went to an hotel, where they stayed three
months, and then they went to another hotel, explaining that they
had left the first because they had waited and waited and couldn't
get the rooms they wanted. These apartments, the rooms they
wanted, were generally very splendid; but fortunately they never
could get them—fortunately, I mean, for Pemberton, who reflected
always that if they had got them there would have been still less
for educational expenses. What Morgan said at last was said
suddenly, irrelevantly, when the moment came, in the middle of a
lesson, and consisted of the apparently unfeeling words: "You ought
to *filer*, you know—you really ought."

Pemberton stared. He had learnt enough French slang from
Morgan to know that to *filer* meant to go away. "Ah, my dear fellow,
don't turn me off!"

Morgan pulled a Greek lexicon toward him (he used a Greek-
German), to look out a word, instead of asking it of Pemberton.
"You can't go on like this, you know."

"Like what, my boy?"

"You know they don't pay you up," said Morgan, blushing and
turning his leaves.

"Don't pay me?" Pemberton stared again and feigned amaze-
ment. "What on earth put that into your head?"

"It has been there a long time," the boy replied, continuing his
search.

Pemberton was silent, then he went on: "I say, what are you hunting for? They pay me beautifully."

"I'm hunting for the Greek for transparent fiction," Morgan
dropped.

"Find that rather for gross impertinence, and disabuse your mind.
What do I want of money?"

"Oh, that's another question!"

Pemberton hesitated—he was drawn in different ways. The
severely correct thing would have been to tell the boy that such
a matter was none of his business and bid him go on with his lines.
But they were really too intimate for that; it was not the way he was
in the habit of treating him; there had been no reason it should be.
On the other hand Morgan had quite lighted on the truth—he
really shouldn't be able to keep it up much longer; therefore why

not let him know one's real motive for forsaking him? At the same time it wasn't decent to abuse to one's pupil the family of one's pupil; it was better to misrepresent than to do that. So in reply to Morgan's last exclamation he just declared, to dismiss the subject, that he had received several payments.

"I say—I say!" the boy ejaculated, laughing.

"That's all right," Pemberton insisted, "Give me your written rendering."

Morgan pushed a copybook across the table, and his companion began to read the page, but with something running in his head that made it no sense. Looking up after a minute or two he found the child's eyes fixed on him, and he saw something strange in them. Then Morgan said: "I'm not afraid of the reality."

" I haven't yet seen the thing that you *are* afraid of—I'll do you that justice!"

This came out with a jump (it was perfectly true), and evidently gave Morgan pleasure. "I've thought of it a long time," he presently resumed.

"Well, don't think of it any more."

The child appeared to comply, and they had a comfortable and even an amusing hour. They had a theory that they were very thorough, and yet they seemed always to be in the amusing part of lessons, the intervals between the tunnels, where there were waysides and views. Yet the morning was brought to a violent end by Morgan's suddenly leaning his arms on the table, burying his head in them and bursting into tears. Pemberton would have been startled at any rate; but he was doubly startled because, as it then occurred to him, it was the first time he had ever seen the boy cry. It was rather awful.

The next day, after much thought, he took a decision and, believing it to be just, immediately acted upon it. He cornered Mr. and Mrs. Moreen again and informed them that if, on the spot, they didn't pay him all they owed him, he would not only leave their house, but would tell Morgan exactly what had brought him to it.

"Oh, you *haven't* told him?" cried Mrs. Moreen, with a pacifying hand on her well-dressed bosom.

"Without warning you? For what do you take me?"

Mr. and Mrs. Moreen looked at each other, and Pemberton could see both that they were relieved and that there was a certain alarm in their relief. "My dear fellow," Mr. Moreen demanded, "what use *can* you have, leading the quiet life we all do, for such a lot of money?"—an inquiry to which Pemberton made no answer, occupied as he was in perceiving that what passed in the mind of his patrons was something like: "Oh, then, if we've felt that the child, dear little angel, has judged us and how he regards us, and we haven't been betrayed, he must have guessed—and, in short, it's *general!*" an idea that rather stirred up Mr. and Mrs. Moreen, as Pemberton had desired that it should. At the same time, if he had thought that his threat would do something towards bringing them round, he was disappointed to find that they had taken for granted (how little they appreciated his delicacy!) that he had already given them away to his pupil. There was a mystic uneasiness in their parental breasts, and that was the way they had accounted for it. None the less his threat did touch them; for if they had escaped it was only to meet a new danger. Mr. Moreen appealed to Pemberton, as usual, as a man of the world; but his wife had recourse, for the first time since the arrival of their inmate, to a fine *hauteur,* reminding him that a devoted mother, with her child, had arts that protected her against gross misrepresentation.

"I should misrepresent you grossly if I accused you of common honesty!" the young man replied; but as he closed the door behind him sharply, thinking he had not done himself much good, while Mr. Moreen lighted another cigarette, he heard Mrs. Moreen shout after him, more touchingly:

"Oh, you do, you *do*, put the knife to one's throat!"

The next morning, very early, she came to his room. He recognised her knock, but he had no hope that she brought him money; as to which he was wrong, for she had fifty francs in her hand. She squeezed forward in her dressing-gown, and he received her in his own, between his bath-tub and his bed. He had been tolerably schooled by this time to the "foreign ways" of his hosts. Mrs. Moreen was zealous, and when she was zealous she didn't care what she did; so she now sat down on his bed, his clothes being on the chairs, and, in her preoccupation, forgot, as she glanced round, to be ashamed of giving him such a nasty room. What Mrs. Moreen was zealous about on this occasion was to persuade him that in the first place she was very good-natured to bring him fifty francs, and, in the second, if he would only see it, he was really too absurd to expect to be *paid*. Wasn't he paid enough, without perpetual money—wasn't he paid by the comfortable, luxurious home that he enjoyed with them all, without a care, an anxiety, a solitary want? Wasn't he sure of his position, and wasn't that everything to a young man like him, quite unknown, with singularly little to show, the ground of whose exorbitant pretensions it was not easy to discover? Wasn't he paid, above all, by the delightful relation he had established with Morgan—quite ideal, as from master to pupil— and by the simple privilege of knowing and living with so amazingly gifted a child, than whom really—she meant literally what she said—there was no better company in Europe? Mrs. Moreen herself took to appealing to him as a man of the world; she said "Voyons, mon cher," and "My dear sir, look here now;" and urged him to be reasonable, putting it before him that it was really a chance for him. She spoke as if, according as he *should* be reasonable, he would prove himself worthy to be her son's tutor and of the extraordinary confidence they had placed in him.

After all, Pemberton reflected, it was only a difference of theory, and the theory didn't matter much. They had hitherto gone on that of remunerated, as now they would go on that of gratuitous, service; but why should they have so many words about it? Mrs. Moreen, however, continued to be convincing; sitting there with her fifty francs she talked and repeated, as women repeat, and bored and irritated him, while he leaned against the wall with his hands in the pockets of his wrapper, drawing it together round his legs and looking over the head of his visitor at the grey negations of his window. She wound up with saying: "You see I bring you a definite proposal."

"A definite proposal?"

"To make our relations regular, as it were—to put them on a comfortable footing."

"I see—it's a system," said Pemberton. "A kind of blackmail."

Mrs. Moreen bounded up, which was what the young man wanted.

"What do you mean by that?"

"You practice on one's fears—one's fears about the child if one should go away."

"And, pray, what would happen to him in that event?" demanded Mrs. Moreen, with majesty.

"Why, he'd be alone with *you*."

"And pray, with whom *should* a child be but with those whom he loves most?"

"If you think that, why don't you dismiss me?"

"Do you pretend that he loves you more than he loves *us?*" cried Mrs. Moreen.

"I think he ought to. I make sacrifices for him. Though I've heard of those *you* make, I don't see them."

Mrs. Moreen stared a moment; then, with emotion, she grasped Pemberton's hand. "*Will* you make it—the sacrifice?"

Pemberton burst out laughing. "I'll see—I'll do what I can—I'll stay a little longer. Your calculation is just—I *do* hate intensely to give him up; I'm fond of him and he interests me deeply, in spite of the inconvenience I suffer. You know my situation perfectly; I haven't a penny in the world, and, occupied as I am with Morgan, I'm unable to earn money."

Mrs. Moreen tapped her undressed arm with her folded bank-note. "Can't you write articles? Can't you translate, as *I* do?"

"I don't know about translating; it's wretchedly paid."

"I am glad to earn what I can," said Mrs. Moreen virtuously, with her head high.

"You ought to tell me who you do it for." Pemberton paused a moment, and she said nothing; so he added: "I've tried to turn off some little sketches, but the magazines won't have them—they're declined with thanks."

"You see then you're not such a phœnix—to have such pretensions," smiled his interlocutress.

"I haven't time to do things properly," Pemberton went on. Then as it came over him that he was almost abjectly good-natured to give these explanations he added: "If I stay on longer it must be on one condition—that Morgan shall know distinctly on what footing I am."

Mrs. Moreen hesitated. "Surely you don't want to show off to a child?"

"To show *you* off, do you mean?"

Again Mrs. Moreen hesitated, but this time it was to produce a still finer flower. "And *you* talk of blackmail!"

"You can easily prevent it," said Pemberton.

"And *you* talk of practicing on fears," Mrs. Moreen continued.

"Yes, there's no doubt I'm a great scoundrel."

His visitor looked at him a moment—it was evident that she was sorely bothered. Then she thrust out her money at him. "Mr. Moreen desired me to give you this on account."

"I'm much obliged to Mr. Moreen; but we have no account."

"You won't take it?"

"That leaves me more free," said Pemberton.

"To poison my darling's mind?" groaned Mrs. Moreen.

"Oh, your darling's mind!" laughed the young man.

She fixed him a moment, and he thought she was going to break out tormentedly, pleadingly: "For God's sake, tell me what *is* in it!" But she checked this impulse—another was stronger. She pocketed the money—the crudity of the alternative was comical— and swept out of the room with the desperate concession: "You may tell him any horror you like!"

VI

A COUPLE of days after this, during which Pemberton had delayed to profit by Mrs. Moreen's permission to tell her son any horror, the two had been for a quarter of an hour walking together in silence when the boy became sociable again with the remark: "I'll tell you how I know it; I know it through Zénobie."

"Zénobie? Who in the world is *she?*"

"A nurse I used to have—ever so many years ago. A charming woman. I liked her awfully, and she liked me."

"There's no accounting for tastes. What is it you know through her?"

"Why, what their idea is. She went away because they didn't pay her. She did like me awfully, and she stayed two years. She told me all about it—that at last she could never get her wages. As soon as they saw how much she liked me they stopped giving her anything. They thought she'd stay for nothing, out of devotion. And she did stay ever so long—as long as she could. She was only a poor girl. She used to send money to her mother. At last she couldn't afford it any longer, and she went away in a fearful rage one night—I mean of course in a rage against *them.* She cried over me tremendously, she hugged me nearly to death. She told me all about it," Morgan repeated. "She told me it was their idea. So I guessed, ever so long ago, that they have had the same idea with you."

"Zénobie was very shrewd," said Pemberton. "And she made you so."

"Oh, that wasn't Zénobie; that was nature. And experience!" Morgan laughed.

"Well, Zénobie was a part of your experience."

"Certainly I was a part of hers, poor dear!" the boy exclaimed. "And I'm a part of yours."

"A very important part. But I don't see how you know that I've been treated like Zénobie."

"Do you take me for an idiot?" Morgan asked. "Haven't I been conscious of what we've been through together?"

"What we've been through?"

"Our privations—our dark days."

"Oh, our days have been bright enough."

Morgan went on in silence for a moment. Then he said: "My dear fellow, you're a hero!"

"Well, you're another!" Pemberton retorted.

"No, I'm not; but I'm not a baby. I won't stand it any longer. You must get some occupation that pays. I'm ashamed, I'm ashamed!" quavered the boy in a little passionate voice that was very touching to Pemberton.

"We ought to go off and live somewhere together," said the young man.

"I'll go like a shot if you'll take me."

"I'd get some work that would keep us both afloat," Pemberton continued.

"So would I. Why shouldn't *I* work? I ain't such a *crétin!*"

"The difficulty is that your parents wouldn't hear of it," said Pemberton. "They would never part with you; they worship the ground you tread on. Don't you see the proof of it? They don't dislike me; they wish me no harm; they're very amiable people; but they're perfectly ready to treat me badly for your sake."

The silence in which Morgan received this graceful sophistry struck Pemberton somehow as expressive. After a moment Morgan repeated: "You *are* a hero!" Then he added: "They leave me with you altogether. You've all the responsibility. They put me off on you from morning till night. Why, then, should they object to my taking up with you completely? I'd help you."

"They're not particularly keen about my being helped, and they delight in thinking of you as *theirs*. They're tremendously proud of you."

"I'm not proud of them. But you know *that*," Morgan returned.

"Except for the little matter we speak of they're charming people," said Pemberton, not taking up the imputation of lucidity, but wondering greatly at the child's own, and especially at this fresh reminder of something he had been conscious of from the first—the strangest thing in the boy's large little composition, a temper, a sensibility, even a sort of ideal, which made him privately resent the general quality of his kinsfolk. Morgan had in secret a small loftiness which begot an element of reflection, a domestic scorn not imperceptible to his companion (though they never had any talk about it), and absolutely anomalous in a juvenile nature, especially when one noted that it had not made this nature "old-fashioned," as the word is of children—quaint or wizened or offensive. It was as if he had been a little gentleman and had paid the penalty by discovering that he was the only such person in the family. This comparison didn't make him vain; but it could make him melancholy and a trifle austere. When Pemberton guessed at these young dimnesses he saw him serious and gallant, and was partly drawn on and partly checked, as if with a scruple, by the charm of attempting to sound the little cool shallows which were quickly growing deeper. When he tried to figure to himself the morning twilight of childhood, so as to deal with it safely, he perceived that it was never fixed, never arrested, that ignorance, at the instant one touched it, was already flushing faintly into knowledge, that there was nothing that at a given moment you could say a clever child didn't know. It seemed to him that *he* both knew too much to imagine Morgan's simplicity and too little to disembroil his tangle.

The boy paid no heed to his last remark; he only went on: "I should have spoken to them about their idea, as I call it, long ago, if I hadn't been sure what they would say."

"And what would they say?"

"Just what they said about what poor Zénobie told me—that it was a horrid, dreadful story, that they had paid her every penny they owed her."

"Well, perhaps they had," said Pemberton.

"Perhaps they've paid you!"

"Let us pretend they have, and *n'en parlons plus*."

"They accused her of lying and cheating," Morgan insisted perversely. "That's why I don't want to speak to them."

"Lest they should accuse me, too?"

To this Morgan made no answer, and his companion, looking

down at him (the boy turned his eyes, which had filled, away), saw that he couldn't have trusted himself to utter.

"You're right. Don't squeeze them," Pemberton pursued. "Except for that, they *are* charming people."

"Except for *their* lying and *their* cheating?"

"I say—I say!" cried Pemberton, imitating a little tone of the lad's which was itself an imitation.

"We must be frank, at the last; we *must* come to an understanding," said Morgan, with the importance of the small boy who lets himself think he is arranging great affairs—almost playing at shipwreck or at Indians. "I know all about everything," he added.

"I daresay your father has his reasons," Pemberton observed, too vaguely, as he was aware.

"For lying and cheating?"

"For saving and managing and turning his means to the best account. He has plenty to do with his money. You're an expensive family."

"Yes, I'm very expensive," Morgan rejoined, in a manner which made his preceptor burst out laughing.

"He's saving for *you*," said Pemberton. "They think of you in everything they do."

"He might save a little——" The boy paused. Pemberton waited to hear what. Then Morgan brought out oddly: "A little reputation."

"Oh, there's plenty of that. That's all right!"

"Enough of it for the people they know, no doubt. The people they know are awful."

"Do you mean the princes? We mustn't abuse the princes."

"Why not? They haven't married Paula—they haven't married Amy. They only clean out Ulick."

"You *do* know everything!" Pemberton exclaimed.

"No, I don't, after all. I don't know what they live on, or how they live, or *why* they live! What have they got and how did they get it? Are they rich, are they poor, or have they a *modeste aisance?* Why are they always chiveying about—living one year like ambassadors and the next like paupers? Who are they, any way, and what are they? I've thought of all that—I've thought of a lot of things. They're so beastly worldly. That's what I hate most—oh, I've *seen* it! All they care about is to make an appearance and to pass for something or other. What do they want to pass for? What *do* they, Mr. Pemberton?"

"You pause for a reply," said Pemberton, treating the inquiry as a joke, yet wondering too, and greatly struck with the boy's intense, if imperfect, vision. "I haven't the least idea."

"And what good does it do? Haven't I seen the way people treat them—the 'nice' people, the ones they want to know? They'll take anything from them—they'll lie down and be trampled on. The nice ones hate that—they just sicken them. You're the only really nice person we know."

"Are you sure? They don't lie down for me!"

"Well, you shan't lie down for them. You've got to go—that's what you've got to do," said Morgan.

"And what will become of you?"

"Oh, I'm growing up. I shall get off before long. I'll see you later."

"You had better let me finish you," Pemberton urged, lending himself to the child's extraordinarily competent attitude.

Morgan stopped in their walk, looking up at him. He had to look up much less than a couple of years before—he had grown, in his loose leanness, so long and high. "Finish me?" he echoed.

"There are such a lot of jolly things we can do together yet. I want to turn you out—I want you to do me credit."

Morgan continued to look at him. "To give you credit—do you mean?"

"My dear fellow, you're too clever to live."

"That's just what I'm afraid you think. No, no; it isn't fair—I can't endure it. We'll part next week. The sooner it's over the sooner to sleep."

"If I hear of anything—any other chance, I promise to go," said Pemberton.

Morgan consented to consider this. "But you'll be honest," he demanded; "you won't pretend you haven't heard?"

"I'm much more likely to pretend I have."

"But what can you hear of, this way, stuck in a hole with us? You ought to be on the spot, to go to England—you ought to go to America."

"One would think you were *my* tutor!" said Pemberton.

Morgan walked on, and after a moment he began again: "Well, now that you know that I know and that we look at the facts and keep nothing back—it's much more comfortable, isn't it?"

"My dear boy, it's so amusing, so interesting, that it surely will be quite impossible for me to forego such hours as these."

This made Morgan stop once more. "You *do* keep something back. Oh, you're not straight—*I* am!"

"Why am I not straight?"

"Oh, you've got your idea!"

"My idea?"

"Why, that I probably sha'n't live, and that you can stick it out till I'm removed."

"You *are* too clever to live!" Pemberton repeated.

"I call it a mean idea," Morgan pursued. "But I shall punish you by the way I hang on."

"Look out or I'll poison you!" Pemberton laughed.

"I'm stronger and better every year. Haven't you noticed that there hasn't been a doctor near me since you came?"

"*I'm* your doctor," said the young man, taking his arm and drawing him on again.

Morgan proceeded, and after a few steps he gave a sigh of mingled weariness and relief. "Ah, now that we look at the facts, it's all right!"

VII

THEY LOOKED at the facts a good deal after this; and one of the first consequences of their doing so was that Pemberton stuck it out, as it were, for the purpose. Morgan made the facts so vivid and so droll, and at the same time so bald and so ugly, that there was fascination in talking them over with him, just as there would have been heartlessness in leaving him alone with them. Now that they had such a number of perceptions in common it was useless for the pair to pretend that they didn't judge such people; but the very judgment, and the exchange of perceptions, created another tie. Morgan had never been so interesting as now that he himself was made plainer by the sidelight of these confidences. What came out in it most was the soreness of his characteristic pride. He had plenty of that, Pemberton felt—so much that it was perhaps well it should have had to take some early bruises. He would have liked his people to be gallant, and he had waked up too soon to the sense that they were perpetually swallowing humble-pie. His mother would consume any amount, and his father would consume even more than his mother. He had a theory that Ulick had wriggled out of an "affair" at Nice: there had once been a flurry at home, a regular panic, after which they all went to bed and took medicine, not to be accounted for on any other supposition. Morgan had a romantic imagination, fed by poetry and history, and he would have liked those who "bore his name" (as he used to say to Pemberton with the humour that made his sensitiveness manly), to have a proper spirit. But their one idea was to get in with people who didn't want them and to take snubs as if they were honourable scars. Why people didn't want them more he didn't know—that was people's own affair; after all they were not superficially repulsive—they were a hundred times cleverer than most of the dreary grandees, the "poor swells" they rushed about Europe to catch up with. "After all, they *are* amusing—they are!" Morgan used to say, with the wisdom of the ages. To which Pemberton always replied: "Amusing—the great Moreen troupe? Why, they're altogether delightful; and if it were not for the hitch that you and I (feeble performers!) make in the *ensemble*, they would carry everything before them."

What the boy couldn't get over was that this particular blight seemed, in a tradition of self-respect, so undeserved and so arbitrary. No doubt people had a right to take the line they liked; but why should *his* people have liked the line of pushing and toadying and lying and cheating? What had their forefathers—all decent folk, so far as he knew—done to them, or what had *he* done to them? Who had poisoned their blood with the fifth-rate social ideal, the fixed idea of making smart acquaintances and getting into the *monde chic*, especially when it was foredoomed to failure and exposure? They showed so what they were after; that was what made the people they wanted not want *them*. And never a movement of dignity, never a throb of shame at looking each other in the face, never any independence or resentment or disgust. If his father or his brother would only knock some one down once or twice a year! Clever as they were they never guessed how they appeared. They were good-natured, yes—as good-natured as Jews at the doors of clothing-shops! But was that the model one wanted one's family to follow? Morgan had dim memories of an old grandfather, the maternal, in New York, whom he had been taken across the ocean to see, at the age of five: a gentleman with a high neckcloth and a good deal of pronunciation, who wore a dress-coat in the morning, which made one wonder what he wore in the evening, and had, or was supposed to have, "property" and something to do with the Bible Society. It couldn't have been but that *he* was a good type. Pemberton himself remembered Mrs. Clancy, a widowed sister of Mr. Moreen's, who was as irritating as a moral tale and had paid a fortnight's visit to the family at Nice shortly after he came to live with them. She was "pure and refined," as Amy said, over the banjo, and had the air of not knowing what they meant and of keeping something back. Pemberton judged that what she kept back was an approval of many of their ways; therefore it was to be supposed that she too was of a good type, and that Mr. and Mrs. Moreen and Ulick and Paula and Amy might easily have been better if they would.

But that they wouldn't was more and more perceptible from day to day. They continued to "chivey," as Morgan called it, and in due time became aware of a variety of reasons for proceeding to Venice. They mentioned a great many of them—they were always strikingly frank, and had the brightest friendly chatter, at the late foreign breakfast in especial, before the ladies had made up their faces, when they leaned their arms on the table, had something to follow the *demi-tasse*, and, in the heat of familiar discussion as to what they "really ought" to do, fell inevitably into the languages in which they could *tutoyer*. Even Pemberton liked them, then; he could endure even Ulick when he heard him give his little flat voice for the "sweet sea-city." That was what made him have a sneaking kindness for them—that they were so out of the workaday world and kept him so out of it. The summer had waned when, with cries of ecstasy, they all passed out on the balcony that overhung the Grand Canal; the sunsets were splendid —the Dorringtons had arrived. The Dorringtons were the only reason they had not talked of at breakfast; but the reasons that they didn't talk of at breakfast always came out in the end. The Dorringtons, on the other hand, came out very little; or else, when they did, they stayed—as was natural—for hours, during which periods Mrs. Moreen and the girls sometimes called at their hotel (to see if they had returned) as many as three times running. The gondola was for the ladies; for in Venice too there were "days," which Mrs. Moreen knew in their order an hour after she arrived. She immediately took one herself, to which the Dorringtons never came, though on a certain occasion when Pemberton and his pupil were together at St. Mark's—where, taking the best walks they had ever had and haunting a hundred churches, they spent a great deal

of time—they saw the old lord turn up with Mr. Moreen and
Ulick, who showed him the dim basilica as if it belonged to them.
Pemberton noted how much less, among its curiosities, Lord Dor-
ington carried himself as a man of the world; wondering too
whether, for such services, his companions took a fee from him.
The autumn, at any rate, waned, the Dorringtons departed, and
Lord Verschoyle, the eldest son, had proposed neither for Amy
nor for Paula.

One sad November day, while the wind roared round the old
palace and the rain lashed the lagoon, Pemberton, for exercise
and even somewhat for warmth (the Moreens were horribly frugal
about fires—it was a cause of suffering to their inmate), walked
up and down the big bare *sala* with his pupil. The scagliola floor
was cold, the high battered casements shook in the storm, and the
stately decay of the place was unrelieved by a particle of furniture.
Pemberton's spirits were low, and it came over him that the fortune
of the Moreens was now even lower. A blast of desolation, a proph-
ecy of disaster and disgrace, seemed to draw through the comfort-
less hall. Mr. Moreen and Ulick were in the Piazza, looking out
for something, strolling drearily, in mackintoshes, under the
arcades; but still, in spite of mackintoshes, unmistakable men of
the world. Paula and Amy were in bed—it might have been
thought they were staying there to keep warm. Pemberton looked
askance at the boy at his side, to see to what extent he was conscious
of these portents. But Morgan, luckily for him, was now mainly
conscious of growing taller and stronger and indeed of being in
his fifteenth year. This fact was intensely interesting to him—it was
the basis of a private theory (which, however, he had imparted to
his tutor) that in a little while he should stand on his own feet.
He considered that the situation would change—that, in short, he
should be "finished," grown up, producible in the world of affairs
and ready to prove himself of sterling ability. Sharply as he was
capable, at times, of questioning his circumstances, there were
happy hours when he was as superficial as a child; the proof of
which was his fundamental assumption that he should presently go
to Oxford, to Pemberton's college, and, aided and abetted by Pemberton, do the most wonderful things. It vexed Pemberton to see
how little, in such a project, he took account of ways and means:
on other matters he was so sceptical about them. Pemberton tried
to imagine the Moreens at Oxford, and fortunately failed; yet un-

less they were to remove there as a family there would be no *modus vivendi* for Morgan. How could he live without an allowance, and where was the allowance to come from? He (Pemberton) might live on Morgan; but how could Morgan live on him? What was to become of him anyhow? Somehow, the fact that he was a big boy now, with better prospects of health, made the question of his future more difficult. So long as he was frail the consideration that he inspired seemed enough of an answer to it. But at the bottom of Pemberton's heart was the recognition of his probably being strong enough to live and not strong enough to thrive. He himself, at any rate, was in a period of natural, boyish rosiness about all this, so that the beating of the tempest seemed to him only the voice of life and the challenge of fate. He had on his shabby little overcoat, with the collar up, but he was enjoying his walk.

It was interrupted at last by the appearance of his mother at the end of the *sala*. She beckoned to Morgan to come to her, and while Pemberton saw him, complacent, pass down the long vista, over the damp false marble, he wondered what was in the air. Mrs. Moreen said a word to the boy and made him go into the room she had quitted. Then, having closed the door after him, she directed her steps swiftly to Pemberton. There *was* something in the air, but his wildest flight of fancy wouldn't have suggested what it proved to be. She signified that she had made a pretext to get Morgan out of the way, and then she inquired—without hesitation —if the young man could lend her sixty francs. While, before bursting into a laugh, he stared at her with surprise, she declared that she was awfully pressed for the money; she was desperate for it—it would save her life.

"Dear lady, *c'est trop fort!*" Pemberton laughed. "Where in the world do you suppose I should get sixty francs, *du train dont vous allez?*"

"I thought you worked—wrote things; don't they pay you?"

"Not a penny."

"Are you such a fool as to work for nothing?"

"You ought surely to know that."

Mrs. Moreen stared an instant, then she coloured a little. Pemberton saw she had quite forgotten the terms—if "terms" they could be called—that he had ended by accepting from herself; they had burdened her memory as little as her conscience. "Oh, yes, I see what you mean—you have been very nice about that; but why go back to it so often?" She had been perfectly urbane with him ever since the rough scene of explanation in his room, the morning he made her accept *his* "terms"—the necessity of his making his case known to Morgan. She had felt no resentment, after seeing that there was no danger of Morgan's taking the matter up with her. Indeed, attributing this immunity to the good taste of his influence with the boy, she had once said to Pemberton: "My dear fellow; it's an immense comfort you're a gentleman." She repeated this, in substance, now. "Of course you're a gentleman—that's a bother the less!" Pemberton reminded her that he had not "gone back" to anything; and she also repeated her prayer that, somewhere and somehow, he would find her sixty francs. He took the liberty of declaring that if he could find them it wouldn't be to lend them to *her*—as to which he consciously did himself injustice, knowing that if he had them he would certainly place them in her hand. He accused himself, at bottom and with some truth, of a fantastic, demoralised sympathy with her. If misery made strange bedfellows it also made strange sentiments. It was moreover a part of the demoralisation and of the general bad effect of living with such people that one had to make rough retorts, quite out of the tradition of good manners. "Morgan, Morgan, to what pass have I come for you?" he privately exclaimed, while Mrs. Moreen floated voluminously down the *sala* again, to liberate the boy; groaning, as she went, that everything was too odious.

Before the boy was liberated there came a thump at the door communicating with the staircase, followed by the apparition of a dripping youth who poked in his head. Pemberton recognised him as the bearer of a telegram and recognised the telegram as addressed to himself. Morgan came back as, after glancing at the signature (that of a friend in London), he was reading the words: "Found jolly job for you—engagement to coach opulent youth on own terms. Come immediately." The answer, happily, was paid, and the messenger waited. Morgan, who had drawn near, waited too, and looked hard at Pemberton; and Pemberton, after a moment, having met his look, handed him the telegram. It was really by wise looks (they knew each other so well), that, while the telegraph-boy, in his waterproof cape, made a great puddle on the floor, the thing was settled between them. Pemberton wrote the answer with a pencil against the frescoed wall, and the messenger departed. When he had gone Pemberton said to Morgan:

"I'll make a tremendous charge; I'll earn a lot of money in a short time, and we'll live on it."

"Well, I hope the opulent youth will be stupid—he probably will—" Morgan parenthesised, "and keep you a long time."

"Of course, the longer he keeps me the more we shall have for our old age."

"But suppose *they* don't pay you!" Morgan awfully suggested.

"Oh, there are not two such—!" Pemberton paused, he was on the point of using an invidious term. Instead of this he said "two such chances."

Morgan flushed—the tears came to his eyes. "*Dites toujours*, two such rascally crews!" Then, in a different tone, he added: "Happy opulent youth!"

"Not if he's stupid!"

"Oh, they're happier then. But you can't have everything, can you?" the boy smiled.

Pemberton held him, his hands on his shoulders. "What will become of *you*, what will you do?" He thought of Mrs. Moreen, desperate for sixty francs.

"I shall turn into a man." And then, as if he recognised all the bearings of Pemberton's allusion: "I shall get on with them better when you're not here."

"Ah, don't say that—it sounds as if I set you against them!"

"You do—the sight of you. It's all right; you know what I mean. I shall be beautiful. I'll take their affairs in hand; I'll marry my sisters."

"You'll marry yourself!" joked Pemberton; as high, rather tense pleasantry would evidently be the right, or the safest, tone for their separation.

It was, however, not purely in this strain that Morgan suddenly asked: "But I say—how will you get to your jolly job? You'll have to telegraph to the opulent youth for money to come on."

Pemberton bethought himself. "They won't like that, will they?"

"Oh, look out for them!"

Then Pemberton brought out his remedy. "I'll go to the American Consul; I'll borrow some money of him—just for the few days, on the strength of the telegram."

Morgan was hilarious. "Show him the telegram—then stay and keep the money!"

Pemberton entered into the joke enough to reply that, for Morgan, he was really capable of that; but the boy, growing more serious, and to prove that he hadn't meant what he said, not only hurried him off to the Consulate (since he was to start that evening, as he had wired to his friend), but insisted on going with him. They splashed through the tortuous perforations and over the humpbacked bridges, and they passed through the Piazza, where they saw Mr. Moreen and Ulick go into a jeweller's shop. The Consul proved accommodating (Pemberton said it wasn't the letter, but Morgan's grand air), and on their way back they went into St. Mark's for a hushed ten minutes. Later they took up and kept up the fun of it to the very end; and it seemed to Pemberton a part of that fun that Mrs. Moreen, who was very angry when he had announced to her his intention, should charge him, grotesquely and vulgarly, and in reference to the loan she had vainly endeavoured to effect, with bolting lest they should "get something out" of him. On the other hand he had to do Mr. Moreen and Ulick the justice to recognise that when, on coming in, *they* heard the cruel news, they took it like perfect men of the world.

VIII

WHEN PEMBERTON got at work with the opulent youth, who was to be taken in hand for Balliol, he found himself unable to say whether he was really an idiot or it was only, on his own part, the long association with an intensely living little mind that made him seem so. From Morgan he heard half-a-dozen times: the boy wrote charming young letters, a patchwork of tongues, with indulgent postscripts in the family Volapuk and, in little squares and rounds and crannies of the text, the drollest illustrations—letters that he was divided between the impulse to show his present disciple, as a kind of wasted incentive, and the sense of something in them that was profanable by publicity. The opulent youth went up, in due course, and failed to pass; but it seemed to add to the presumption that brilliancy was not expected of him all at once that his parents, condoning the lapse, which they good-naturedly treated as little as possible as if it were Pemberton's, should have sounded the rally again, begged the young coach to keep his pupil in hand another year.

The young coach was now in a position to lend Mrs. Moreen sixty francs, and he sent her a post-office order for that amount. In return for this favour he received a frantic, scribbled line from her: "Implore you to come back instantly—Morgan dreadfully ill." They were on the rebound, once more in Paris—often as Pemberton had seen them depressed he had never seen them crushed—and communication was therefore rapid. He wrote to the boy to ascertain the state of his health, but he received no answer to his letter. Accordingly he took an abrupt leave of the opulent youth and, crossing the Channel, alighted at the small hotel, in the quarter of the Champs Elysées, of which Mrs. Moreen had given him the address. A deep if dumb dissatisfaction with this lady and her companions bore him company: they couldn't be vulgarly honest, but they could live at hotels, in velvety *entresols,* amid a smell of burnt pastilles, in the most expensive city in Europe. When he had left them, in Venice, it was with an irrepressible suspicion that something was going to happen; but the only thing that had happened was that they succeeded in getting away. "How is he? where is he?" he asked of Mrs. Moreen; but before she could speak, these questions were answered by the pressure round his neck of a pair of arms, in shrunken sleeves, which were perfectly capable of an effusive young foreign squeeze.

"Dreadfully ill—I don't see it!" the young man cried. And then, to Morgan: "Why on earth didn't you relieve me? Why didn't you answer my letter?"

Mrs. Moreen declared that when she wrote he was very bad, and Pemberton learned at the same time from the boy that he had answered every letter he had received. This led to the demonstration that Pemberton's note had been intercepted. Mrs. Moreen was prepared to see the fact exposed, as Pemberton perceived, the moment he faced her, that she was prepared for a good many other things. She was prepared above all to maintain that she had acted from a sense of duty, that she was enchanted she had got him over, whatever they might say; and that it was useless of him to pretend that he didn't *know,* in all his bones, that his place at such a time was with Morgan. He had taken the boy away from them, and now he had no right to abandon him. He had created for himself the gravest responsibilities; he must at least abide by what he had done.

"Taken him away from you?" Pemberton exclaimed indignantly.

"Do it—do it, for pity's sake; that's just what I want. I can't stand *this*—and such scenes. They're treacherous!" These words broke from Morgan, who had intermitted his embrace, in a key which made Pemberton turn quickly to him, to see that he had suddenly seated himself, was breathing with evident difficulty and was very pale.

"*Now* do you say he's not ill—my precious pet?" shouted his mother, dropping on her knees before him with clasped hands, but touching him no more than if he had been a gilded idol. "It will pass—it's only for an instant; but don't say such dreadful things!"

"I'm all right—all right," Morgan panted to Pemberton, whom he sat looking up at with a strange smile, his hands resting on either side on the sofa.

"Now do you pretend I've been treacherous—that I've deceived?" Mrs. Moreen flashed at Pemberton as she got up.

"It isn't *he* says it, it's I!" the boy returned, apparently easier, but sinking back against the wall; while Pemberton, who had sat down beside him, taking his hand, bent over him.

"Darling child, one does what one can; there are so many things to consider," urged Mrs. Moreen. "It's his *place*—his only place. You see *you* think it is now."

"Take me away—take me away," Morgan went on, smiling to Pemberton from his white face.

"Where shall I take you, and how—oh, *how*, my boy?" the young man stammered, thinking of the rude way in which his friends in London held that, for his convenience, and without a pledge of instantaneous return, he had thrown them over; of the just resentment with which they would already have called in a successor, and of the little help as regarded finding fresh employment that resided for him in the flatness of his having failed to pass his pupil.

"Oh, we'll settle that. You used to talk about it," said Morgan. "If we can only go, all the rest's a detail."

"Talk about it as much as you like, but don't think you can attempt it. Mr. Moreen would never consent—it would be so precarious," Pemberton's hostess explained to him. Then to Morgan she explained: "It would destroy our peace, it would break our hearts. Now that he's back it will be all the same again. You'll have your life, your work and your freedom, and we'll all be happy as we used to be. You'll bloom and grow perfectly well, and we won't have any more silly experiments, will we? They're too absurd. It's Mr. Pemberton's place—every one in his place. You in yours, your

papa in his, me in mine—*n'est-ce pas, chéri?* We'll all forget how
foolish we've been, and we'll have lovely times."

She continued to talk and to surge vaguely about the little
draped, stuffy *salon*, while Pemberton sat with the boy, whose
colour gradually came back; and she mixed up her reasons, dropping that there were going to be changes, that the other children
might scatter (who knew?—Paula had her ideas), and that then
it might be fancied how much the poor old parent-birds would
want the little nestling. Morgan looked at Pemberton, who wouldn't
let him move; and Pemberton knew exactly how he felt at hearing
himself called a little nestling. He admitted that he had had one or
two bad days, but he protested afresh against the iniquity of his
mother's having made them the ground of an appeal to poor Pemberton. Poor Pemberton could laugh now, apart from the comicality
of Mrs. Moreen's producing so much philosophy for her defence
(she seemed to shake it out of her agitated petticoats, which
knocked over the light gilt chairs), so little did the sick boy strike
him as qualified to repudiate any advantage.

He himself was in for it, at any rate. He should have Morgan on
his hands again indefinitely; though indeed he saw the lad had a
private theory to produce which would be intended to smooth this
down. He was obliged to him for it in advance; but the suggested
amendment didn't keep his heart from sinking a little, any more
than it prevented him from accepting the prospect on the spot, with
some confidence moreover that he would do so even better if he
could have a little supper. Mrs. Moreen threw out more hints about
the changes that were to be looked for, but she was such a mixture
of smiles and shudders (she confessed she was very nervous), that
he couldn't tell whether she were in high feather or only in hysterics.
If the family were really at last going to pieces why shouldn't she
recognise the necessity of pitching Morgan into some sort of life-
boat? This presumption was fostered by the fact that they were
established in luxurious quarters in the capital of pleasure; that
was exactly where they naturally *would* be established in view of
going to pieces. Moreover didn't she mention that Mr. Moreen and
the others were enjoying themselves at the opera with Mr. Granger,
and wasn't *that* also precisely where one would look for them on the
eve of a smash? Pemberton gathered that Mr. Granger was a rich,
vacant American—a big bill with a flourishy heading and no items;
so that one of Paula's "ideas" was probably that this time she had

really done it, which was indeed an unprecedented blow to the general cohesion. And if the cohesion was to terminate what was to become of poor Pemberton? He felt quite enough bound up with them to figure, to his alarm, as a floating spar in case of a wreck.

It was Morgan who eventually asked if no supper had been ordered for him; sitting with him below, later, at the dim, delayed meal, in the presence of a great deal of corded green plush, a plate of ornamental biscuit and a langour marked on the part of the waiter. Mrs. Moreen had explained that they had been obliged to secure a room for the visitor out of the house; and Morgan's consolation (he offered it while Pemberton reflected on the nastiness of lukewarm sauces), proved to be, largely, that this circumstance would facilitate their escape. He talked of their escape (recurring to it often afterwards), as if they were making up a "boy's book" together. But he likewise expressed his sense that there was something in the air, that the Moreens couldn't keep it up much longer. In point of fact, as Pemberton was to see, they kept it up for five or six months. All the while, however, Morgan's contention was designed to cheer him. Mr. Moreen and Ulick, whom he had met the day after his return, accepted that return like perfect men of the world. If Paula and Amy treated it even with less formality an allowance was to be made for them, inasmuch as Mr. Granger had not come to the opera after all. He had only placed his box at their service, with a bouquet for each of the party; there was even one apiece, embittering the thought of his profusion, for Mr. Moreen and Ulick. "They're all like that," was Morgan's comment; "at the very last, just when we think we've got them fast, we're chucked!"

Morgan's comments, in these days, were more and more free; they even included a large recognition of the extraordinary tenderness with which he had been treated while Pemberton was away. Oh, yes, they couldn't do enough to be nice to him, to show him they had him on their mind and make up for his loss. That was just what made the whole thing so sad, and him so glad, after all, of Pemberton's return—he had to keep thinking of their affection less, had less sense of obligation. Pemberton laughed out at this last reason, and Morgan blushed and said: "You know what I mean." Pemberton knew perfectly what he meant; but there were a good many things it didn't make any clearer. This episode of his second sojourn in Paris stretched itself out wearily, with their resumed readings and wanderings and maunderings, their potterings on

the quays, their hauntings of the museums, their occasional linger-
ings in the Palais Royal, when the first sharp weather came on and
there was a comfort in warm emanations, before Chevet's wonderful succulent window. Morgan wanted to hear a great deal about
the opulent youth—he took an immense interest in him. Some of the
details of his opulence—Pemberton could spare him none of them
—evidently intensified the boy's appreciation of all his friend had
given up to come back to him; but in addition to the greater rec-
iprocity established by such a renunciation he had always his
little brooding theory, in which there was a frivolous gaiety too,
that their long probation was drawing to a close. Morgan's conviction that the Moreens couldn't go on much longer kept pace
with the unexpended impetus with which, from month to month,
they did go on. Three weeks after Pemberton had rejoined them
they went on to another hotel, a dingier one than the first; but
Morgan rejoiced that his tutor had at least still not sacrificed the
advantage of a room outside. He clung to the romantic utility of
this when the day, or rather the night, should arrive for their
escape.

For the first time, in this complicated connection, Pemberton
felt sore and exasperated. It was, as he had said to Mrs. Moreen in
Venice, *trop fort*—everything was *trop fort*. He could neither really
throw off his blighting burden nor find in it the benefit of a pacified
conscience or of a rewarded affection. He had spent all the money
that he had earned in England, and he felt that his youth was going and that he was getting nothing back for it. It was all very well
for Morgan to seem to consider that he would make up to him for all
inconveniences by settling himself upon him permanently—there
was an irritating flaw in such a view. He saw what the boy had in
his mind; the conception that as his friend had had the generosity
to come back to him he must show his gratitude by giving him his
life. But the poor friend didn't desire the gift—what could he do
with Morgan's life? Of course at the same time that Pemberton
was irritated he remembered the reason, which was very honourable to Morgan and which consisted simply of the fact that he was
perpetually making one forget that he was after all only a child.
If one dealt with him on a different basis one's misadventures were
one's own fault. So Pemberton waited in a queer confusion of yearning and alarm for the catastrophe which was held to hang over the
house of Moreen, of which he certainly at moments felt the symp-

toms brush his cheek and as to which he wondered much in what form it would come.

Perhaps it would take the form of dispersal—a frightened *sauve qui peut*, a scuttling into selfish corners. Certainly they were less elastic than of yore; they were evidently looking for something they didn't find. The Dorringtons hadn't reappeared, the princes had scattered; wasn't that the beginning of the end? Mrs. Moreen had lost her reckoning of the famous "days"; her social calendar was blurred—it had turned its face to the wall. Pemberton suspected that the great, the cruel, discomfiture had been the extraordinary behaviour of Mr. Granger, who seemed not to know what he wanted, or, what was much worse, what *they* wanted. He kept sending flowers, as if to bestrew the path of his retreat, which was never the path of return. Flowers were all very well, but—Pemberton could complete the proposition. It was now positively conspicuous that in the long run the Moreens were a failure; so that the young man was almost grateful the run had not been short. Mr. Moreen, indeed, was still occasionally able to get away on business, and, what was more surprising, he was also able to get back. Ulick had no club, but you could not have discovered it from his appearance, which was as much as ever that of a person looking at life from the window of such an institution; therefore Pemberton was doubly astonished at an answer he once heard him make to his mother, in the desperate tone of a man familiar with the worst privations. Her question Pemberton had not quite caught; it appeared to be an appeal for a suggestion as to whom they could get to take Amy. "Let the devil take her!" Ulick snapped; so that Pemberton could see that not only they had lost their amiability, but had ceased to believe in themselves. He could also see that if Mrs. Moreen was trying to get people to take her children she might be regarded as closing the hatches for the storm. But Morgan would be the last she would part with.

One winter afternoon—it was a Sunday—he and the boy walked far together in the Bois de Boulogne. The evening was so splendid, the cold lemon-coloured sunset so clear, the stream of carriages and pedestrians so amusing and the fascination of Paris so great, that they stayed out later than usual and became aware that they would have to hurry home to arrive in time for dinner. They hurried accordingly, arm-in-arm, good-humoured and hungry, agreeing that there was nothing like Paris after all and that after all, too, that had come and gone they were not yet sated with innocent pleasures. When they reached the hotel they found that, though scandalously late, they were in time for all the dinner they were likely to sit down to. Confusion reigned in the apartments of the Moreens (very shabby ones this time, but the best in the house), and before the interrupted service of the table (with objects displaced almost as if there had been a scuffle, and a great wine stain from an overturned bottle), Pemberton could not blink the fact that there had been a scene of proprietary mutiny. The storm had come—they were all seeking refuge. The hatches were down—Paula and Amy were invisible (they had never tried the most casual art upon Pemberton, but he felt that they had enough of an eye to him not to wish to meet him as young ladies whose frocks had been confiscated), and Ulick appeared to have jumped overboard. In a word, the host and his staff had ceased to "go on" at the pace of their guests, and the air of embarrassed detention, thanks to a pile of gaping trunks in the passage, was strangely commingled with the air of indignant withdrawal.

When Morgan took in all this—and he took it in very quickly—he blushed to the roots of his hair. He had walked, from his infancy, among difficulties and dangers, but he had never seen a public exposure. Pemberton noticed, in a second glance at him, that the tears had rushed into his eyes and that they were tears of bitter shame. He wondered for an instant, for the boy's sake, whether he might successfully pretend not to understand. Not successfully, he felt, as Mr. and Mrs. Moreen, dinnerless by their extinguished hearth, rose before him in their little dishonoured *salon,* considering apparently with much intensity what lively capital would be next on their list. They were not prostrate, but they were very pale, and Mrs. Moreen had evidently been crying. Pemberton quickly learned however that her grief was not for the loss of her dinner, much as she usually enjoyed it, but on account of a necessity much more tragic. She lost no time in laying this necessity bare, in telling him how the change had come, the bolt had fallen, and how they would all have to turn themselves about. Therefore cruel as it was to them to part with their darling she must look to him to carry a little further the influence he had so fortunately acquired with the boy—to induce his young charge to follow him into some modest retreat. They depended upon him, in a word, to take their delightful child temporarily under his protection—it would leave

Mr. Moreen and herself so much more free to give the proper attention (too little, alas! had been given), to the readjustment of their affairs.

"We trust you—we feel that we can," said Mrs. Moreen, slowly rubbing her plump white hands and looking, with compunction, hard at Morgan, whose chin, not to take liberties, her husband stroked with a tentative paternal forefinger.

"Oh, yes; we feel that we can. We trust Mr. Pemberton fully, Morgan," Mr. Moreen conceded.

Pemberton wondered again if he might pretend not to understand; but the idea was painfully complicated by the immediate perception that Morgan had understood.

"Do you mean that he may take me to live with him—for ever and ever?" cried the boy. "Away, away, anywhere he likes?"

"For ever and ever? *Comme vous-y-allez!*" Mr. Moreen laughed indulgently. "For as long as Mr. Pemberton may be so good."

"We've struggled, we've suffered," his wife went on; "but you've made him so your own that we've already been through the worst of the sacrifice."

Morgan had turned away from his father—he stood looking at Pemberton with a light in his face. His blush had died out, but something had come that was brighter and more vivid. He had a moment of boyish joy, scarcely mitigated by the reflection that, with this unexpected consecration of his hope—too sudden and too violent; the thing was a good deal less like a boy's book—the "escape" was left on their hands. The boyish joy was there for an instant, and Pemberton was almost frightened at the revelation of gratitude and affection that shone through his humiliation. When Morgan stammered "My dear fellow, what do you say to *that?*" he felt that he should say something enthusiastic. But he was still more frightened at something else that immediately followed and that made the lad sit down quickly on the nearest chair. He had turned very white and had raised his hand to his left side. They were all three looking at him, but Mrs. Moreen was the first to bound forward. "Ah, his darling little heart!" she broke out; and this time, on her knees before him and without respect for the idol, she caught him ardently in her arms. "You walked him too far, you hurried him too fast!" she tossed over her shoulder at Pemberton. The boy made no protest, and the next instant his mother, still holding him, sprang up with her face convulsed and with the terrified cry "Help, help!

he's going, he's gone!" Pemberton saw, with equal horror, by Morgan's own stricken face, that he *was* gone. He pulled him half out of his mother's hands, and for a moment, while they held him together, they looked, in their dismay, into each other's eyes. "He couldn't stand it, with his infirmity," said Pemberton—"the shock, the whole scene, the violent emotion."

"But I thought he *wanted* to go to you!" wailed Mrs. Moreen.

"I *told* you he didn't, my dear," argued Mr. Moreen. He was trembling all over, and he was, in his way, as deeply affected as his wife. But, after the first, he took his bereavement like a man of the world.

STUDY

What Maisie Knew and Other Tales

HENRY JAMES*
Preface [1907–1909]

My urchin of "The Pupil" (1891) has sensibility in abundance, it would seem—and yet preserves in spite of it, I judge, his strong little male quality. . . .

[A] friend . . . who had come from a far country to settle in Florence, happened to speak to me [during a railroad trip] of a wonderful American family, an odd adventurous, extravagant band, of high but rather unauthenticated pretensions, the most interesting member of which was a small boy, acute and precocious, afflicted with a heart of weak action, but beautifully intelligent, who saw their prowling precarious life exactly as it was, and measured and judged it, and measured and judged *them*, all round, ever so quaintly; presenting himself in short as an extraordinary little person. . . . I *saw*, on the spot, little Morgan Moreen, I saw all the rest of the Moreens; I felt, to the last delicacy, the nature of my young friend's relation with them (he had become at once my young friend) and, by the same stroke, to its uttermost fine

* Copyright, 1908, 1909, Charles Scribner's Sons; renewal copyright, 1936, 1937, Henry James. Reprinted from *The Art of the Novel*, by Henry James, with the permission of Charles Scribner's Sons.

throb, the subjection to *him* of the beguiled, bewildered, defrauded, unremunerated, yet after all richly repaid youth who would to a certainty, under stress of compassion, embark with the tribe on tutorship, and whose edifying connexion with it would be my leading document. . . .

Why, somehow . . . did one see the Moreens, whom I place at Nice, at Venice, in Paris, as of the special essence of the little old miscellaneous cosmopolitan Florence, the Florence of other, or irrecoverable years, the restless yet withal so convenient scene of a society that has passed away for ever with all its faded ghosts and fragile relics; immaterial presences that have quite ceased to revisit . . . walks and prospects once sacred and shaded, but now laid bare, gaping wide, despoiled of their past and unfriendly to any appreciation of it?—through which the unconscious Barbarians troop. . . .

They had nothing to do, the dear Moreens, with this dreadful period, any more than I, as occupied and charmed with them, was humiliatingly subject to it; we were, all together, of a better romantic age and faith; we referred ourselves, with our highest complacency, to the classic years of the great Americano-European legend; the years of limited communication, of monstrous and unattenuated contrast, of prodigious and unrecorded adventure. . . .

The Moreens were of the family . . . of the great unstudied precursors ["of the great Americano-European legend; . . . of prodigious and unrecorded adventure"]—poor and shabby members, no doubt; dim and superseded types. I must add indeed that, such as they were, or as they may at present incoherently appear, I don't pretend really to have "done" them: all I have given in "The Pupil" is little Morgan's troubled vision of them as reflected in the vision, also troubled enough, of his devoted friend. The manner of the thing may thus illustrate [my] incorrigible taste for gradations and superpositions of effect; [my] love, when it is a question of a picture, of anything that makes for proportion and perspective, that contributes to a view of *all* the dimensions. Addicted to seeing "through"—one thing through another, accordingly, and still other things through *that*—[I take], too greedily perhaps, on any errand, as many things as possible by the way. It is after this fashion that [I incur] the stigma of labouring uncannily for a certain fulness of truth—truth diffused, distributed and, as it were, atmospheric. . . .

[Like the "portentous little Hyacinth" of *The Princess Casamassima*, Morgan Moreen is] tainted to the core . . . with the trick of mental reaction on the things about him and fairly staggering under the appropriations . . . that he owes to the critical spirit.

The Wind Blew from the East

FERNER NUHN*

[T]here are scores of places in James's works where only a reference to abnormal psychology could explain the intensity of certain emotions. Consider for example . . . *The Pupil*. . . . Such a story begs at once for Freud, or one of his colleagues. People do not ruin their lives for other people unless deep emotional centers are involved, and when the case is that of an adult young man and a precocious small boy, we may be excused for sensing something off the normal pattern. Did James want to suggest an abnormal passion between the two? It is much to be doubted. He makes no effort to hide the fact of great affection between the man and the boy, displayed once or twice by an embrace, but this very circumstance makes us question any further implication.

This is not to say that the reader may not deduce, as something of which James himself may have been unaware, the presence of an unusual emotional substratum in the very nature of the story. The deduction seems inevitable. But it does not follow that this is the point of the story—James's point.

. . . James's point . . . has to do with the intangible compulsions of the spirit rather than with those of instinct, normal or not. The plight of the precocious youngster is a spiritual plight and calls for a spiritual response. Whatever reward there may be to offset the sacrifice of the tutor comes from the knowledge that a fine little spirit, found struggling in sordid surroundings, has not been left in the lurch. If there is fatality here, it is the fatality of imagination. The young man, once aware of the pitiful call for understanding, and aware that he alone has heard and can meet it, simply cannot fail his knowledge.

Something of this sort, you gather from the story and from James's preface, is James's own "point." It may or may not be

* (New York, Harper & Bros., 1942). By permission.

adequate to explain the actual events of the story—I think it is not
—but that is another question.

The Great Short Novels of Henry James
Philip Rahv (ed.)*

The Pupil . . . is converted by its rare measure of objectivity and
insight into a piece of modern poetry pure and simple—a poetry
not of the lyrical impulse but of the psychological faculty.

The objectivity is of a quality peculiar to James, which is quite
unlike the objectivity of the naturalist school of fiction. It depends
neither on exhaustive documentation nor on the author's assumption of an attitude of seemingly scientific detachment toward his
material. For the Jamesian objectivity is not a calculated method
but the result, rather, of an unusually concrete and close understanding of the characters and situation. So close and concrete
is this understanding that it is transformed into a kind of self-con-
tained irony which leaves us with no "problem" on our hands, no
general issue or topic which we can extract from the work for
purposes of discussion. . . . [Readers] who are accustomed to
judge literature by the ideological stimulus it provides, by the
range and profundity of the questions raised, may be unable to
appreciate the qualities of a *nouvelle* like *The Pupil*. . . .

In *The Pupil* James again turns to account his method of presenting characters indirectly, through a perspective of the most
careful design. His effort is to make us see the characters "through"
those among them who possess the gift of consciousness, or . .
"who are capable of a certain high lucidity." He believed that the
human predicament dealt with in a work of fiction needs to be or-
ganized around a nucleus of "irrepressible appreciation"—that is
to say, that it needs a central intelligence to bring out its finer possibilities. Hence his emphasis on what seems like a purely technical
issue—the issue of the "point of view" from which the action of a
story is seen by the reader. For the choice of the "point of view"
and its structural placing in the story are not only its available
means of unity and coherence but also the means of securing for it
the maximum amount of consciousness. Given this approach, it is
obvious that a good deal of the drama of those who are consciou

* FROM *The Great Short Novels of Henry James*, edited by Philip Rahv
(New York, The Dial Press, Inc., 1944). By permission.

and who do "appreciate" what happens to them must consist of
their relation to those who don't—the fools, as James called them.
In *The Pupil* it is little Morgan Moreen and his tutor who stand at
the post of observation and awareness, while the other figures are
"the fools who minister to the free spirits engaged with them."

Henry James

F. W. DUPEE[*]

About even the boy-hero of "The Pupil" there is something rather
elderly and gentlemanly; he is hustled and humiliated by his shady
parents, life fails to materialize for him at all, he dies on the verge
of it. . . .

In [so many of James's stories about "poor gentlemen" there is]
an implicit desire of being loved. A kind of fraternal-homosexual
affection unites boy and tutor in "The Pupil."

The Short Story

SEAN O'FAOLAIN[†]

This is a wonderfully promising situation, though for a novel rather
than a short story. It ends with the final collapse of the rickety
fortunes of the family and the death of the child: a climax, to be
sure, but the climax of a novel rather than a short story. We can
only be grateful that no effort has been made here to develop
a plot: instead we move contentedly from one slight incident to
another until it becomes evident that some catastrophe must bring
down the house-of-cards, which is what so satisfactorily occurs.

"James's 'The Pupil': The Art of Seeing Through"

TERENCE MARTIN[‡]

. . James's method of characterizing the Moreens begins typically
enough with their name; identity and characterization are one in

[*] Copyright ©, 1951, 1956, by William Sloane Associates Inc.

[†] Quoted from *The Short Story*, by Sean O'Faolain, published 1951, by
The Devin-Adair Co., New York; Copyright, 1951, by Devin-Adair.

[‡] FROM *Modern Fiction Studies*, IV (Winter, 1958–1959). By permission
of the copyright owners, Purdue Research Foundation.

the name. Moreen is a fabric of coarse, stout wool or wool and cotton; usually it is watered or embossed. In short, it presents one kind of surface to the eye when underneath it is intrinsically coarse. The description fits the Moreen family precisely. . . .

In the name Ulick, James adds a far less subtle name characterization. . . .

The details of the daily life of the Moreens support James's initial name-characterization. . . . It becomes clear that they glitter on the surface, that their ways—as seen by Pemberton—are seductive and winning, but that the glitter is a part of their essential hypocrisy. . . .

Morgan, as we know, is entirely out of place in so mendacious a family. . . . Literally, the name Morgan signifies a dweller on the sea, and such a literal meaning applies to Morgan Moreen. Condemned to being with his family but not of them, to being in their world but not of it, Morgan is a nomad, a person eternally homeless. But the same might also suggest something further about his relationship to his family, for with the addition of a suffix the [word] becomes morganatic. In this form the name suggests a richly ironic relationship which is supported by the dramatic context of the story. In a morganatic relationship (usually marriage) the inferior partner does not acquire the rank, the title, the worldly position of the superior: in "The Pupil" Morgan does not acquire the heritage of moreen that belongs by right of identity to the rest of the family: . . . he is not, that is, growing up to be a hypocrite and a fraud. But the word morganatic suggests a fuller meaning if one inverts the relationship: clearly Morgan is the superior member of the family; he alone possesses honesty and wisdom, he alone has insight, he alone is the pupil. And just as these traits are age-old ideals, so by possessing them is Morgan much older than his family. He feels this himself and makes others feel it. . . . They are *hi* people; he wonders what *he* has done to them. Morgan has an ancestral view of the family. He is a child who embodies tradition an old child, wise but perplexed at what *his* family has become. . .

To Morgan, Pemberton seems to offer the fullest chance at life and love that he has ever had. For Pemberton loves Morgan, and when he comes to see the way in which the family uses his pupil and Morgan's own knowledge of this, he stays on without pay as long as he can out of love or what seems to be love. But he . .

has a "sneaking kindness" for the Moreens; their undeniable surface charm engages him. . . .

In the context of [Pemberton's] love and attention Morgan's
health blooms. . . .

Pemberton returns to the Moreens from England in response to
an urgent and fraudulent appeal from Moreen. . . . At this point
there is a curious change in his relationship to Morgan; for the
remainder of the story he is a passive figure, no longer talking of
the future, simply waiting to see what will happen. . . . What
appeared to be love (which is what Morgan is counting on) is gone.

I believe that this change in attitude further defines Pemberton's initial attitude toward Morgan; in the light of his later passivity we may see the terms of his earlier apparently more aggressive affection. After Pemberton returns to the family, Morgan
repeatedly refers to the future (their future); he reiterates what
he takes to be their mutual desire, that Pemberton take him away.
He thus forces Pemberton to think practically of these matters. But
this is something that, despite his words, Pemberton has never
really been able to do, and Morgan's insistence serves only to force
him into passivity. Pemberton loves Morgan as Morgan exists
in one particular situation; he loves the victimized Morgan. For
the object of his love to insist on the chance of not being a victim,
and to look to Pemberton to save (de-victimize) him, is to challenge the whole basis of the love relationship.

. . . Pemberton is a successor to the nurse Zénobie; his functions throughout are more those of a nurse than of a doctor. He
would be a doctor, he claims to be, but he is not: he emerges, finally,
as a passive and dependent figure—one whose function it is to
nurse rather than to doctor. Indeed, his lack of independence
breeds his "sneaking kindness" toward the Moreens, for "they
were so out of the workaday world and kept him so out of it." He
has, we recall, been unable to conceive of supporting Morgan,
though he can conceive of Morgan supporting him. Mrs. Moreen
quite rightly senses his role of nursemaid when she says that Pemberton's place is with Morgan and the family, that he belongs in
his place. Her insight increases his dissatisfaction, for he now sees
the limitation, the self-sacrificing nature of such a role; at the same
time he realizes that Morgan is urging him to be a rescuer, an alternative which because it would entail masculine, aggressive action
and the confidence of being able to support Morgan) is not open

to him. His dilemma, and the explanation of his passivity, is that he cannot happily resume the old relationship, as Mrs. Moreen would have him do, nor can he conceive of rescuing Morgan and having Morgan, no longer a victim, become absolutely dependent on him. He has suggested and flirted with the latter alternative but he is unable and unwilling to project it in practical terms. Morgan is trying to take their love out of its original context on the assumption that it is independent of context, but, since everything depends on Pemberton, such a change is not possible. Furthermore, it is obvious to Pemberton that the Moreens will not be able to stave off "public exposure" much longer and that disaster will bring about change. Thus he waits "in a queer confusion of yearning and alarm for the catastrophe." . . .

All of the seeing through culminates in the brilliant final scene of the story. . . . At this point the meaning of his mother's gesture strikes Morgan (appropriately enough, in the heart). . . . His parents have no more use for him; they will give him away. Morgan suffers a fatal heart attack, for he has seen through to the fact that without identity there is no basis for life or for love. In the moment before his death Morgan is held by the hands of Pemberton and Mrs. Moreen; at this moment Morgan and Pemberton (or is it Pemberton and Mrs. Moreen?) "look all their dismay into each other's eyes." It is the dismay of the final seeing through, a silent recognition that for Morgan there is nothing.

But it is a dismay and a seeing through that involves Pemberton as well as the Moreen family. . . . He is now being urged by the Moreen family to take away a de-victimized Morgan. And although he is not forced to reject Morgan overtly, it is obvious that he does not want Morgan. . . . Pemberton has returned and waited . . . for Morgan's death. . . .

Pemberton has indeed poisoned Morgan by his suggestion that Morgan could depend on him, by his failure to be a savior of any kind. Powerless to devise an antidote to his poison, he has waited to see what will happen. And thus when the action of the Moreens causes Morgan's heart attack, Pemberton—still the would-be but inadequate doctor—can offer only a diagnosis. He shares the responsibility for the hopelessness of Morgan's death.

Exactly how much of this Morgan knows James does not spell out for us. . . . At this point, I believe, Morgan sees through Pemberton—indeed, all the evidence of the story, his sensitive ness, his devotion to and dependence on Pemberton, his intelligence, points to this. Morgan sees through to the quality of Pemberton's failure, to the fact that there will be no rescue by Pemberton, and no attempt at rescue. It would follow that he sees, too, exactly what his family would do with him. It is the logical last link of the story: Morgan and Pemberton confront each other; and the pupil sees through. . . .

By seeing into the chaos of self that is his world, Morgan has gained the ultimate vision and has been destroyed by it. . . . Blind to the full significance of what they have done, the Moreens and Pemberton thus survive. But the pupil is dead—the pupil who mastered the art and paid the price of seeing through.

"Seeing Through 'The Pupil' Again"

John V. Hagopian[*]

Terence Martin's analysis . . . is possibly mistaken in making Pemberton the ultimate villain of the piece. Pemberton may, indeed, be a villain, but . . . not out of spite or hatred, but out of desperate need to preserve his own vitality—to reject and in effect consign to death someone he pities, because such a pity makes demands on him that are absolutely unbearable.

It is true, as Martin observes, that at the climax "Morgan and Pemberton confront each other; and the pupil sees through." However, this pupil . . . was by no means the first or the only character to achieve a tragically-charged vision in this magnificently-wrought little tale. In the beginning of his relationship with young Morgan (a relationship that parallels in development the usual processes of *heterosexual* courtship and marriage) Pemberton responds with embarrassment to Morgan's affectionate remark, "You're a jolly old humbug!" . . .

The shadowy question first glimpsed here and destined to play an unprecedented role gradually becomes clear as the story proceeds. Pemberton soon realizes that [he has been victimized by the Moreens], from whom he becomes willing to accept as sole payment for his services "the sweet relation he had established with Morgan." But as that relationship grows, so does Pemberton's resentment and fear of it. . . . And along with his sense of respon-

[*] From *Modern Fiction Studies*, V (Summer, 1959). By permission of the copyright owners, Purdue Research Foundation.

sibility for the sickly lad grows a subconscious aggression against him for draining off the best years of his life. . . . The precocious boy clings to Pemberton like a leech, and, far from getting worse, actually thrives on the unnatural alliance with the tutor. It becomes apparent, however, that he will never be well enough to confront life on his own. . . .

Hard upon the heels of this recognition comes Pemberton's break, his departure for London, cushioned by forced pleasantry and his jocular injunction to Morgan to get married. Tricked into returning to the Moreens, he realizes that "he had created for himself the gravest responsibilities and must at least abide by what he had done" in alienating Morgan from his family and then abandoning him. He was now "in for it. . . . He should have Morgan on his hands again indefinitely." Pemberton here is heroic in assuming his moral responsibility, ready to martyr himself for the pathetic boy. But as time goes by . . ., Pemberton "felt his collar gall him." His own natural, healthy drive for self-assertion and his vitality demand that he throw off "his blighting burden." It is clear that he has not taken on this obligation out of love but out of moral duty, and it is hardly fair or perceptive of Martin to describe his feelings as "a radical change. . . ." His resentment had been indicated quite early and had gradually developed until "he saw his youth going and . . . he was getting nothing back for it. . . . *What could he do with Morgan's dreadful little life?*"

What, indeed? Can it be anything but a deep longing for normal manhood that makes Pemberton wait "in a queer confusion of yearning and alarm for the catastrophe"? It is understandable, too, that he does not wait passively, as Martin asserts he does. His healthy urge to be rid of the blighting burden leads him, on that last tragic winter day, to take his young cardiac case for a walk far into the Bois de Boulogne, keep him out later than usual, and then hurry him home to the wine-stained dinner table. It is not only "the action of the Moreens [that] causes Morgan's heart attack." There is truth in the accusation that Mrs. Moreen hurls over her shoulder at Pemberton: "You walked him too far, you hurried him too fast."

Martin is perfectly correct in observing that Morgan's "seeing through . . . to the fact that there will be no rescue by Pemberton, and no attempt at rescue" is the final blow that kills him. But to label this Pemberton's 'failure' and to equate him with the despicable Moreens is to betray a lack of psychological insight and a lack of moral compassion for Pemberton's own terrible plight. Years later when Pemberton fingers the lock of Morgan's hair and the half-dozen letters . . ., he is recalling a tragic decision and a tragic act committed out of stern necessity.

" 'The Pupil' : The Education of a Prude"

WILLIAM BYSSHE STEIN[*]

We must see the collective image of the Moreens through, I calculate, three dimensions of esthetic distance; for James's execution of this work shows him "Addicted to seeing 'through'—one thing through another, accordingly, and still other things through *that*." This narrative mode prohibits our taking the expressed opinion of any single character in the story as the arbitrary standard of the truth of the reality under re-creation. . . . James is concerned with projecting "their [Pemberton's and Morgan's] moral vibrations"; but this does not necessarily indicate that these impressions of experience are not defiled by too much sensibility. . . .

[T]hree definable lenses of aesthetic distance *in the story* reflect the image of the [Moreens'] Bohemianism. A fourth, operative but unobtrusive, controls the reader's degree of subjective involvement in the adjudicative function of the first three. In order, James screens the unique flavor of this period of American social history through the various states of sensibility of his central intelligence. He exhibits Pemberton, for instance, in moments of unrehearsed and spontaneous reaction to events. At another time he is presented in mechanical response to concrete occurrences on which occasions we witness his natively conditioned moral reflexes. Finally we view him in acts of perception of incidents in which Morgan is his eyes. But the young boy, even though he is precocious and hypersensitive, is the agent and the victim of "a *good* boy's book" of morality, a code of make-believe honor and dignity. . . . This "private ideal" is also the product of "a romantic imagination, fed by poetry and history"; for "he would have liked those who 'bore his name' . . . to carry themselves with an air."

This is the sensibility, we must keep in mind, which is constantly at the service of Pemberton. It is arbitrary, pedantic, au-

[*] FROM *Arizona Quarterly*, XV (Spring, 1959).

thoritarian, and imaginary. It is hostile to the reality of the environment in which it is found. But, as James would have us see it, it is a capacity for receptivity that has to be indulged but not necessarily applied to lived experience. Ironically, however, Pemberton begins to share the values of this world of fantasy because these infantile aspirations move in the orbit of his moral universe, which is influenced by the gravitation of Puritanism from his native land. In the preface James makes it quite clear that, with his timidity and unsophistication, it is he who is actually the pupil. . . . And James traces this surrender of adult to childish values to the paradox of an innate Puritanism that European cosmopolitanism intensifies. . . . The composite sensibility of Pemberton is hardly depicted to arouse the reader's admiration. Rather James subtly unveils it in order to excite our laughter. For though it is a delicate and highly receptive faculty, it is prudish. Its addiction to self-renunciation and self-sacrifice is motivated by a staunch but comical self-righteousness. In this sense, as a scale of dramatic proportion, it is the antithesis of the Bohemian excesses of the Moreens.

Appropriately, then, the fourth dimension of aesthetic distance substantiates, I think, this observation. This is the "through" lens of tone, a narrative ingredient not unfamiliar to the readers of James's prefaces. In this case it is an emotional quality that permeates his treatment of the subject. It may be said to constitute the "atmospheric" character of the story, for, consistent with this reconstitution of a phase of American social history, it is romantic and nostalgic. And, as an *a priori* condition of the creative act, it determines his preconceptions of the moral timbre of the adult Moreens. They represent for him "the family then of the great unstudied precursors" who boldly invaded Europe in quest of its treasures. They are not, it is significant, to be associated with the modern pilgrims, "the unconscious barbarians." . . . [W]e have *William Wetmore Story and his Friends* to establish the validity of James's feeling on the topic of these early Americans.

As he says in this biography, "We have more things than they, but we have less and less room for them, either in our lives or in our minds; so that even if our taste is superior we have less use for it, and thereby, to our loss, less enjoyment of our relations." With all of their mistakes, their ignorance and presumption, we are indebted to them for "the price they paid." In the humiliation, the frustration, and the shame of the Moreens, James totals such an account for us. At any rate, it is in this light that I view the final scene of the story. The confiscation of the clothes and the defeat of social play entailed are the devices of slapstick comedy, and they are hilarious. True, Morgan's death occurs in the same context, but for a purpose. The two events taken together constitute the climax of Pemberton's education. James seems to say that the European pilgrim is under obligation to bring his sensibilities into free and perceptive relationship with the personal, social, aesthetic, and moral forces of the old world. Only this kind of immersion in experience can bring self-knowledge. Pemberton, with almost feminine fastidiousness, shrinks from this full encounter with truth. Yet, as James argues so often in his novels, too great a refinement of the sensibilities . . . is self-defeating. And it seems to me that readers of "The Pupil" are too prone to convert the social gaucherie of the Moreens into egregious immorality. James himself, however, generously excuses these excesses [in his Preface]. In sum, the Moreens in their perhaps too callous social resilience are not wholly admirable, but, on the other hand, neither are they moral criminals. They are simply the earliest victims of the fever of social aspiration that afflicted Americans, great and small, in their first intercourse with European culture. . . .

In this perspective the Moreen clan ought to elicit our pity, though not our compassion. We can reserve this latter feeling for Morgan and Pemberton with their excessive moral vibrations. . . . James carefully delineates the various stages of Pemberton's revulsion against the behavior of the Moreens, a revulsion that, at its peak, proclaims the resurgence of the Puritan moral fervor that underlay his timid, inhibited quest for identity in the old world. In his first encounter with the Moreens, he immediately labels the father "a man of the world." At this particular moment the epithet has not any definite signification except social manners. But thereafter, as his animosity for him and his family increases, the same epithet is invoked whenever he makes his entry into a scene. But gradually the term evolves into a curse, an anathema of righteous wrath. And at the end of the story, the last phrase as a matter of fact, Pemberton uses it again to support his belief in the immorality of the parents, especially Mr. Moreen. But in a drastic failure of self-insight, he refuses to recognize that it is his reluctant response to the boy's plan of escape that causes Morgan to collapse in despair. . . . This is a fatal betrayal, unexpected as it is. He [Morgan] knew his parents, but he did not know Pemberton's moral involvement in their affairs had become self-protective. Reverting to an atavistic Puritanism, he had to escape the man of the world—the devil—at any cost.

. . . [T]he extension of "man of the world" leitmotif is also attended by another pattern of adjudicative imagery. This one is initiated in his first attempt to assimilate the bizarre antics of the Moreens into his framework of values: "He had thought himself very sharp that first day in hitting them all off in his mind with the 'cosmopolite' label. Later it seemed feeble and colorless—confessedly helplessly provisional." A little more than a year later this social valuation changes radically. It is now converted into a pompous moral judgment in consonance with his dependence upon the principles of his Puritan conscience: "He had simply given himself away to a band of adventurers. The idea, the word itself, wore a romantic horror for him—he had always lived on such safe lines. Later it assumed a more interesting, almost a soothing, sense: it pointed a moral, and Pemberton could enjoy a moral." The nature of this moral is illogical and absurd, but it divulges his surrender to the theology of his forebears: "Oh they were 'respectable,' and that made them more *immondes!*" This French term is fashioned from the biblical attribute of uncleanliness and impurity. It is, as it were, a contemptuous pejorative reserved for the use of the chosen people. By its rhetorical candor, the word shows James in the process of disrobing Pemberton of all tolerance, of all humanity. Hence it is no great surprise that at a later time this moral superiority becomes a habit, comically accentuated by his conversations with Morgan about his parents: "the real problem came up—the problem of how far it was excusable to discuss the *turpitude* of parents with a child of twelve, of thirteen, of fourteen." (italics mine) This sequence of the boy's age indicates how obsessive the tutor's concern with the evilness of the Moreens' social mores had become. Their behavior was no longer a matter of cosmopolitan eccentricity; it now was a manifestation of depravity, of inherent baseness, of original sin. Moreover, what they did was indistinguishable from European culture, its power to corrupt the innocent . . . : "She squeezed forward in her dressing gown, and he received her in his own, between his bath-tub and his bed. He had been tolerably schooled by this time to the 'foreign ways' of his hosts." The marshalling of all this indelicate imagery, though it is part of the setting, emphasizes the state of Pemberton's consciousness, its prudishness, its sin-centeredness. In the final analysis it likewise explains his servitude to the private ideal of Morgan whose inveterate condemnation of his family pivots on the colloquial usage of beastly: "They're so beastly worldly." The repetition of this metaphor impinges upon the mind of the tutor in its animalistic connotations, leading him to associate the Moreens with a "view of life, dim and confused and instinctive, like that of clever colour-blind animals." From another angle of vision, of course, we see in operation here James's addiction to seeing one thing through another and still another. This is to say that we observe here an image of the Moreens subtly filtered through the boy's ingenuous code, through his tutor's impression of it, and finally through the sin-screening conscience of the latter. Surely, we cannot take this composite impression of the Moreens as any more than a distorted reflection of reality—the comic adumbration of an unappreciative American pilgrim in Europe.

In contrast with Pemberton's moralizing propensities, it is interesting to note his spontaneous reactions to the behavior of his employers. At the beginning of their association he immediately senses their piquant difference from conventional people, their lack of inhibition, their delight in life. . . . Even several years later he is still able to muster some admiration for them, and mind you, despite Morgan's insidious deprecations. . . . In these pictures James seeks to warn the reader that he must maintain "proportion and perspective" in regard to these "candid children of the West." However incongruous and incredible their actions may appear to Pemberton, they do not deliberately attempt to deceive the tutor. They are incapable of this sort of deception. Their social deceit is another thing. They are forced into it by their preposterous ambitions and by the society in which they move. . . . Pemberton's ambivalence in this situation is derived from his inability to reconcile their personal candor to their manneristic affectations. This is the inward conflict that, from the standpoint of James's narrative execution, is designed to clarify his function in the story. He is its comic center.

Ultimately, in his loss of generosity and tolerance, he is converted into a scapegoat. He is sacrificed on the cross of his dogmatic seriousness. And, paradoxically, it is Morgan who thus victimizes him. As I have argued, Pemberton is the dupe of a fanciful code of respectability, one which Morgan reiterates because he instinctively knows that this is his major appeal to the tutor. In this way he converts the latter into "the hero" of his fantasy world. . . . [O]ne facet of the ambiguity of his fiction lies in the ostensible rapport of individuals in terms of sensibility; yet we discover . . . that the seeming equipoise of mutual interests is effected by the excessive sensibility of one of the characters. The failure to perceive this incongruity generates the pathos of defeat in which so many of James's characters find themselves. In "The Pupil" we can call this outcome the failure of education. The prude, because he attempts to write the book of life in the idiom of his own subjective life, ends up holding an untranslatable form of experience. This is Pemberton's fate: "Indeed the whole mystic volume in which the boy had been amateurishly bound demanded some practice in translation. Today, after a considerable interval, there is something phantasmagoric, like a prismatic reflexion or a serial novel, in Pemberton's memory of the queerness of the Moreens." In this single passage James sums up, not only the topic of the tutor's self-deception, but his mode of dramatizing this experience.

The Beast in the Jungle

[1903]

❧⟡❧

I

WHAT DETERMINED the speech that startled him in the course of their encounter scarcely matters, being probably but some words spoken by himself quite without intention—spoken as they lingered and slowly moved together after their renewal of acquaintance. He had been conveyed by friends an hour or two before to the house at which she was staying; the party of visitors at the other house, of whom he was one, and thanks to whom it was his theory, as always, that he was lost in the crowd, had been invited over to luncheon. There had been after luncheon much dispersal, all in the interest of the original motive, a view of Weatherend itself and the fine things, intrinsic features, pictures, heirlooms, treasures of all the arts, that made the place almost famous; and the great rooms were so numerous that guests could wander at their will, hang back from the principal group and in cases where they took such matters with the last seriousness give themselves up to mysterious appreciations and measurements. There were persons to be observed, singly or in couples, bending toward objects in out-of-the-way corners with their hands on their knees and their heads nodding quite as with the emphasis of an excited sense of smell. When they were two they either mingled their sounds of ecstasy or melted into silences of even deeper import, so that there were aspects of the occasion that gave it for Marcher much the air of the "look round," previous to a sale highly advertised, that excites or quenches, as may be, the dream of acquisition. The dream of acquisition at Weatherend would have had to be wild indeed, and John Marcher found himself, among such suggestions, disconcerted almost equally by the presence of those who knew too much and by that of those who knew nothing. The great

FROM *The Better Sort* (New York, Charles Scribner's Sons, 1903).

rooms caused so much poetry and history to press upon him that he needed some straying apart to feel in a proper relation with them, though this impulse was not, as happened, like the gloating of some of his companions, to be compared to the movements of a dog sniffing a cupboard. It had an issue promptly enough in a direction that was not to have been calculated.

It led, briefly, in the course of the October afternoon, to his closer meeting with May Bartram, whose face, a reminder, yet not quite a remembrance, as they sat much separated at a very long table, had begun merely by troubling him rather pleasantly. It affected him as the sequel of something of which he had lost the beginning. He knew it, and for the time quite welcomed it, as a continuation, but didn't know what it continued, which was an interest or an amusement the greater as he was also somehow aware—yet without a direct sign from her—that the young woman herself hadn't lost the thread. She hadn't lost it, but she wouldn't give it back to him, he saw, without some putting forth of his hand for it; and he not only saw that, but saw several things more, things odd enough in the light of the fact that at the moment some accident of grouping brought them face to face he was still merely fumbling with the idea that any contact between them in the past would have had no importance. If it had had no importance he scarcely knew why his actual impression of her should so seem to have so much; the answer to which, however, was that in such a life as they all appeared to be leading for the moment one could but take things as they came. He was satisfied, without in the least being able to say why, that this young lady might roughly have ranked in the house as a poor relation; satisfied also that she was not there on a brief visit, but was more or less a part of the establishment—almost a working, a remunerated part. Didn't she enjoy at periods a protection that she paid for by helping, among other services, to show the place and explain it, deal with the tiresome people, answer questions about the dates of the building, the styles of the furniture, the authorship of the pictures, the favourite haunts of the ghost? It wasn't that she looked as if you could have given her shillings—it was impossible to look less so. Yet when she finally drifted toward him, distinctly handsome, though ever so much older—older than when he had seen her before—it might have been as an effect of her guessing that he had, within the couple of hours, devoted more imagination to her than to all the others put together, and had thereby penetrated to a kind of truth that the others were too stupid for. She *was* there on harder terms than any one; she was there as a consequence of things suffered, one way and another, in the interval of years; and she remembered him very much as she was remembered—only a good deal better.

By the time they at last thus came to speech they were alone in one of the rooms—remarkable for a fine portrait over the chimney-place—out of which their friends had passed, and the charm of it was that even before they had spoken they had practically arranged with each other to stay behind for talk. The charm, happily, was in other things too—partly in there being scarce a spot at Weatherend without something to stay behind for. It was in the way the autumn day looked into the high windows as it waned; the way the red light, breaking at the close from under a low sombre sky, reached out in a long shaft and played over old wainscots, old tapestry, old gold, old colour. It was most of all perhaps in the way she came to him as if, since she had been turned on to deal with the simpler sort, he might, should he choose to keep the whole thing down, just take her mild attention for a part of her general business. As soon as he heard her voice, however, the gap was filled up and the missing link supplied; the slight irony he divined in her attitude lost its advantage. He almost jumped at it to get there before her. "I met you years and years ago in Rome. I remember all about it." She confessed to disappointment—she had been so sure he didn't; and to prove how well he did he began to pour forth the particular recollections that popped up as he called for them. Her face and her voice, all at his service now, worked the miracle—the impression operating like the torch of a lamplighter who touches into flame, one by one, a long row of gas-jets. Marcher flattered himself the illumination was brilliant, yet he was really still more pleased on her showing him, with amusement, that in his haste to make everything right he had got most things rather wrong. It hadn't been at Rome—it had been at Naples; and it hadn't been eight years before—it had been more nearly ten. She hadn't been, either, with her uncle and aunt, but with her mother and her brother; in addition to which it was not with the Pembles *he* had been, but with the Boyers, coming down in their company from Rome—a point on which she insisted, a little to his confusion, and as to which she had her evidence in hand. The Boyers she had known, but didn't know the Pembles, though she had heard of them, and it was the people he was with who had made them acquainted. The incident of the thunderstorm that had raged round them with such violence as to drive them for refuge into an excavation—this incident had not occurred at the Palace of the Cæsars, but at Pompeii, on an occasion when they had been present there at an important find.

He accepted her amendments, he enjoyed her corrections, though the moral of them was, she pointed out, that he *really* didn't remember the least thing about her; and he only felt it as a drawback that when all was made strictly historic there didn't appear much of anything left. They lingered together still, she neglecting her office—for from the moment he was so clever she had no proper right to him—and both neglecting the house, just waiting as to see if a memory or two more wouldn't again breathe on them. It hadn't taken them many minutes, after all, to put down on the table, like the cards of a pack, those that constituted their respective hands; only what came out was that the pack was unfortunately not perfect—that the past, invoked, invited, encouraged, could give them, naturally, no more than it had. It had made them anciently meet—her at twenty, him at twenty-five; but nothing was so strange, they seemed to say to each other, as that, while so occupied, it hadn't done a little more for them. They looked at each other as with the feeling of an occasion missed; the present would have been so much better if the other, in the far distance, in the foreign land, hadn't been so stupidly meagre. There weren't apparently, all counted, more than a dozen little old things that had succeeded in coming to pass between them; trivialities of youth, simplicities of freshness, stupidities of ignorance, small possible germs, but too deeply buried—too deeply (didn't it seem?) to sprout after so many years. Marcher could only feel he ought to have rendered her some service—saved her from a capsized boat in the Bay or at least recovered her dressing-bag, filched from her cab in the streets of Naples by a lazzarone with a stiletto. Or it would have been nice if he could have been taken with fever all alone at his hotel, and she could have come to look after him, to write to his people, to drive him out in convalescence. *Then* they would be in possession of the something or other that their actual show seemed to lack. It yet somehow presented itself, this show, as too good to be spoiled; so that they were reduced for a few minutes more to wondering a little helplessly why—since they seemed to know a certain number of the same people—their reunion had been so long averted. They didn't use that name for it, but their delay from minute to minute to join the others was a kind of confession that they didn't quite want it to be a failure. Their attempted supposition of reasons for their not having met but showed how little they knew of each other. There came in fact a moment when Marcher felt a positive pang. It was vain to pretend she was an old friend, for all the communities were wanting, in spite of which it was as an old friend that he saw she would have suited him. He had new ones enough—was surrounded with them for instance on the stage of the other house; as a new one he probably wouldn't have so much as noticed her. He would have liked to invent something, get her to make-believe with him that some passage of a romantic or critical kind *had* originally occurred. He was really almost reaching out in imagination—as against time —for something that would do, and saying to himself that if it didn't come this sketch of a fresh start would show for quite awkwardly bungled. They would separate, and now for no second or no third chance. They would have tried and not succeeded. Then it was, just at the turn, as he afterwards made it out to himself, that, everything else failing, she herself decided to take up the case and, as it were, save the situation. He felt as soon as she spoke that she had been consciously keeping back what she said and hoping to get on without it; a scruple in her that immensely touched him when, by the end of three or four minutes more, he was able to measure it. What she brought out, at any rate, quite cleared the air and supplied the link—the link it was so odd he should frivolously have managed to lose.

"You know you told me something I've never forgotten and that again and again has made me think of you since; it was that tremendously hot day when we went to Sorrento, across the bay, for the breeze. What I allude to was what you said to me, on the way back, as we sat under the awning of the boat enjoying the cool. Have you forgotten?"

He had forgotten and was even more surprised than ashamed. But the great thing was that he saw in this no vulgar reminder of any "sweet" speech. The vanity of women had long memories, but she was making no claim on him of a compliment or a mistake. With another woman, a totally different one, he might have feared the recall possibly even of some imbecile "offer." So, in having to say that he had indeed forgotten, he was conscious rather of a loss than of a gain; he already saw an interest in the matter of her mention. "I try to think—but I give it up. Yet I remember the Sorrento day."

"I'm not very sure you do," May Bartram after a moment said; "and I'm not very sure I ought to want you to. It's dreadful to bring a person back at any time to what he was ten years before. If you've lived away from it," she smiled, "so much the better."

"Ah if *you* haven't why should I?" he asked.

"Lived away, you mean, from what I myself was?"

"From what *I* was. I was of course an ass," Marcher went on; "but I would rather know from you just the sort of ass I was than —from the moment you have something in your mind—not know anything."

Still, however, she hesitated. "But if you've completely ceased to be that sort—?"

"Why I can then all the more bear to know. Besides, perhaps I haven't."

"Perhaps. Yet if you haven't," she added, "I should suppose you'd remember. Not indeed that *I* in the least connect with my impression the invidious name you use. If I had only thought you foolish," she explained, "the thing I speak of wouldn't so have remained with me. It was about yourself." She waited as if it might come to him; but as, only meeting her eyes in wonder, he gave no sign, she burnt her ships. "Has it ever happened?"

Then it was that, while he continued to stare, a light broke for him and the blood slowly came to his face, which began to burn with recognition. "Do you mean I told you—?" But he faltered, lest what came to him shouldn't be right, lest he should only give himself away.

"It was something about yourself that it was natural one shouldn't forget—that is if one remembered you at all. That's why I ask you," she smiled, "if the thing you then spoke of has ever come to pass?"

Oh then he saw, but he was lost in wonder and found himself embarrassed. This, he also saw, made her sorry for him, as if her allusion had been a mistake. It took him but a moment, however, to feel it hadn't been, much as it had been a surprise. After the first little shock of it her knowledge on the contrary began, even if rather strangely, to taste sweet to him. She was the only other person in the world then who would have it, and she had had it all these years, while the fact of his having so breathed his secret had unaccountably faded from him. No wonder they couldn't have met as if nothing had happened. "I judge," he finally said, "that I know what you mean. Only I had strangely enough lost any sense of having taken you so far into my confidence."

"Is it because you've taken so many others as well?"

"I've taken nobody. Not a creature since then."

"So that I'm the only person who knows?"

"The only person in the world."

"Well," she quickly replied, "I myself have never spoken. I've never, never repeated of you what you told me." She looked at him so that he perfectly believed her. Their eyes met over it in such a way that he was without a doubt. "And I never will."

She spoke with an earnestness that, as if almost excessive, put him at ease about her possible derision. Somehow the whole question was a new luxury to him—that is from the moment she was in possession. If she didn't take the sarcastic view she clearly took the sympathetic, and that was what he had had, in all the long time, from no one whomsoever. What he felt was that he couldn't at present have begun to tell her, and yet could profit perhaps exquisitely by the accident of having done so of old. "Please don't then. We're just right as it is."

"Oh I am," she laughed, "if you are!" To which she added: "Then you do still feel in the same way?"

It was impossible he shouldn't take to himself that she was really interested, though it all kept coming as perfect surprise. He had thought of himself so long as abominably alone, and lo he wasn't alone a bit. He hadn't been, it appeared, for an hour—since those moments on the Sorrento boat. It was *she* who had been, he seemed to see as he looked at her—she who had been made so by the graceless fact of his lapse of fidelity. To tell her what he had told her—what had it been but to ask something of her? something that she had given, in her charity, without his having, by a remembrance, by a return of the spirit, failing another encounter, so much as thanked her. What he had asked of her had been simply at first not to laugh at him. She had beautifully not done so for ten years, and she was not doing so now. So he had endless gratitude to make up. Only for that he must see just how he had figured to her. "What, exactly, was the account I gave—?"

"Of the way you did feel? Well, it was very simple. You said you had had from your earliest time, as the deepest thing within you, the sense of being kept for something rare and strange, possibly prodigious and terrible, that was sooner or later to happen to you, that you had in your bones the foreboding and the conviction of, and that would perhaps overwhelm you."

"Do you call that very simple?" John Marcher asked.

She thought a moment. "It was perhaps because I seemed, as you spoke, to understand it."

"You do understand it?" he eagerly asked.

Again she kept her kind eyes on him. "You still have the belief?"

"Oh!" he exclaimed helplessly. There was too much to say.

"Whatever it's to be," she clearly made out, "it hasn't yet come."

He shook his head in complete surrender now. "It hasn't yet come. Only, you know, it isn't anything I'm to *do*, to achieve in the world, to be distinguished or admired for. I'm not such an ass as *that*. It would be much better, no doubt, if I were."

"It's to be something you're merely to suffer?"

"Well, say to wait for—to have to meet, to face, to see suddenly break out in my life; possibly destroying all further consciousness, possibly annihilating me; possibly, on the other hand, only altering everything, striking at the root of all my world and leaving me to the consequences, however they shape themselves."

She took this in, but the light in her eyes continued for him not to be that of mockery. "Isn't what you describe perhaps but the expectation—or at any rate the sense of danger, familiar to so many people—of falling in love?"

John Marcher wondered. "Did you ask me that before?"

"No—I wasn't so free-and-easy then. But it's what strikes me now."

"Of course," he said after a moment, "it strikes you. Of course it strikes *me*. Of course what's in store for me may be no more than that. The only thing is," he went on, "that I think if it had been that I should by this time know."

"Do you mean because you've *been* in love?" And then as he but looked at her in silence: "You've been in love, and it hasn't meant such a cataclysm, hasn't proved the great affair?"

"Here I am, you see. It hasn't been overwhelming."

"Then it hasn't been love," said May Bartram.

"Well, I at least thought it was. I took it for that—I've taken it till now. It was agreeable, it was delightful, it was miserable," he explained. "But it wasn't strange. It wasn't what *my* affair's to be."

"You want something all to yourself—something that nobody else knows or *has* known?"

"It isn't a question of what I 'want'—God knows I don't want anything. It's only a question of the apprehension that haunts me —that I live with day by day."

He said this so lucidly and consistently that he could see it further impose itself. If she hadn't been interested before she'd have been interested now. "Is it a sense of coming violence?"

Evidently now too again he liked to talk of it. "I don't think of it as—when it does come—necessarily violent. I only think of it as natural and as of course above all unmistakeable. I think of it simply as *the* thing. *The* thing will of itself appear natural."

"Then how will it appear strange?"

Marcher bethought himself. "It won't—to *me*."

"To whom then?"

"Well," he replied, smiling at last, "say to you."

"Oh then I'm to be present?"

"Why you *are* present—since you know."

"I see." She turned it over. "But I mean at the catastrophe."

At this, for a minute, their lightness gave way to their gravity; it was as if the long look they exchanged held them together. "It will only depend on yourself—if you'll watch with me."

"Are you afraid?" she asked.

"Don't leave me *now*," he went on.

"Are you afraid?" she repeated.

"Do you think me simply out of my mind?" he pursued instead of answering. "Do I merely strike you as a harmless lunatic?"

"No," said May Bartram. "I understand you. I believe you."

"You mean you feel how my obsession—poor old thing!—may correspond to some possible reality?"

"To some possible reality."

"Then you *will* watch with me?"

She hesitated, then for the third time put her question. "Are you afraid?"

"Did I tell you I was—at Naples?"

"No, you said nothing about it."

"Then I don't know. And I should *like* to know," said John Marcher. "You'll tell me yourself whether you think so. If you'll watch with me you'll see."

"Very good then." They had been moving by this time across the room, and at the door, before passing out, they paused as for the full wind-up of their understanding. "I'll watch with you," said May Bartram.

II

THE fact that she "knew"—knew and yet neither chaffed him nor betrayed him—had in a short time begun to constitute between them a goodly bond, which became more marked when, within the year that followed their afternoon at Weatherend, the opportunities for meeting multiplied. The event that thus promoted these occasions was the death of the ancient lady her great-aunt, under whose wing, since losing her mother, she had to such an extent found shelter, and who, though but the widowed mother of the new successor to the property, had succeeded—thanks to a high tone and a high temper—in not forfeiting the supreme position at the great house. The deposition of this personage arrived but with her death, which, followed by many changes, made in particular a difference for the young woman in whom Marcher's expert attention had recognised from the first a dependent with a pride that might ache though it didn't bristle. Nothing for a long time had made him easier than the thought that the aching must have been much soothed by Miss Bartram's now finding herself able to set up a small home in London. She had acquired property, to an amount that made that luxury just possible, under her aunt's extremely complicated will, and when the whole matter began to be straightened out, which indeed took time, she let him know that the happy issue was at last in view. He had seen her again before that day, both because she had more than once accompanied the ancient lady to town and because he had paid another visit to the friends who so conveniently made of Weatherend one of the charms of their own hospitality. These friends had taken him back there; he had achieved there again with Miss Bartram some quiet detachment; and he had in London succeeded in persuading her to more than one brief absence from her aunt.

They went together, on these latter occasions, to the National Gallery and the South Kensington Museum, where, among vivid reminders, they talked of Italy at large—not now attempting to recover, as at first, the taste of their youth and their ignorance. That recovery, the first day at Weatherend, had served its purpose well, had given them quite enough; so that they were, to Marcher's sense, no longer hovering about the headwaters of their stream, but had felt their boat pushed sharply off and down the current.

They were literally afloat together; for our gentleman this was marked, quite as marked as that the fortunate cause of it was just the buried treasure of her knowledge. He had with his own hands dug up this little hoard, brought to light—that is to within reach of the dim day constituted by their discretions and privacies—the object of value the hiding-place of which he had, after putting it into the ground himself, so strangely, so long forgotten. The rare luck of his having again just stumbled on the spot made him indifferent to any other question; he would doubtless have devoted more time to the odd accident of his lapse of memory if he hadn't been moved to devote so much to the sweetness, the comfort, as he felt, for the future, that this accident itself had helped to keep fresh. It had never entered into his plan that any one should "know," and mainly for the reason that it wasn't in him to tell any one. That would have been impossible, for nothing but the amusement of a cold world would have waited on it. Since, however, a mysterious fate had opened his mouth betimes, in spite of him, he would count that a compensation and profit by it to the utmost. That the right person *should* know tempered the asperity of his secret more even than his shyness had permitted him to imagine; and May Bartram was clearly right, because—well, because there she was. Her knowledge simply settled it; he would have been sure enough by this time had she been wrong. There was that in his situation, no doubt, that disposed him too much to see her as a mere confidant, taking all her light for him from the fact—the fact only—of her interest in his predicament; from her mercy, sympathy, seriousness, her consent not to regard him as the funniest of the funny. Aware, in fine, that her price for him was just in her giving him this constant sense of his being admirably spared, he was careful to remember that she had also a life of her own, with things that might happen to *her*, things that in friendship one should likewise take account of. Something fairly

remarkable came to pass with him, for that matter, in this connexion—something represented by a certain passage of his consciousness, in the suddenest way, from one extreme to the other.

He had thought himself, so long as nobody knew, the most disinterested person in the world, carrying his concentrated burden,
his perpetual suspense, ever so quietly, holding his tongue about
it, giving others no glimpse of it nor of its effect upon his life, asking of them no allowance and only making on his side all those
that were asked. He hadn't disturbed people with the queerness
of their having to know a haunted man, though he had had moments of rather special temptation on hearing them say they were
forsooth "unsettled." If they were as unsettled as he was—he who
had never been settled for an hour in his life—they would know
what it meant. Yet it wasn't, all the same, for him to make them,
and he listened to them civilly enough. This was why he had such
good—though possibly such rather colourless—manners; this was
why, above all, he could regard himself, in a greedy world, as decently—as in fact perhaps even a little sublimely—unselfish. Our
point is accordingly that he valued this character quite sufficiently
to measure his present danger of letting it lapse, against which he
promised himself to be much on his guard. He was quite ready,
none the less, to be selfish just a little, since surely no more charming occasion for it had come to him. "Just a little," in a word,
was just as much as Miss Bartram, taking one day with another,
would let him. He never would be in the least coercive, and would
keep well before him the lines on which consideration for her—
the very highest—ought to proceed. He would thoroughly establish the heads under which her affairs, her requirements, her peculiarities—he went so far as to give them the latitude of that
name—would come into their intercourse. All this naturally was a
sign of how much he took the intercourse itself for granted. There
was nothing more to be done about *that*. It simply existed; had
sprung into being with her first penetrating question to him in the
autumn light there at Weatherend. The real form it should have
taken on the basis that stood out large was the form of their marrying. But the devil in this was that the very basis itself put marrying out of the question. His conviction, his apprehension, his
obsession, in short, wasn't a privilege he could invite a woman to
share; and that consequence of it was precisely what was the matter with him. Something or other lay in wait for him, amid the

twists and the turns of the months and the years, like a crouching beast in the jungle. It signified little whether the crouching beast were destined to slay him or to be slain. The definite point was the inevitable spring of the creature; and the definite lesson from that was that a man of feeling didn't cause himself to be accompanied by a lady on a tiger-hunt. Such was the image under which he had ended by figuring his life.

They had at first, none the less, in the scattered hours spent together, made no allusion to that view of it; which was a sign he was handsomely alert to give that he didn't expect, that he in fact didn't care, always to be talking about it. Such a feature in one's outlook was really like a hump on one's back. The difference it made every minute of the day existed quite independently of discussion. One discussed of course *like* a hunchback, for there was always, if nothing else, the hunchback face. That remained, and she was watching him; but people watched best, as a general thing, in silence, so that such would be predominantly the manner of their vigil. Yet he didn't want, at the same time, to be tense and solemn; tense and solemn was what he imagined he too much showed for with other people. The thing to be, with the one person who knew, was easy and natural—to make the reference rather than be seeming to avoid it, to avoid it rather than be seeming to make it, and to keep it, in any case, familiar, facetious even, rather than pedantic and portentous. Some such consideration as the latter was doubtless in his mind for instance when he wrote pleasantly to Miss Bartram that perhaps the great thing he had so long felt as in the lap of the gods was no more than this circumstance, which touched him so nearly, of her acquiring a house in London. It was the first allusion they had yet again made, needing any other hitherto so little; but when she replied, after having given him the news, that she was by no means satisfied with such a trifle as the climax to so special a suspense, she almost set him wondering if she hadn't even a larger conception of singularity for him than he had for himself. He was at all events destined to become aware little by little, as time went by, that she was all the while looking at his life, judging it, measuring it, in the light of the thing she knew, which grew to be at last, with the consecration of the years, never mentioned between them save as "the real truth" about him. That had always been his own form of reference to it, but she adopted the form so quietly that, looking back at the end of a period, he knew there was no moment at which it was traceable that she had, as he might say, got inside his idea, or exchanged the attitude of beautifully indulging for that of still more beautifully believing him.

It was always open to him to accuse her of seeing him but as the most harmless of maniacs, and this, in the long run—since it covered so much ground—was his easiest description of their friendship. He had a screw loose for her, but she liked him in spite of it and was practically, against the rest of the world, his kind wise keeper, unremunerated but fairly amused and, in the absence of other near ties, not disreputably occupied. The rest of the world of course thought him queer, but she, she only, knew how, and above all why, queer; which was precisely what enabled her to dispose the concealing veil in the right folds. She took his gaiety from him—since it had to pass with them for gaiety—as she took everything else; but she certainly so far justified by her unerring touch his finer sense of the degree to which he had ended by convincing her. *She* at least never spoke of the secret of his life except as "the real truth about you," and she had in fact a wonderful way of making it seem, as such, the secret of her own life too. That was in fine how he so constantly felt her as allowing for him; he couldn't on the whole call it anything else. He allowed for himself, but she, exactly, allowed still more; partly because, better placed for a sight of the matter, she traced his unhappy perversion through reaches of its course into which he could scarce follow it. He knew how he felt, but, besides knowing that, she knew how he *looked* as well; he knew each of the things of importance he was insidiously kept from doing, but she could add up the amount they made, understand how much, with a lighter weight on his spirit, he might have done, and thereby establish how, clever as he was, he fell short. Above all she was in the secret of the difference between the forms he went through—those of his little office under Government, those of caring for his modest patrimony, for his library, for his garden in the country, for the people in London whose invitations he accepted and repaid—and the detachment that reigned beneath them and that made of all behaviour, all that could in the least be called behaviour, a long act of dissimulation. What it had come to was that he wore a mask painted with the social simper, out of the eye-holes of which there looked eyes of an expression not in the least matching the other features. This the stupid world, even after years, had never more than half-discovered. It was only May Bartram who had, and she achieved, by an art indescribable, the feat of at once—or perhaps it was only alternately—meeting the eyes from in front and mingling her own vision, as from over his shoulder, with their peep through the apertures.

So while they grew older together she did watch with him, and so she let this association give shape and colour to her own existence. Beneath *her* forms as well detachment had learned to sit, and behaviour had become for her, in the social sense, a false account of herself. There was but one account of her that would have been true all the while and that she could give straight to nobody, least of all to John Marcher. Her whole attitude was a virtual statement, but the perception of that only seemed called to take its place for him as one of the many things necessarily crowded out of his consciousness. If she had moreover, like himself, to make sacrifices to their real truth, it was to be granted that her compensation might have affected her as more prompt and more natural. They had long periods, in this London time, during which, when they were together, a stranger might have listened to them without in the least pricking up his ears; on the other hand the real truth was equally liable at any moment to rise to the surface, and the auditor would then have wondered indeed what they were talking about. They had from an early hour made up their minds that society was, luckily, unintelligent, and the margin allowed them by this had fairly become one of their commonplaces. Yet there were still moments when the situation turned almost fresh—usually under the effect of some expression drawn from herself. Her expressions doubtless repeated themselves, but her intervals were generous. "What saves us, you know, is that we answer so completely to so usual an appearance: that of the man and woman whose friendship has become such a daily habit—or almost—as to be at last indispensable." That for instance was a remark she had frequently enough had occasion to make, though she had given it at different times different developments. What we are especially concerned with is the turn it happened to take from her one afternoon when he had come to see her in honour of her birthday. This anniversary had fallen on a Sunday, at a season of thick fog and general outward gloom; but he had brought her his customary offering, having known her now long enough to have established a hundred small traditions. It was one of his proofs to himself, the present he made her on her birthday, that he hadn't sunk into real selfishness. It was mostly nothing more than a small trinket, but it was always fine of its kind, and he was regularly careful to pay for it more than he thought he could afford. "Our habit saves you at least, don't you see? because it makes you, after all, for the vulgar, indistinguishable from other men. What's the most inveterate mark of men in general? Why the capacity to spend endless time with dull women—to spend it I won't say without being bored, but without minding that they are, without being driven off at a tangent by it; which comes to the same thing. I'm your dull woman, a part of the daily bread for which you pray at church. That covers your tracks more than anything."

"And what covers yours?" asked Marcher, whom his dull woman could mostly to this extent amuse. "I see of course what you mean by your saving me, in this way and that, so far as other people are concerned—I've seen it all along. Only what is it that saves *you?* I often think, you know, of that."

She looked as if she sometimes thought of that too, but rather in a different way. "Where other people, you mean, are concerned?"

"Well, you're really so in with me, you know—as a sort of result of my being so in with yourself. I mean of my having such an immense regard for you, being so tremendously mindful of all you've done for me. I sometimes ask myself if it's quite fair. Fair I mean to have so involved and—since one may say it—interested you. I almost feel as if you hadn't really had time to do anything else."

"Anything else but be interested?" she asked. "Ah what else does one ever want to be? If I've been 'watching' with you, as we long ago agreed I was to do, watching's always in itself an absorption."

"Oh certainly," John Marcher said, "if you hadn't had your curiosity—! Only doesn't it sometimes come to you as time goes on that your curiosity isn't being particularly repaid?"

May Bartram had a pause. "Do you ask that, by any chance, because you feel at all that yours isn't? I mean because you have to wait so long."

Oh he understood what she meant! "For the thing to happen that never does happen? For the beast to jump out? No, I'm just where I was about it. It isn't a matter as to which I can *choose,* I can decide for a change. It isn't one as to which there *can* be a change. It's in the lap of the gods. One's in the hands of one's law —there one is. As to the form the law will take, the way it will operate, that's its own affair."

"Yes," Miss Bartram replied; "of course one's fate's coming, of course it *has* come in its own form and its own way, all the while. Only, you know, the form and the way in your case were to have been—well, something so exceptional and, as one may say, so particularly *your* own."

Something in this made him look at her with suspicion. "You say 'were to *have* been,' as if in your heart you had begun to doubt."

"Oh!" she vaguely protested.

"As if you believe," he went on, "that nothing will now take place."

She shook her head slowly but rather inscrutably. "You're far from my thought."

He continued to look at her. "What then is the matter with you?"

"Well," she said after another wait, "the matter with me is simply that I'm more sure than ever my curiosity, as you call it, will be but too well repaid."

They were frankly grave now; he had got up from his seat, had turned once more about the little drawing-room to which, year after year, he brought his inevitable topic; in which he had, as he might have said, tasted their intimate community with every sauce, where every object was as familiar to him as the things of his own house and the very carpets were worn with his fitful walk very much as the desks in old counting-houses are worn by the elbows of generations of clerks. The generations of his nervous moods had been at work there, and the place was the written history of his whole middle life. Under the impression of what his friend had just said he knew himself, for some reason, more aware of these things; which made him, after a moment, stop again before her. "Is it possibly that you've grown afraid?"

"Afraid?" He thought, as she repeated the word, that his question had made her, a little, change colour; so that, lest he should have touched on a truth, he explained very kindly: "You remember that that was what you asked *me* long ago—that first day at Weatherend."

"Oh yes, and you told me you didn't know—that I was to see for myself. We've said little about it since, even in so long a time."

"Precisely," Marcher interposed—"quite as if it were too delicate a matter for us to make free with. Quite as if we might find, on pressure, that I *am* afraid. For then," he said, "we shouldn't, should we? quite know what to do."

She had for the time no answer to this question. "There have been days when I thought you were. Only, of course," she added, "there have been days when we have thought almost anything."

"Everything. Oh!" Marcher softly groaned as with a gasp, half-spent, at the face, more uncovered just then than it had been for a long while, of the imagination always with them. It had always had its incalculable moments of glaring out, quite as with the very eyes of the very Beast, and, used as he was to them, they could still draw from him the tribute of a sigh that rose from the depths of his being. All they had thought, first and last, rolled over him; the past seemed to have been reduced to mere barren speculation. This in fact was what the place had just struck him as so full of—the simplification of everything but the state of suspense. That remained only by seeming to hang in the void surrounding it. Even his original fear, if fear it had been, had lost itself in the desert. "I judge, however," he continued, "that you see I'm not afraid now."

"What I see, as I make it out, is that you've achieved something almost unprecedented in the way of getting used to danger. Living with it so long and so closely you've lost your sense of it; you know it's there, but you're indifferent, and you cease even, as of old, to have to whistle in the dark. Considering what the danger is," May Bartram wound up, "I'm bound to say I don't think your attitude could well be surpassed."

John Marcher faintly smiled. "It's heroic?"

"Certainly—call it that."

It was what he would have liked indeed to call it. "I *am* then a man of courage?"

"That's what you were to show me."

He still, however, wondered. "But doesn't the man of courage know what he's afraid of—or *not* afraid of? I don't know *that,* you see. I don't focus it. I can't name it. I only know I'm exposed."

"Yes, but exposed—how shall I say?—so directly. So intimately. That's surely enough."

"Enough to make you feel then—as what we may call the end and the upshot of our watch—that I'm not afraid?"

"You're not afraid. But it isn't," she said, "the end of our watch. That is it isn't the end of yours. You've everything still to see."

"Then why haven't *you?*" he asked. He had had, all along, today, the sense of her keeping something back, and he still had it. As this was his first impression of that it quite made a date. The case was the more marked as she didn't at first answer; which in turn made him go on. "You know something I don't." Then his voice, for that of a man of courage, trembled a little. "You know what's to happen." Her silence, with the face she showed, was almost a confession—it made him sure. "You know, and you're afraid to tell me. It's so bad that you're afraid I'll find out."

All this might be true, for she did look as if, unexpectedly to her, he had crossed some mystic line that she had secretly drawn round her. Yet she might, after all, not have worried; and the real climax was that he himself, at all events, needn't. "You'll never find out."

III

It was all to have made, none the less, as I have said, a date; which came out in the fact that again and again, even after long intervals, other things that passed between them wore in relation to this hour but the character of recalls and results. Its immediate effect had been indeed rather to lighten insistence—almost to provoke a reaction; as if their topic had dropped by its own weight and as if moreover, for that matter, Marcher had been visited by one of his occasional warnings against egotism. He had kept up, he felt, and very decently on the whole, his consciousness of the importance of not being selfish, and it was true that he had never sinned in that direction without promptly enough trying to press the scales the other way. He often repaired his fault, the season permitting, by inviting his friend to accompany him to the opera; and it not infrequently thus happened that, to show he didn't wish her to have but one sort of food for her mind, he was the cause of her appearing there with him a dozen nights in the month. It even happened that, seeing her home at such times, he occasionally went in with her to finish, as he called it, the evening, and, the bet-

ter to make his point, sat down to the frugal but always careful
little supper that awaited his pleasure. His point was made, he
thought, by his not eternally insisting with her on himself; made
for instance, at such hours, when it befell that, her piano at hand
and each of them familiar with it, they went over passages of the
opera together. It chanced to be on one of these occasions, however, that he reminded her of her not having answered a certain
question he had put to her during the talk that had taken place
between them on her last birthday. "What is it that saves *you?*"
—saved her, he meant, from that appearance of variation from
the usual human type. If he had practically escaped remark,
as she pretended, by doing, in the most important particular,
what most men do—find the answer to life in patching up an alliance of a sort with a woman no better than himself—how had she
escaped it, and how could the alliance, such as it was, since they
must suppose it had been more or less noticed, have failed to make
her rather positively talked about?

"I never said," May Bartram replied, "that it hadn't made me
a good deal talked about."

"Ah well then you're not 'saved.'"

"It hasn't been a question for me. If you've had your woman,
I've had," she said, "my man."

"And you mean that makes you all right?"

Oh it was always as if there were so much to say! "I don't know
why it shouldn't make me—humanly, which is what we're speaking of—as right as it makes you."

"I see," Marcher returned. " 'Humanly,' no doubt, as showing
that you're living for something. Not, that is, just for me and my
secret."

May Bartram smiled. "I don't pretend it exactly shows that
I'm not living for you. It's my intimacy with you that's in question."

He laughed as he saw what she meant. "Yes, but since, as you
say, I'm only, so far as people make out, ordinary, you're—
aren't you?—no more than ordinary either. You help me to pass
for a man like another. So if I *am*, as I understand you, you're not
compromised. Is that it?"

She had another of her waits, but she spoke clearly enough.
"That's it. It's all that concerns me—to help you to pass for a man
like another."

He was careful to acknowledge the remark handsomely. "How kind, how beautiful, you are to me! How shall I ever repay you?"

She had her last grave pause, as if there might be a choice of ways. But she chose. "By going on as you are."

It was into this going on as he was that they relapsed, and really for so long a time that the day inevitably came for a further sounding of their depths. These depths, constantly bridged over by a structure firm enough in spite of its lightness and of its occasional oscillation in the somewhat vertiginous air, invited on occasion, in the interest of their nerves, a dropping of the plummet and a measurement of the abyss. A difference had been made moreover, once for all, by the fact that she had all the while not appeared to feel the need of rebutting his charge of an idea within her that she didn't dare to express—a charge uttered just before one of the fullest of their later discussions ended. It had come up for him then that she "knew" something and that what she knew was bad—too bad to tell him. When he had spoken of it as visibly so bad that she was afraid he might find it out, her reply had left the matter too equivocal to be let alone and yet, for Marcher's special sensibility, almost too formidable again to touch. He circled about it at a distance that alternately narrowed and widened and that still wasn't much affected by the consciousness in him that there was nothing she could "know," after all, any better than he did. She had no source of knowledge he hadn't equally—except of course that she might have finer nerves. That was what women had where they were interested; they made out things, where people were concerned, that the people often couldn't have made out for themselves. Their nerves, their sensibility, their imagination, were conductors and revealers, and the beauty of May Bartram was in particular that she had given herself so to his case. He felt in these days what, oddly enough, he had never felt before, the growth of a dread of losing her by some catastrophe—some catastrophe that yet wouldn't at all be *the* catastrophe: partly because she had almost of a sudden begun to strike him as more useful to him than ever yet, and partly by reason of an appearance of uncertainty in her health, coincident and equally new. It was characteristic of the inner detachment he had hitherto so successfully cultivated and to which our whole account of him is a reference, it was characteristic that his complications, such as they were, had never yet seemed so as at this crisis to thicken about him, even to the point of making him ask himself if he were, by any chance, of a truth, within sight or sound, within touch or reach, within the immediate jurisdiction, of the thing that waited.

When the day came, as come it had to, that his friend confessed to him her fear of a deep disorder in her blood, he felt somehow the shadow of a change and the chill of a shock. He immediately began to imagine aggravations and disasters, and above all to think of her peril as the direct menace for himself of personal privation. This indeed gave him one of those partial recoveries of equanimity that were agreeable to him—it showed him that what was still first in his mind was the loss she herself might suffer. "What if she should have to die before knowing, before seeing—?" It would have been brutal, in the early stages of her trouble, to put that question to her; but it had immediately sounded for him to his own concern, and the possibility was what most made him sorry for her. If she did "know," moreover, in the sense of her having had some—what should he think?—mystical irresistible light, this would make the matter not better, but worse, inasmuch as her original adoption of his own curiosity had quite become the basis of her life. She had been living to see what would *be* to be seen, and it would quite lacerate her to have to give up before the accomplishment of the vision. These reflexions, as I say, quickened his generosity; yet, make them as he might, he saw himself, with the lapse of the period, more and more disconcerted. It lapsed for him with a strange steady sweep, and the oddest oddity was that it gave him, independently of the threat of much inconvenience, almost the only positive surprise his career, if career it could be called, had yet offered him. She kept the house as she had never done; he had to go to her to see her—she could meet him nowhere now, though there was scarce a corner of their loved old London in which she hadn't in the past, at one time or another done so; and he found her always seated by her fire in the deep old-fashioned chair she was less and less able to leave. He had been struck one day, after an absence exceeding his usual measure, with her suddenly looking much older to him than he had ever thought of her being; then he recognised that the suddenness was all on his side—he had just simply and suddenly noticed. She looked older because inevitably, after so many years, she *was* old, or almost; which was of course true in still greater measure of her companion. If she was old, or almost, John Marcher assuredly was, and yet it was her showing of the lesson, not his own, that brought the truth home to him. His surprises began here; when once they had begun they multiplied; they came rather with a rush: it was as if, in the oddest way in the world, they had all been kept back, sown in a thick cluster, for the late afternoon of life, the time at which for people in general the unexpected has died out.

One of them was that he should have caught himself—for he *had* so done—*really* wondering if the great accident would take form now as nothing more than his being condemned to see this charming woman, this admirable friend, pass away from him. He had never so unreservedly qualified her as while confronted in thought with such a possibility; in spite of which there was small doubt for him that as an answer to his long riddle the mere efface-ment of even so fine a feature of his situation would be an abject anti-climax. It would represent, as connected with his past atti-tude, a drop of dignity under the shadow of which his existence could only become the most grotesque of failures. He had been far from holding it a failure—long as he had waited for the appear-ance that was to make it a success. He had waited for quite an-other thing, not for such a thing as that. The breath of his good faith came short, however, as he recognised how long he had waited, or how long at least his companion had. That she, at all events, might be recorded as having waited in vain—this affected him sharply, and all the more because of his at first having done little more than amuse himself with the idea. It grew more grave as the gravity of her condition grew, and the state of mind it pro-duced in him, which he himself ended by watching as if it had been some definite disfigurement of his outer person, may pass for another of his surprises. This conjoined itself still with another, the really stupefying consciousness of a question that he would have allowed to shape itself had he dared. What did everything mean—what, that is, did *she* mean, she and her vain waiting and her probable death and the soundless admonition of it all—unless that, at this time of day, it was simply, it was overwhelmingly too late? He had never at any stage of his queer consciousness ad-mitted the whisper of such a correction; he had never till within these last few months been so false to his conviction as not to hold that what was to come to him had time, whether *he* struck him-self as having it or not. That at last, at last, he certainly hadn't it, to speak of, or had it but in the scantiest measure—such, soon enough, as things went with him, became the inference with which his old obsession had to reckon: and this it was not helped to do by the more and more confirmed appearance that the great vagueness casting the long shadow in which he had lived had, to attest itself, almost no margin left. Since it was in Time that he was to have met his fate, so it was in Time that his fate was to have acted; and as he waked up to the sense of no longer being young, which was exactly the sense of being stale, just as that, in turn, was the sense of being weak, he waked up to another matter beside. It all hung together; they were subject, he and the great vagueness, to an equal and indivisible law. When the possibilities themselves had accordingly turned stale, when the secret of the gods had grown faint, had perhaps even quite evaporated, that, and that only, was failure. It wouldn't have been failure to be bankrupt, dishonoured, pilloried, hanged; it was failure not to be anything. And so, in the dark valley into which his path had taken its unlooked-for twist, he wondered not a little as he groped. He didn't care what awful crash might overtake him, with what ignominy or what monstrosity he might yet be associated—since he wasn't after all too utterly old to suffer—if it would only be decently proportionate to the posture he had kept, all his life, in the threatened presence of it. He had but one desire left—that he shouldn't have been "sold."

IV

THEN IT WAS that, one afternoon, while the spring of the year was young and new she met all in her own way his frankest betrayal of these alarms. He had gone in late to see her, but evening hadn't settled and she was presented to him in that long fresh light of waning April days which affects us often with a sadness sharper than the greyest hours of autumn. The week had been warm, the spring was supposed to have begun early, and May Bartram sat, for the first time in the year, without a fire; a fact that, to Marcher's sense, gave the scene of which she formed part a smooth and ultimate look, an air of knowing, in its immaculate order and cold meaningless cheer, that it would never see a fire again. Her own aspect—he could scarce have said why—intensified this note. Almost as white as wax, with the marks and signs in her face as nu merous and as fine as if they had been etched by a needle, with soft white draperies relieved by a faded green scarf on the delicate tone of which the years had further refined, she was the picture of a serene and exquisite but impenetrable sphinx, whose head, or indeed all whose person, might have been powdered with silver. She was a sphinx, yet with her white petals and green fronds she might have been a lily too—only an artificial lily, wonderfully imitated and constantly kept, without dust or stain, though not exempt from a slight droop and a complexity of faint creases, under some clear glass bell. The perfection of household care, of high polish and finish, always reigned in her rooms, but they now looked most as if everything had been wound up, tucked in, put away, so that she might sit with folded hands and with nothing more to do. She was "out of it," to Marcher's vision; her work was over; she communicated with him as across some gulf or from some island of rest that she had already reached, and it made him feel strangely abandoned. Was it—or rather wasn't it—that if for so long she had been watching with him the answer to their question must have swum into her ken and taken on its name, so that her occupation was verily gone? He had as much as charged her with this in saying to her, many months before, that she even then knew something she was keeping from him. It was a point he had never since ventured to press, vaguely fearing as he did that it might become a difference, perhaps a disagreement, between them. He had in this later time turned nervous, which was what he in all the other years had never been; and the oddity was that his nervousness should have waited till he had begun to doubt, should have held off so long as he was sure. There was something, it seemed to him, that the wrong word would bring down on his head, something that would so at least ease off his tension. But he wanted not to speak the wrong word; that would make everything ugly. He wanted the knowledge he lacked to drop on him, if drop it could, by its own august weight. If she was to forsake him it was surely for her to take leave. This was why he didn't directly ask her again what she knew; but it was also why, approaching the matter from another side, he said to her in the course of his visit: "What do you regard as the very worst that at this time of day *can* happen to me?"

He had asked her that in the past often enough; they had, with the odd irregular rhythm of their intensities and avoidances, exchanged ideas about it and then had seen the ideas washed away by cool intervals, washed like figures traced in sea-sand. It had ever been the mark of their talk that the oldest allusions in it required but a little dismissal and reaction to come out again, sounding for the hour as new. She could thus at present meet his enquiry quite freshly and patiently. "Oh yes, I've repeatedly thought, only it always seemed to me of old that I couldn't quite make up my mind. I thought of dreadful things, between which it was difficult to choose; and so must you have done."

"Rather! I feel now as if I had scarce done anything else. I appear to myself to have spent my life in thinking of nothing *but* dreadful things. A great many of them I've at different times named to you, but there were others I couldn't name."

"They were too, too dreadful?"

"Too, too dreadful—some of them."

She looked at him a minute, and there came to him as he met it an inconsequent sense that her eyes, when one got their full clearness, were still as beautiful as they had been in youth, only beautiful with a strange cold light—a light that somehow was a part of the effect, if it wasn't rather a part of the cause, of the pale hard sweetness of the season and the hour. "And yet," she said at last, "there are horrors we've mentioned."

It deepened the strangeness to see her, as such a figure in such a picture, talk of "horrors," but she was to do in a few minutes something stranger yet—though even of this he was to take the full measure but afterwards—and the note of it already trembled. It was, for the matter of that, one of the signs that her eyes were having again the high flicker of their prime. He had to admit, however, what she said. "Oh yes, there were times when we did go far." He caught himself in the act of speaking as if it all were over. Well, he wished it were; and the consummation depended for him clearly more and more on his friend.

But she had now a soft smile. "Oh far—!"

It was oddly ironic. "Do you mean you're prepared to go further?"

She was frail and ancient and charming as she continued to look at him, yet it was rather as if she had lost the thread. "Do you consider that we went far?"

"Why I thought it the point you were just making—that we *had* looked most things in the face."

"Including each other?" She still smiled. "But you're quite right. We've had together great imaginations, often great fears; but some of them have been unspoken."

"Then the worst—we haven't faced that. I *could* face it, I believe, if I knew what you think it. I feel," he explained, "as if I had lost my power to conceive such things." And he wondered if he looked as blank as he sounded. "It's spent."

"Then why do you assume," she asked, "that mine isn't?"

"Because you've given me signs to the contrary. It isn't a question for you of conceiving, imagining, comparing. It isn't a question now of choosing." At last he came out with it. "You know something I don't. You've shown me that before."

These last words had affected her, he made out in a moment, exceedingly, and she spoke with firmness. "I've shown you, my dear, nothing."

He shook his head. "You can't hide it."

"Oh, oh!" May Bartram sounded over what she couldn't hide. It was almost a smothered groan.

"You admitted it months ago, when I spoke of it to you as of something you were afraid I should find out. Your answer was that I couldn't, that I wouldn't, and I don't pretend I have. But you had something therefore in mind, and I now see how it must have been, how it still is, the possibility that, of all possibilities, has settled itself for you as the worst. This," he went on, "is why I appeal to you. I'm only afraid of ignorance to-day—I'm not afraid of knowledge." And then as for a while she said nothing: "What makes me sure is that I see in your face and feel here, in this air and amid these appearances, that you're out of it. You've done. You've had your experience. You leave me to my fate."

Well, she listened, motionless and white in her chair, as on a decision to be made, so that her manner was fairly an avowal, though still, with a small fine inner stiffness, an imperfect surrender. "It *would* be the worst," she finally let herself say. "I mean the thing I've never said."

It hushed him a moment. "More monstrous than all the monstrosities we've named?"

"More monstrous. Isn't that what you sufficiently express," she asked, "in calling it the worst?"

Marcher thought. "Assuredly—if you mean, as I do, something that includes all the loss and all the shame that are thinkable."

"It would if it *should* happen," said May Bartram. "What we're speaking of, remember, is only my idea."

"It's your belief," Marcher returned. "That's enough for me. I feel your beliefs are right. Therefore if, having this one, you give me no more light on it, you abandon me."

"No, no!" she repeated. "I'm with you—don't you see?—still." And as to make it more vivid to him she rose from her chair—a movement she seldom risked in these days—and showed herself, all draped and all soft, in her fairness and slimness. "I haven't forsaken you."

It was really, in its effort against weakness, a generous assurance, and had the success of the impulse not, happily, been great, it would have touched him to pain more than to pleasure. But the cold charm in her eyes had spread, as she hovered before him, to all the rest of her person, so that it was for the minute almost a recovery of youth. He couldn't pity her for that; he could only take her as she showed—as capable even yet of helping him. It was as if, at the same time, her light might at any instant go out; wherefore he must make the most of it. There passed before him with intensity the three or four things he wanted most to know; but the question that came of itself to his lips really covered the others. "Then tell me if I shall consciously suffer."

She promptly shook her head. "Never!"

It confirmed the authority he imputed to her, and it produced on him an extraordinary effect. "Well, what's better than that? Do you call that the worst?"

"You think nothing is better?" she asked.

She seemed to mean something so special that he again sharply wondered, though still with the dawn of a prospect of relief. "Why not, if one doesn't *know?*" After which, as their eyes, over his question, met in a silence, the dawn deepened and something to his purpose came prodigiously out of her very face. His own, as he took it in, suddenly flushed to the forehead, and he gasped with the force of a perception to which, on the instant, everything fitted. The sound of his gasp filled the air; then he became articulate. "I see—if I don't suffer!"

In her own look, however, was doubt. "You see what?"

"Why what you mean—what you've always meant."

She again shook her head. "What I mean isn't what I've always meant. It's different."

"It's something new?"

She hung back from it a little. "Something new. It's not what you think. I see what you think."

His divination drew breath then; only her correction might be wrong. "It isn't that I *am* a blockhead?" he asked between faintness and grimness. "It isn't that it's all a mistake?"

"A mistake?" she pityingly echoed. *That* possibility, for her, he saw, would be monstrous; and if she guaranteed him the immunity from pain it would accordingly not be what she had in mind. "Oh no," she declared; "it's nothing of that sort. You've been right."

Yet he couldn't help asking himself if she weren't, thus pressed, speaking but to save him. It seemed to him he should be most in a hole if his history should prove all a platitude. "Are you telling me the truth, so that I shan't have been a bigger idiot than I can bear to know? I *haven't* lived with a vain imagination, in the most besotted illusion? I haven't waited but to see the door shut in my face?"

She shook her head again. "However the case stands *that* isn't the truth. Whatever the reality, it *is* a reality. The door isn't shut. The door's open," said May Bartram.

"Then something's to come?"

She waited once again, always with her cold sweet eyes on him. "It's never too late." She had, with her gliding step, diminished the distance between them, and she stood nearer to him, close to him, a minute, as if still charged with the unspoken. Her movement might have been for some finer emphasis of what she was at once hesitating and deciding to say. He had been standing by the chimney-piece, fireless and sparely adorned, a small perfect old French clock and two morsels of rosy Dresden constituting all its furniture; and her hand grasped the shelf while she kept him waiting, grasped it a little as for support and encouragement. She only kept him waiting, however; that is he only waited. It had become suddenly, from her movement and attitude, beautiful and vivid to him that she had something more to give him; her wasted face delicately shone with it—it glittered almost as with the white lustre of silver in her expression. She was right, incontestably, for what he saw in her face was the truth, and strangely, without consequence, while their talk of it as dreadful was still in the air, she appeared to present it as inordinately soft. This, prompting bewilderment, made him but gape the more gratefully for her revelation, so that they continued for some minutes silent, her face shining at him, her contact imponderably pressing, and his stare all kind but all expectant. The end, none the less, was that what he had expected failed to come to him. Something else took place instead, which seemed to consist at first in the mere closing of her eyes. She gave way at the same instant to a slow fine shudder, and though he remained staring—though he stared in fact but the harder—turned off and regained her chair. It was the end of what she had been intending, but it left him thinking only of that.

"Well, you don't say—?"

She had touched in her passage a bell near the chimney and had sunk back strangely pale. "I'm afraid I'm too ill."

"Too ill to tell me?" It sprang up sharp to him, and almost to his lips, the fear she might die without giving him light. He checked himself in time from so expressing his question, but she answered as if she had heard the words.

"Don't you know—now?"

"'Now'—?" She had spoken as if some difference had been made within the moment. But her maid, quickly obedient to her bell, was already with them. "I know nothing." And he was afterwards to say to himself that he must have spoken with odious impatience, such an impatience as to show that, supremely disconcerted, he washed his hands of the whole question.

"Oh!" said May Bartram.

"Are you in pain?" he asked as the woman went to her.

"No," said May Bartram.

Her maid, who had put an arm round her as if to take her to her room, fixed on him eyes that appealingly contradicted her; in spite of which, however, he showed once more his mystification. "What then has happened?"

She was once more, with her companion's help, on her feet, and, feeling withdrawal imposed on him, he had blankly found his hat and gloves and had reached the door. Yet he waited for her answer. "What *was* to," she said.

V

HE CAME back the next day, but she was then unable to see him, and as it was literally the first time this had occurred in the long stretch of their acquaintance he turned away, defeated and sore, almost angry—or feeling at least that such a break in their custom was really the beginning of the end—and wandered alone with his thoughts, especially with the one he was least able to keep down. She was dying and he would lose her; she was dying and his life would end. He stopped in the Park, into which he had passed, and stared before him at his recurrent doubt. Away from her the doubt pressed again; in her presence he had believed her, but as he felt his forlornness he threw himself into the explanation that, nearest at hand, had most of a miserable warmth for him and least of a cold torment. She had deceived him to save him—to put him off with something in which he should be able to rest. What could the thing that was to happen to him be, after all, but just this thing that had begun to happen? Her dying, her death, his consequent solitude—*that* was what he had figured as the Beast in the Jungle, that was what had been in the lap of the gods. He had had her word for it as he left her—what else on earth could she have meant? It wasn't a thing of a monstrous order; not a fate rare and distinguished; not a stroke of fortune that overwhelmed and immortalised; it had only the stamp of the common doom. But poor Marcher at this hour judged the common doom sufficient. It would serve his turn, and even as the consummation of infinite waiting he would bend his pride to accept it. He sat down on a bench in the twilight. He hadn't been a fool. Something had *been,* as she had said, to come. Before he rose indeed it had quite struck him that the final fact really matched with the long avenue through which he had had to reach it. As sharing his suspense and as giving herself all, giving her life, to bring it to an end, she had come with him every step of the way. He had lived by her aid, and to leave her behind would be cruelly, damnably to miss her. What could be more overwhelming than that?

Well, he was to know within the week, for though she kept him a while at bay, left him restless and wretched during a series of days on each of which he asked about her only again to have to turn away, she ended his trial by receiving him where she had always received him. Yet she had been brought out at some hazard into the presence of so many of the things that were, consciously, vainly, half their past, and there was scant service left in the gentleness of her mere desire, all too visible, to check his obsession and wind up his long trouble. That was clearly what she wanted, the one thing more for her own peace while she could still put out her hand. He was so affected by her state that, once seated by her chair, he was moved to let everything go; it was she herself therefore who brought him back, took up again, before she dismissed him, her last word of the other time. She showed how she wished to leave their business in order. "I'm not sure you understood. You've nothing to wait for more. It *has* come."

Oh how he looked at her! "Really?"

"Really."

"The thing that, as you said, *was* to?"

"The thing that we began in our youth to watch for."

Face to face with her once more he believed her; it was a claim to which he had so abjectly little to oppose. "You mean that it has come as a positive definite occurrence, with a name and a date?"

"Positive. Definite. I don't know about the 'name,' but oh with a date!"

He found himself again too helplessly at sea. "But come in the night—come and passed me by?"

May Bartram had her strange faint smile. "Oh no, it hasn't passed you by!"

"But if I haven't been aware of it and it hasn't touched me—?"

"Ah your not being aware of it"—and she seemed to hesitate an instant to deal with this—"your not being aware of it is the strangeness *in* the strangeness. It's the wonder *of* the wonder." She spoke as with the softness almost of a sick child, yet now at last, at the end of all, with the perfect straightness of a sibyl. She visibly knew that she knew, and the effect on him was of something co-ordinate, in its high character, with the law that had ruled him. It was the true voice of the law; so on her lips would the law itself have sounded. "It *has* touched you," she went on. "It has done its office. It has made you all its own."

"So utterly without my knowing it?"

"So utterly without your knowing it." His hand, as he leaned to her, was on the arm of her chair, and, dimly smiling always now, she placed her own on it. "It's enough if *I* know it."

"Oh!" he confusedly breathed, as she herself of late so often had done.

"What I long ago said is true. You'll never know now, and I think you ought to be content. You've *had* it," said May Bartram.

"But had what?"

"Why what was to have marked you out. The proof of your

law. It has acted. I'm too glad," she then bravely added, "to have been able to see what it's *not*."

He continued to attach his eyes to her, and with the sense that it was all beyond him, and that *she* was too, he would still have sharply challenged her hadn't he so felt it an abuse of her weakness to do more than take devoutly what she gave him, take it hushed as to a revelation. If he did speak, it was out of the foreknowledge of his loneliness to come. "If you're glad of what it's 'not' it might then have been worse?"

She turned her eyes away, she looked straight before her; with which after a moment: "Well, you know our fears."

He wondered. "It's something then we never feared?"

On this slowly she turned to him. "Did we ever dream, with all our dreams, that we should sit and talk of it thus?"

He tried for a little to make out that they had; but it was as if their dreams, numberless enough, were in solution in some thick cold mist through which thought lost itself. "It might have been that we couldn't talk?"

"Well"—she did her best for him—"not from this side. This, you see," she said, "is the *other* side."

"I think," poor Marcher returned, "that all sides are the same to me." Then, however, as she gently shook her head in correction: "We mightn't, as it were, have got across—?"

"To where we are—no. We're *here*"—she made her weak emphasis.

"And much good does it do us!" was her friend's frank comment.

"It does us the good it can. It does us the good that *it* isn't here. It's past. It's behind," said May Bartram. "Before—" but her voice dropped.

He had got up, not to tire her, but it was hard to combat his yearning. She after all told him nothing but that his light had failed—which he knew well enough without her. "Before—?" he blankly echoed.

"Before, you see, it was always to *come*. That kept it present."

"Oh I don't care what comes now! Besides," Marcher added, "it seems to me I liked it better present, as you say, than I can like it absent with *your* absence."

"Oh mine!"—and her pale hands made light of it.

"With the absence of everything." He had a dreadful sense of standing there before her for—so far as anything but this proved, this bottomless drop was concerned—the last time of their life. It rested on him with a weight he felt he could scarce bear, and this weight it apparently was that still pressed out what remained in him of speakable protest. "I believe you; but I can't begin to pretend I understand. *Nothing*, for me, is past; nothing *will* pass till I pass myself, which I pray my stars may be as soon as possible. Say, however," he added, "that I've eaten my cake, as you contend, to the last crumb—how can the thing I've never felt at all be the thing I was marked out to feel?"

She met him perhaps less directly, but she met him unperturbed. "You take your 'feelings' for granted. You were to suffer your fate. That was not necessarily to know it."

"How in the world—when what is such knowledge but suffering?"

She looked up at him a while in silence. "No—you don't understand."

"I suffer," said John Marcher.

"Don't, don't!"

"How can I help at least *that*?"

"*Don't!*" May Bartram repeated.

She spoke it in a tone so special, in spite of her weakness, that he stared an instant—stared as if some light, hitherto hidden, had shimmered across his vision. Darkness again closed over it, but the gleam had already become for him an idea. "Because I haven't the right—?"

"Don't *know*—when you needn't," she mercifully urged. "You needn't—for we shouldn't."

"Shouldn't?" If he could but know what she meant!

"No—it's too much."

"Too much?" he still asked but, with a mystification that was the next moment of a sudden to give way. Her words, if they meant something, affected him in this light—the light also of her wasted face—as meaning *all*, and the sense of what knowledge had been for herself came over him with a rush which broke through into a question. "Is it of that then you're dying?"

She but watched him, gravely at first, as to see, with this, where he was, and she might have seen something or feared something that moved her sympathy. "I would live for you still—if I could." Her eyes closed for a little, as if, withdrawn into herself, she were for a last time trying. "But I can't!" she said as she raised them again to take leave of him.

She couldn't indeed, as but too promptly and sharply appeared, and he had no vision of her after this that was anything but darkness and doom. They had parted for ever in that strange talk; access to her chamber of pain, rigidly guarded, was almost wholly forbidden him; he was feeling now moreover, in the face of doctors, nurses, the two or three relatives attracted doubtless by the presumption of what she had to "leave," how few were the rights, as they were called in such cases, that he had to put forward, and how odd it might even seem that their intimacy shouldn't have given him more of them. The stupidest fourth cousin had more, even though she had been nothing in such a person's life. She had been a feature of features in *his*, for what else was it to have been so indispensable? Strange beyond saying were the ways of existence, baffling for him the anomaly of his lack, as he felt it to be, of producible claim. A woman might have been, as it were, everything to him, and it might yet present him in no connexion that any one seemed held to recognise. If this was the case in these closing weeks it was the case more sharply on the occasion of the last offices rendered, in the great grey London cemetery, to what had been mortal, to what had been precious, in his friend. The concourse at her grave was not numerous, but he saw himself treated as scarce more nearly concerned with it than if there had been a thousand others. He was in short from this moment face to face with the fact that he was to profit extraordinarily little by the interest Mary Bartram had taken in him. He couldn't quite have said what he expected, but he hadn't surely expected this approach to a double privation. Not only had her interest failed him, but he seemed to feel himself unattended—and for a reason he couldn't seize—by the distinction, the dignity, the propriety, if nothing else, of the man markedly bereaved. It was as if in the view of society he had not *been* markedly bereaved, as if there still failed some sign or proof of it, and as if none the less his character could never be affirmed nor the deficiency ever made up. There were moments as the weeks went by when he would have liked by some almost aggressive act, to take his stand on the intimacy of his loss, in order that it *might* be questioned and his retort, to the relief of his spirit, so recorded; but the moments of an irritation more helpless followed fast on these, the moments during which, turning things over with a good conscience but with a bare horizon, he found himself wondering if he oughtn't to have begun, so to speak, further back.

He found himself wondering indeed at many things, and this last speculation had others to keep it company. What could he have done, after all, in her lifetime, without giving them both, as it were, away? He couldn't have made known she was watching him, for that would have published the superstition of the Beast. This was what closed his mouth now—now that the Jungle had been threshed to vacancy and that the Beast had stolen away. It sounded too foolish and too flat; the difference for him in this particular, the extinction in his life of the element of suspense, was such as in fact to surprise him. He could scarce have said what the effect resembled; the abrupt cessation, the positive prohibition, of music perhaps, more than anything else, in some place all adjusted and all accustomed to sonority and to attention. If he could at any rate have conceived lifting the veil from his image at some moment of the past (what had he done, after all, if not lift it to *her?*) so to do this to-day, to talk to people at large of the Jungle cleared and confide to them that he now felt it as safe, would have been not only to see them listen as to a goodwife's tale, but really to hear himself tell one. What it presently came to in truth was that poor Marcher waded through his beaten grass, where no life stirred, where no breath sounded, where no evil eye seemed to gleam from a possible lair, very much as if vaguely looking for the Beast, and still more as if acutely missing it. He walked about in an existence that had grown strangely more spacious, and, stopping fitfully in places where the undergrowth of life struck him as closer, asked himself yearningly, wondered secretly and sorely, if it would have lurked here or there. It would have at all events *sprung;* what was at least complete was his belief in the truth itself of the assurance given him. The change from his old sense to his new was absolute and final: what was to happen *had* so absolutely and finally happened that he was as little able to know a fear for his future as to know a hope; so absent in short was any question of anything still to come. He was to live entirely with the other question, that of his unidentified past, that of his having to see his fortune impenetrably muffled and masked.

The torment of this vision became then his occupation; he couldn't perhaps have consented to live but for the possibility of guessing. She had told him, his friend, not to guess; she had forbidden him, so far as he might, to know, and she had even in a sort denied the power in him to learn: which were so many things, precisely, to deprive him of rest. It wasn't that he wanted, he argued for fairness, that anything past and done should repeat itself; it was only that he shouldn't, as an anticlimax, have been taken sleeping so sound as not to be able to win back by an effort of thought the lost stuff of consciousness. He declared to himself at moments that he would either win it back or have done with consciousness for ever; he made this idea his one motive in fine, made it so much his passion that none other, to compare with it, seemed ever to have touched him. The lost stuff of consciousness became thus for him as a strayed or stolen child to an unappeasable father; he hunted it up and down very much as if he were knocking at doors and enquiring of the police. This was the spirit in which, inevitably, he set himself to travel; he started on a journey that was to be as long as he could make it; it danced before him that, as the other side of the globe couldn't possibly have less to say to him, it might, by a possibility of suggestion, have more. Before he quitted London, however, he made a pilgrimage to May Bartram's grave, took his way to it through the endless avenues of the grim suburban metropolis, sought it out in the wilderness of tombs, and, though he had come but for the renewal of the act of farewell, found himself, when he had at last stood by it, beguiled into long intensities. He stood for an hour, powerless to turn away and yet powerless to penetrate the darkness of death; fixing with his eyes her inscribed name and date, beating his forehead against the fact of the secret they kept, drawing his breath, while he waited, as if some sense would in pity of him rise from the stones. He kneeled on the stones, however, in vain; they kept what they concealed; and if the face of the tomb did become a face for him it was because her two names became a pair of eyes that didn't know him. He gave them a last long look, but no palest light broke.

VI

HE STAYED AWAY, after this, for a year; he visited the depths of Asia, spending himself on scenes of romantic interest, of superlative sanctity; but what was present to him everywhere was that for a man who had known what *he* had known the world was vul-

gar and vain. The state of mind in which he had lived for so many
years shone out to him, in reflexion, as a light that coloured and
refined, a light beside which the glow of the East was garish, cheap
and thin. The terrible truth was that he had lost—with everything
else—a distinction as well; the things he saw couldn't help being
common when he had become common to look at them. He was
simply now one of them himself—he was in the dust, without a
peg for the sense of difference; and there were hours when, before
the temples of gods and the sepulchres of kings, his spirit turned
for nobleness of association to the barely discriminated slab in the
London suburb. That had become for him, and more intensely with
time and distance, his one witness of a past glory. It was all that
was left to him for proof or pride, yet the past glories of Pharaohs
were nothing to him as he thought of it. Small wonder then that
he came back to it on the morrow of his return. He was drawn
there this time as irresistibly as the other, yet with a confidence,
almost, that was doubtless the effect of the many months that had
elapsed. He had lived, in spite of himself, into his change of feeling, and in wandering over the earth had wandered, as might be
said, from the circumference to the centre of his desert. He had
settled to his safety and accepted perforce his extinction; figuring
to himself, with some colour, in the likeness of certain little old
men he remembered to have seen, of whom, all meagre and
wizened as they might look, it was related that they had in their
time fought twenty duels or been loved by ten princesses. They
indeed had been wondrous for others while he was but wondrous
for himself; which, however, was exactly the cause of his haste to
renew the wonder by getting back, as he might put it, into his
own presence. That had quickened his steps and checked his delay.
If his visit was prompt it was because he had been separated so
long from the part of himself that alone he now valued.

It's accordingly not false to say that he reached his goal with
a certain elation and stood there again with a certain assurance.
The creature beneath the sod *knew* of his rare experience, so that,
strangely now, the place had lost for him its mere blankness of
expression. It met him in mildness—not, as before, in mockery; it
wore for him the air of conscious greeting that we find, after
absence, in things that have closely belonged to us and which seem
to confess of themselves to the connexion. The plot of ground, the
graven tablet, the tended flowers affected him so as belonging to

him that he resembled for the hour a contented landlord reviewing a piece of property. Whatever had happened—well, had happened. He had not come back this time with the vanity of that question, his former worrying "what, *what?*" now practically so spent. Yet he would none the less never again so cut himself off from the spot; he would come back to it every month, for if he did nothing else by its aid he at least held up his head. It thus grew for him, in the oddest way, a positive resource; he carried out his idea of periodical returns, which took their place at last among the most inveterate of his habits. What it all amounted to, oddly enough, was that in his finally so simplified world this garden of death gave him the few square feet of earth on which he could still most live. It was as if, being nothing anywhere else for any one, nothing even for himself, he were just everything here, and if not for a crowd of witnesses or indeed for any witness but John Marcher, then by clear right of the register that he could scan like an open page. The open page was the tomb of his friend, and *there* were the facts of the past, there the truth of his life, there the backward reaches in which he could lose himself. He did this from time to time with such effect that he seemed to wander through the old years with his hand in the arm of a companion who was, in the most extraordinary manner, his other, his younger self; and to wander, which was more extraordinary yet, round and round a third presence—not wandering she, but stationary, still, whose eyes, turning with his revolution, never ceased to follow him, and whose seat was his point, so to speak, of orientation. Thus in short he settled to live—feeding all on the sense that he once *had* lived, and dependent on it not alone for a support but for an identity.

It sufficed him in its way for months and the year elapsed; it would doubtless even have carried him further but for an accident, superficially slight, which moved him, quite in another direction, with a force beyond any of his impressions of Egypt or of India. It was a thing of the merest chance—the turn, as he afterwards felt, of a hair, though he was indeed to live to believe that if light hadn't come to him in this particular fashion it would still have come in another. He was to live to believe this, I say, though he was not to live, I may not less definitely mention, to do much else. We allow him at any rate the benefit of the conviction, struggling up for him at the end, that, whatever might have happened or not happened, he would have come round of himself to the light. The incident of an autumn day had put the match to the train laid from of old by his misery. With the light before him he knew that even of late his ache had only been smothered. It was strangely drugged, but it throbbed; at the touch it began to bleed. And the touch, in the event, was the face of a fellow mortal. This face, one grey afternoon when the leaves were thick in the alleys, looked into Marcher's own, at the cemetery, with an expression like the cut of a blade. He felt it, that is, so deep down that he winced at the steady thrust. The person who so mutely assaulted him was a figure he had noticed, on reaching his own goal, absorbed by a grave a short distance away, a grave apparently fresh, so that the emotion of the visitor would probably match it for frankness. This fact alone forbade further attention, though during the time he stayed he remained vaguely conscious of his neighbour, a middle-aged man apparently, in mourning, whose bowed back, among the clustered monuments and mortuary yews, was constantly presented. Marcher's theory that these were elements in contact with which he himself revived, had suffered, on this occasion, it may be granted, a marked, an excessive check. The autumn day was dire for him as none had recently been, and he rested with a heaviness he had not yet known on the low stone table that bore May Bartram's name. He rested without power to move, as if some spring in him, some spell vouchsafed, had suddenly been broken for ever. If he could have done that moment as he wanted he would simply have stretched himself on the slab that was ready to take him, treating it as a place prepared to receive his last sleep. What in all the wide world had he now to keep awake for? He stared before him with the question, and it was then that, as one of the cemetery walks passed near him, he caught the shock of the face.

His neighbour at the other grave had withdrawn, as he himself, with force enough in him, would have done by now, and was advancing along the path on his way to one of the gates. This brought him close, and his pace was slow, so that—and all the more as there was a kind of hunger in his look—the two men were for a minute directly confronted. Marcher knew him at once for one of the deeply stricken—a perception so sharp that nothing else in the picture comparatively lived, neither his dress, his age, nor his presumable character and class; nothing lived but the deep ravage of the features he showed. He *showed* them—that was the point; he was moved, as he passed, by some impulse that was either a signal for sympathy or, more possibly, a challenge to an opposed sorrow. He might already have been aware of our friend, might at some previous hour have noticed in him the smooth habit of the scene, with which the state of his own senses so scantly consorted, and might thereby have been stirred as by an overt discord. What Marcher was at all events conscious of was in the first place that the image of scarred passion presented to him was conscious too—of something that profaned the air; and in the second that, roused, startled, shocked, he was yet the next moment looking after it, as it went, with envy. The most extraordinary thing that had happened to him—though he had given that name to other matters as well—took place, after his immediate vague stare, as a consequence of this impression. The stranger passed, but the raw glare of his grief remained, making our friend wonder in pity what wrong, what wound it expressed, what injury not to be healed. What had the man *had*, to make him by the loss of it so bleed and yet live?

Something—and this reached him with a pang—that *he*, John Marcher, hadn't; the proof of which was precisely John Marcher's arid end. No passion had ever touched him, for this was what passion meant; he had survived and maundered and pined, but where had been *his* deep ravage? The extraordinary thing we speak of was the sudden rush of the result of this question. The sight that had just met his eyes named to him, as in letters of quick flame, something he had utterly, insanely missed, and what he had missed made these things a train of fire, made them mark themselves in an anguish of inward throbs. He had seen *outside* of his life, not learned it within, the way a woman was mourned when she had been loved for herself: such was the force of his conviction of the meaning of the stranger's face, which still flared for him as a smoky torch. It hadn't come to him, the knowledge, on the wings of experience; it had brushed him, jostled him, upset him, with the disrespect of chance, the insolence of accident. Now that the illumination had begun, however, it blazed to the zenith, and what he presently stood there gazing at was the sounded void of his life. He gazed, he drew breath, in pain; he turned in his dismay, and, turning, he had before him in sharper incision than ever the open page of his story. The name on the table smote him as the passage of his neighbour had done, and what it said to him, full in the face, was that *she* was what he had missed. This was

the awful thought, the answer to all the past, the vision at the
dread clearness of which he grew as cold as the stone beneath
him. Everything fell together, confessed, explained, overwhelmed;
leaving him most of all stupefied at the blindness he had cherished.
The fate he had been marked for he had met with a vengeance—
he had emptied the cup to the lees; he had been the man of his
time, *the* man, to whom nothing on earth was to have happened.
That was the rare stroke—that was his visitation. So he saw it,
as we say, in pale horror, while the pieces fitted and fitted. So *she*
had seen it while he didn't, and so she served at this hour to drive
the truth home. It was the truth, vivid and monstrous, that all the
while he had waited the wait was itself his portion. This the
companion of his vigil had at a given moment made out, and she
had then offered him the chance to baffle his doom. One's doom,
however, was never baffled, and on the day she told him his own
had come down she had seen him but stupidly stare at the escape
she offered him.

The escape would have been to love her; then, *then* he would
have lived. *She* had lived—who could say now with what passion?
—since she had loved him for himself; whereas he had never
thought of her (ah how it hugely glared at him!) but in the chill
of his egotism and the light of her use. Her spoken words came
back to him—the chain stretched and stretched. The Beast had
lurked indeed, and the Beast, at its hour, had sprung; it had sprung
in that twilight of the cold April when, pale, ill, wasted, but all
beautiful, and perhaps even then recoverable, she had risen from
her chair to stand before him and let him imaginably guess. It had
sprung as he didn't guess; it had sprung as she hopelessly turned
from him, and the mark, by the time he left her, had fallen where
it *was* to fall. He had justified his fear and achieved his fate; he
had failed, with the last exactitude, of all he was to fail of; and a
moan now rose to his lips as he remembered she had prayed he
mightn't know. This horror of waking—*this* was knowledge,
knowledge under the breath of which the very tears in his eyes
seemed to freeze. Through them, none the less, he tried to fix it
and hold it; he kept it there before him so that he might feel the
pain. That at least, belated and bitter, had something of the taste
of life. But the bitterness suddenly sickened him, and it was as
if, horribly, he saw, in the truth, in the cruelty of his image, what
had been appointed and done. He saw the Jungle of his life and

saw the lurking Beast; then, while he looked, perceived it, as by a stir of the air, rise, huge and hideous, for the leap that was to settle him. His eyes darkened—it was close; and, instinctively turning, in his hallucination, to avoid it, he flung himself, face down, on the tomb.

STUDY

❦

The Notebooks of Henry James

F. O. MATTHIESSEN AND KENNETH B. MURDOCK (eds.)*

[Entry dated August 27, 1901]

. . . a man haunted by the fear, more and more, throughout life, that *something will happen to him:* he doesn't know quite what. His life *seems* safe and ordered, his liabilities and exposures (as a *result* of the fear) a good deal curtailed and cut down, so that the years go by and the stroke doesn't fall. Yet "It *will* come, it will still come," he finds himself believing—and indeed saying to some one, some second-consciousness. Mustn't indeed the "2nd consciousness" be some woman, and it be she who *helps* him to see? She has always loved him—yes, *that,* for the story, "pretty," and he, saving, protecting, exempting his life (always, really, with and *for* the fear), has never known it. He likes her, talks to her, confides in her, sees her often—*la côtoie,* as to her hidden passion, but never guesses. She meanwhile, all the time, sees his life as it is. It is to her that he tells his fear—yes, she is the "2nd consciousness." At first she *feels,* herself, for him, his feeling of his fear, and is tender, reassuring, protective. Then she reads, as I say, his real case, and is, though unexpressedly, *lucid.* The years go by and *she sees the thing not happen.* At last one day they are somehow, some day, face to face over it, and then she speaks. "It *has,* the great thing, you've always lived in dread of, had the foreboding of—it *has* happened to you." He wonders—when, how, what? "What is it?—

* FROM *The Notebooks of Henry James,* edited by F. O. Matthiessen and Kenneth B. Murdock. Copyright, 1947, by Oxford University Press, Inc. Reprinted by permission.

why, it is *nothing* has happened!" Then, later on, I think to keep
up the prettiness, it must be that HE sees, that he understands. She
has loved him always—and *that* might have happened. But it's
too late—she's dead. That, I think, at least, he comes to later on,
after an interval, after her death. She is dying, or ill, when she says
it. He *then* DOESN'T understand, doesn't see—or so far, only, as
to agree with her, ruefully, that that very well *may* be it: that nothing has happened. He goes back; she is gone; she is dead. *What*
she has said to him has in a way, by its truth, created the need for
her, made him want her, *positively* want her, more. But she is gone,
he has lost her, and *then* he sees all she has meant. She has loved
him. (*It must come for the* READER *thus, at this moment.*) With
his base safety and shrinkage he never knew. That was what might
have happened, and what *has* happened is that it didn't.

The Altar of the Dead and Other Tales

HENRY JAMES*

Preface [1907–1909]

[John Marcher] was to have been, after a strange fashion and from
the threshold of his career, condemned to keep counting with the
unreasoned prevision of some extraordinary fate; the conviction,
lodged in his brain, part and parcel of his imagination from far
back, that experience would be marked for him, and whether for
good or for ill, by some rare distinction, some incalculable violence
or unprecedented stroke. . . . Therefore as each item of experience comes, with its possibilities, into view, he can but dismiss it
under this sterilising habit of the failure to find it good enough and
thence to appropriate it.

His one desire remains of course to meet his fate, or at least to
divine it . . .; but none of its harbingers . . . speak his ear in the
true voice . . . and the years ebb while he holds his breath and
stays his hand. . . . He perforce lets everything go—leaving all
the while his general presumption disguised and his general abstention unexplained; since he's ridden by the idea of what things
may lead to, since they mostly always lead to human communities
. . . of experience, and since, above all, in his uncertainty, he

musn't compromise others. Like the blinded seeker in the old-fashioned game he "burns," on occasion, as with the sense of the hidden thing near—only to deviate again however into the chill; the chill that indeed settles on him as the striking of his hour is deferred. His career thus resolves itself into a great negative adventure, my report of which presents, for its centre, the fine case that has caused him most tormentedly to "burn," and then most unprofitably to stray. He is afraid to recognise what he incidentally misses, since what his high belief amounts to is . . . that he shall have felt and vibrated more [than anyone else]; which no acknowledgment of the minor loss must conflict with. Such a course of existence naturally involves a climax—the final flash of the light under which he reads his lifelong riddle and sees his conviction proved. He has indeed been marked and indeed suffered his fortune—which is precisely to have been the man in the world to whom nothing whatever was to happen. My picture leaves him overwhelmed. . . .

"Henry James and the Trapped Spectator"

L. C. KNIGHTS*

The Beast in the Jungle (1903) will serve to show that in James's later period subtlety is sometimes far from being evidence of evasiveness, hesitancy or scrupulosity. . . . [A]ll that an admirer needs to do is to indicate the subtle firmness with which James presents his "case," to demonstrate, that is, the mode which he established for the telling. Things are "seen" largely through the eyes of Marcher, but the seeing is flecked with unobtrusive irony so that we are aware of two views—Marcher's, and that of James himself—existing simultaneously. . . . "His concentrated burden," "his perpetual suspense," "a haunted man"—these phrases, and a good deal besides, represent Marcher's view. James only allows himself a few asides—"'Just a little,' in a word, was just as much as Miss Bartram, taking one day with another, would let him"—but these are sufficient to give an angle on Marcher's attitude towards himself, on his egotism, his calculated unselfishness, and on his exalted view of his own refinements, even when we are given what are, apparently, his own thoughts: "A man of feeling didn't cause himself to be accompanied by a lady on a tiger hunt." And the two

* FROM *The Southern Review,* IV (Winter, 1939).

points of view—the subjective and the objectively critical—not only alternate swiftly and with almost unnoticed transitions, they are often presented simultaneously. . . . Almost every word [at times] bears the double burden. And the advantage of this method is not merely that it enables James to extract the maximum of horror from his theme. It allows him to present Marcher's case with a degree of sympathy—for the theme is a common human feeling, isolated and magnified but not in any other way distorted; and the reader is made to share Marcher's horror—and at the same time to give a detached and penetrating analysis of the ravages of an obsession. . . .

What this account of *The Beast in the Jungle* is intended to bring out is the sureness, the relevance, and coherence of the minute particulars of the style—of James's art . . . which, at its best, is a medium for projecting the immediate awareness if not of "opposite and discordant" qualities at all events of varied and (in most minds) contradictory impulses, so that the reader's consciousness is enlarged to admit a new relationship. . . . "[T]he amount of felt life" informing *any* work is in exact correspondence with the "art," [and] depends entirely on the fullness and fineness with which the subject is presented.

This, in turn, suggests the dangers inherent in the attempt to find a simple "explanation" of an author's work in terms of his life. . . . *The Beast in the Jungle* [is] personal in inspiration, but here the personal motive serves only as the spring which releases the achieved work of art.

Of course James was isolated—and he knew it; but . . . he sensed also the forces that, in his time, were making for "the awful doom of general dishumanisation." And in his apprehension of the isolation of the individual . . . he showed himself the first of the "modern novelists."

"The Beast in the Jungle: The Limits of Method"

Francis E. Smith[*]

[J]ames's concern with technique was a dangerous thing, as he well knew. When a novelist sets himself the task of constructing and resolving psychological puzzles in artistic patterns, he can

[*] From *Perspective,* I (Autumn, 1947).

achieve his effect best in an untrammeled fictional world where the abstract is free to operate. Our initial assumptions upon entering such a world enable its characters to side-step the obstacles of every-day life and arrange themselves according to the artist's rarified logic without becoming incredible. There is no reason to question James's eminent success in the use of this method. But we can usefully illustrate the inherent limits of this method by considering how in *The Beast in the Jungle* James hampers rather than enriches the effectiveness of the theme which his story propounds. . . .

[The] difficulty is this, that the story must take as its hero a man who can do or perform nothing. The original nature of a hero was that he was to perform heroic deeds. In modern fiction his deeds are often more sordid than heroic but they are deeds. . . . [These] are denied to John Marcher. The obvious conclusion is that since the hero cannot act he must think. Thought is after all—and especially to James—a mode of action. But . . . the hero is forbidden by his fate even to think with any remarkable perception. Hence the author is forced to rely not on the greatness of thought but on the smallness of it, on the intricacies, the delicacies, and the nuances of it. The fascination of watching it glance and reflect from the hero and his partner in kaleidoscopic combinations must be sufficient to maintain the reader's suspense as he watches Marcher grope through a jungle of inaction to learn the identity of its lurking tiger.

The central theme, then, is the changing relationship between Marcher and May Bartram. . . . The history of this relationship . . . is the movement of the story. The six chapters each contain one vital scene in which Marcher faces his obsession and his friendship in an attempt to come nearer the truth. These scenes, however, taken together, form but a small portion of the story, for it is part of James's method to present everything inside an elaborately contrived frame. The very first sentence is a suggestion of *in medias res* which is abandoned at once for the filling-in of the background. . . . But this sentence also states the theme of the chapter. Marcher will be "startled." And that, after some pages, is the first confrontation of himself, his friend, and his beast. Early in each chapter there is a statement of theme that will be dramatically presented in the scene to follow. The scene of the second chapter, for instance, will present "a certain passage of his consciousness in the suddenest way from one extreme to the other." The third scene will "recall" the second and show its "results." Each scene, however, is separated from the others by long analyses of the thoughts and motives that will determine what will take place when the scene occurs or will show the results of the past.

Not only is this true of the scenes but the speeches themselves are further set off from one another by intricate tracing of thought that makes them seem far apart, as if spoken over a period of hours rather than minutes. James's characters to a peculiar extent in this story communicate not only by speech but by analysis of speech aided by sight which is everywhere stressed as the final means to truth. "Their eyes met in such a way that he was without doubt." "He knew how he felt, but besides knowing that, he knew how he looked, as well." "Her whole attitude was a virtual statement." "Her silence with the face she showed, was almost a confession." Silence is indeed golden; speech is a point of departure, a sort of map leading to buried treasure. These maps are extremely precious and must be carefully prepared and read. James realizes that people talking about important things both for reasons of protective delicacy and because of knowledge commonly possessed seldom speak all of their thoughts; but in this story the speech is so fragmentary and the thoughts so detailed that there is sort of a hyperbole of the minute which appears, even *in* its context, rather laughable. . . . While it is true that great revelations may spring from minutest sources, still the delicacy of feeling and introspection displayed in such passages is, because it can only be acquired by strenuous practice for which even the most sensitive people are hardly allowed time, too foreign to ordinary experience to be completely convincing. The psychological stumbling blocks these people build for themselves seem too fatuously fabricated. Half a kick would burst them to splinters. One waits impatiently for the blow.

Of course such precision of thought is one of Marcher's dire traits of character, and by strategic parenthetical statements James makes this clear. Marcher is largely blinded to his own best course by the very legalistic quibbling he indulges in in his ethical thinking. His integrity is established upon a sort of moral etiquette, which like social etiquette becomes the more false the more rigorously it is insisted upon. It is this insistence which causes him to reject marriage to May Bartram as an impossibly selfish act, whereas a larger view, plunging carelessly through the ordered surface, would have faith in the value of those paradoxes that have force in the moral world, that make life happy in part as it is pursued through sacrifice and in the face of danger. Here again, however, precious speculation is over-developed not merely in Marcher but in the story itself so that it impedes the progress of the action, weighting down almost sentence by sentence the reader's attention to the point of exhaustion. . . .

Of actual physical setting there is almost none in the story except in the first scene. . . . The fact is that James is telling a psychological story in which it is not the thing seen that is important, but the attitude of the person who sees; and it is in describing this attitude that James elicits graphic images. . . . The familiarity of May's face and voice when he first speaks to her operates in his mind "like the torch of a lamplighter who touches into flame, one by one, a long row of gas jets," and the near approach of the beast is given a surgical image that James extends over a page. . . .

Of physical action there is almost less in the scenes that make up this story than there is of physical setting. . . .

But if there is something too abstract in the method of James's art in *The Beast in the Jungle*, . . . it must be remembered that this defect arises out of his choice of a story and that choice, difficult and dangerous, yet has the advantage of engendering a fascinating study in irony—a study which only a mature artist could create. Because of the underlying irony of a man who waits for something and finds that his waiting had made that something nothing, almost every thought and development in the story is cut by paradox and undermined by irony. Marcher tried to be ordinary to hide his uniqueness, but his uniqueness is that he is ordinary. His exaltation of moral precision has left him immoral. His regrettable accident in having told May Bartram his obsession is the best thing that could have happened to him, but his attempt to spare her from sharing his fate makes her the first victim of it. He thinks of her as interested in him as a harmless maniac when actually she cannot outlive the shock of seeing his mania.

These contradictions all depend on the basic irony which gives the story its title, the symbol of the beast in the jungle. The beast is made of thin air; its substance is fantasy; in one sense it represents nothing. Yet it is as powerful as its flesh-and-blood cousin. The beast is a tiger and it has all of a tiger's attributes. Chief among these is the combination of beauty and ferocity, a combination which has always been attached to destructive forces [as witness the Blake poem]. This beauty is thought of as a snare leading to destruction. . . . Marcher has felt this tiger as destined to spring upon him, but though he is apprehensive he does not realize the beast's deadly potentiality; and when he suggests that it may "destroy all further consciousness" he is not feeling that as a possibility. Really he is looking for something that will give his life special meaning which the mere fact of death, without some ineffable revelation, could hardly do. As he grows older he cares for his beast, feeds him and keeps him clean. Nursing the tiger becomes the occupation of his life. And as he does so, the tiger becomes his familiar, exerting its baneful influence the most when it is most merged with himself. May realizes that he is living with a pet that has grown to terrible proportions, and she tries first to get him to face the beast and drive it out. When that fails she tries by mental sleight-of-hand to convince him that the tiger has sprung upon him harmlessly in his sleep and so to avert his day of reckoning. But he is shocked to think of losing the beast which has by this time changed for him into something as harmless as a piece of cake: "Say, however," he added, "that I've eaten my cake, as you contend to the last crumb,—how can the thing I've never felt at all be the thing I've been marked out to feel?" He will not give it up. . . .

Thus Marcher commits suicide by refusing to act. . . . James is not advocating a doctrine of work for work's sake, nor are we asked to feel that Marcher has wasted his life because he is one of a crowd or because he has never done anything to make a name for himself, but simply that he refuses to forget himself, fall in love, and learn through emotional experience something of the abundance possible to life. . . .

[Like] all rather pathetic figures, Marcher does not make a good subject for a story. The motif of irony, the complicated processes of thought, the lurking of the beast, the desire to know what the beast is and how it will spring, these are the centers of the reader's interest. One must admit when he considers the subject matter of *The Beast in the Jungle* and these consequent foci, that James has here performed a *tour de force* in the genre of psychological mystery. And the final irony is that he has preached his lesson too well, that his method here is too specialized, too barren of action, too empty of emotion, that his characters lose what life they have in the maze of logical inference until they have more of the nature of propositions than of human beings.

The World Within: Fiction Illuminating Neuroses of Our Time

MARY L. ASWELL (ed.)

[Analysis by Fredric Wertham, M.D.]*

The term "neurosis," which is far too often used indiscriminately, does not have so precise a meaning as one would think. But to the extent that it does mean something definite, "The Beast in the Jungle" is the best story ever written about the subject. It is *the* neurosis in pure culture. . . .

The Beast in the Jungle is the symbol of nameless dread, nameless because it has no conscious substance in reality. Self-centered, fascinated by the past and anxious about the future, the hero loses the present. Embedded in vague anxiety is the anticipation that something will happen some day that will change the whole direction of his life. He does not live in reality, but in a prereality. Finally it comes to him with "the emotion of recognition" . . . that nothing will happen and the Beast is just an abstraction derived from the reality which is the Jungle of his unconscious. . . . "The Beast in the Jungle" . . . has a special message in these days for people who do nothing about their lives and think it is all laid out for them.

"A Note on 'The Beast in the Jungle' "

DAVID KERNER†

[No] one apparently has been puzzled by the mystery which opens the story. . . .

[A summary of the opening part] leads us to three questions.

First, James writes that although May Bartram at Weatherend "clearly took the sympathetic" view of Marcher's case, Marcher "couldn't at present have begun to tell her." If Marcher couldn't

---

* By permission of the Author (New York, Whittlesly House: McGraw-Hill Book Co., 1947).

† FROM *The University of Kansas City Review*, XVII (Winter, 1950).

confess now, to a person of perfect sympathy, how did he confess at Sorrento? Suppose we grant the early confession. Once having found May, how could Marcher have let her go? This time he holds her for the rest of her life; logically, he should have held her the first time. What happens now, after the renewal of acquaintance, at Weatherend, should have happened ten years ago at Sorrento— but it didn't. And finally, if Marcher did confess, once in his life, the most important fact in his life, how was he able to forget it? . . . A man as lonely as Marcher does not forget his one experience of perfect sympathy—yet Marcher has forgotten it. Nothing we know of Marcher allows us to assume that at Sorrento he could have confessed the idea of his life to May Bartram only to leave her and then forget her. Is it possible that Marcher never confessed? . . . [If so], how does May know his secret? She could hardly have guessed it. . . .

[Any] reader of James might begin to suspect that she is a ghost or at least a hallucination, and when, for lack of evidence, he dismisses the first possibility, he faces the question, can a hallucination last for thirty years?

To deal with May Bartram as a hallucination we must review the character of John Marcher. It is a character founded on self-deception. Marcher will believe any fantasy about himself as long as it helps to conceal from him the fact that he is afraid to live. He is a blind man, blind to May's love. . . . His arrogance he considers intelligence. . . . His detachment from life he considers good manners. . . . Few men could lie to themselves so much and live, but Marcher is a raging success. . . . Early in his life, to dike the floods of [sexual] instinct pressing out and of society pressing in, Marcher's personality of lies is walled around by the obsession that he must do nothing but wait. As he grows older, instinct and society grow importunate, and when he is thiry-five, to reinforce the wall, Marcher again enters the mirror of his mind. He returns with May Bartram, who preserves him from instinct and society for the remainder of his self-deluding strength. Marcher has, now, not one hallucination but two—the beast and the beauty. . . . [May] . . . *is* Marcher. Both of them are proudly remote, masters of evasion and delay, practically sexless, and self-detached. . . . May is incredibly faithful for one so prophetic; she is identified as part of Marcher, and her two roles are reconcilable only as projections of different parts of Marcher's mind, which lives on solitude and

fantasy; but none of this is conclusive proof that May is a hallucination.

Of course May Bartram is a person. Weatherend guests, her
great-aunt, her maid, and relatives at her funeral testify to her
actuality. Then, James at times writes about May from outside
Marcher's consciousness. And further, May has her own character,
she is proud and self-effacing, so that the saintly self-denial she
offers Marcher is consistent with the few other things we know
about her.

To admit this, however, does not answer the questions raised by
the first part of the story. . . . Can it be that May is both a person and a hallucination?

Let us suppose that May is a person. The reader wonders, in the
first section of the story, whether Marcher will marry May, and, in
the fourth section, whether Marcher will put out his hand to touch
May's shoulder; at the end the reader sympathizes with Marcher
because he has seen what Marcher lost.

Let us suppose now that May is a dream. The drama is inside
Marcher: the reader does not share Marcher's hopes but knows
the nature of the beast at once; knowing May not as a person but
as a delusion, the reader need not feel that May is the woman
Marcher might have loved. . . . There is a middle order of existence between the natural and the supernatural. May Bartram represents ideal love, and the problem of her mode of existence is the
problem of the nature of the ideal.

It was James's custom to represent such a reality by means of a
ghost. A ghost was the embodiment of a real person's hallucination;
it was both real and imagined. . . . Like the ghost in *The Jolly
Corner,* May is the Road Not Taken. She is a combination, however,
not of ghost and hallucination but of person and hallucination.
. . . May Bartram . . . is the projection of Marcher's realizable
nature by which he can judge his failure to live. Are such projections real? What is the middle order of existence, neither natural nor supernatural? What is May? The reader is twitted by her
name: May is *may*-be. . . .

[But the question of what May is] can sensibly be regarded as
a curiosity which is not essential to the meaning of the story
[for, after all] May Bartram is [merely] a ficelle. Ficelles are dramatic catalysts. When his stories concerned only one character,
James invented other characters, whom he called ficelles, in order

to expose the essential character. For example, Maria Gostrey in *The Ambassadors.* . . .

Ficelles solve one problem but raise two new ones. First, ficelles must be disguised. In order to cover their bones James must create the illusion of a consequential relation between the ficelles and the main character. . . . This raises the second problem. Whatever the relation is between the ficelles and the main character, it can lead nowhere: . . . James's second problem is how to get the main character out of relation with the ficelle without making the hoaxed reader feel unfriendly.

Since May Bartram is essentially the hoax which turns a statement of character into a scenic exposition or drama, the question of her mode of reality loses much of its importance.

There is another reason for not pursuing the question. The story is a parable, and parables are not concerned with questions of verisimilitude. A parable is an illustration of a law of human conduct. . . . The law illustrated [here] is: "It is not good for man to live alone." Time, place and so on are specified but shadowy; the story is composed of disembodied voices. Marcher is fear; May is love. By isolating ingrownness, James wishes to terrify the reader out of wasting his humanity.

"Three Commentaries: Poe, James, and Joyce"

ALLEN TATE[*]

[Here] we have the embodiment of the great contemporary subject: the isolation and the frustration of personality. . . .

The story is laid out in six sections, and the point of view is consistently of Marcher. The two first sections constitute a long foreground or "complication." . . . There are only two short-view scenes in the story. . . . Yet one can see that he could not allow himself to get too deeply into Marcher's consciousness, at the stage of the complication, or Marcher himself would have had to examine his illusion too closely, and the story would have collapsed. The reader may well wonder whether the two brief scenic moments, when they finally come, are adequately prepared for, in spite of the length of preparation. James has not, in the first three sections, made either Marcher or Miss Bartram a *visible* char-

[*] FROM *The Sewanee Review*, LVIII (Winter, 1950)

acter; he has merely presented their enveloping fate, as it *could* have been seen from Marcher's point of view; but we have seen them not quite credibly.

The excessive foreground is an instance of what James called the Indirect Approach to the objective situation through the trial-and-error of a Central Intelligence; but the Receptive Lucidity of a Strether, in *The Ambassadors*, is not at Marcher's command. Are we to conclude that the very nature of James's problem in "The Beast in the Jungle," the problem of dramatizing the insulated ego, of making active what in its essence is incapable of action, excluded the use of an active and searching intelligence in the main character?

The first of the two scenes appears in part IV when years of waiting have driven May Bartram to something like desperation. She cannot overtly break the frame of their intercourse, which permits her only to affirm and reaffirm her loyalty to the role of asking nothing for herself; in the act of a new reaffirmation,

"No, no!" she repeated. "I'm with you—don't you see—still." And as to make it more vivid to him she rose from her chair—a movement she seldom risked in these days—and showed herself, all draped and all soft, in her fairness and slimness. "I haven't forsaken you."

. . . Here we get a special case of James's Operative Irony, which "implies and projects the possible other case." But the "possible other case" is not in the awareness of Marcher . . .; it is manipulated by James himself standing beside Marcher and moving May Bartram up close to imply her virtual offer of herself, her very body—an offer of which Marcher is not aware, so deeply concerned is he with his "problem." As May Bartram stands before him, "all soft," it is Marcher's Beast which has leaped at him from his jungle; and he doesn't know it.

It is a fine scene, unobtrusively arrived at, and it has a certain power. It is perhaps sounder in its structure than the second and climactic scene. Marcher's frequent visits to Miss Bartram's grave are occasions of a developing insight into his loss, his failure to see that his supreme experience had been there for him day after day through many years. But James must have known that, to make the insight dramatically credible, it must reach the reader through a scene; and to have a "scene" there must be at least two persons and an interchange between them. He thus suddenly introduces, at the last moment, what he called in the Preface *ficelle,* a character not in the action but brought in to elicit some essential quality from the involved characters. The stranger haunting the other grave is such a *ficelle;* but not having been "planted" earlier and disguised, he appears with the force of a shock, and could better be described as a *deus ex machina*—a device for ending an action by means of a force outside it; here it serves to render scenically, for the eye and ear, what had otherwise been a reported insight of Marcher's. James could not let himself merely tell us that Marcher had at last seen his tragic flaw; he must contrive to show him seeing it.

. . . If we look at [this story] in terms of the visible material— the material *made* visible—it is much too long; the foreground is too elaborate, and the structure suffers from the disproportion of the Misplaced Middle (James's phrase); that is, he has not been able to render dramatically parts I and II and "confer on the false quantity the brave appearance of the true." If the grief-stricken stranger at the end was to be more than a palpable trick, should not James have planted him (or his equivalent) somewhere in the foreground?

These questions do not exhaust the story, which remains one of the great stories in the language. In the long run its effect is that of tone, even of lyric meditation. . . .

Henry James

F. W. DUPEE*

If a pathos not altogether earned is sometimes the fault of James's poor-gentlemen stories, it is here richly justified by Marcher's ultimate recognition; and here everything in the tale falls into place. The very abstractness of it, the absence of reinforcing and qualifying circumstances, the vague airless unfurnished, unpeopled medium in which the action, consisting mostly of low-toned conversations between Marcher and a woman friend, takes place, is all in the spirit of the subject. And the woman, so often merely a confidante in these stories, is here brought squarely into the picture. Weary of waiting for Marcher to perceive the truth, which she has long since discovered just as she has long been in love with him, May Bartram

* (New York, William Sloane Associates, 1951).

at last dies. So tenuous, so secret, has their intimacy been that he is not even asked to her funeral. This episode, one of James's great images of exclusion, is swiftly followed by as impassioned a scene as any he ever wrote. Marcher can at least visit May Bartram's grave; which he does; and it is in the cemetery that light finally comes to him. She was not merely his confidante but his lover, whom he has sacrificed to his delusion. . . . The failure of love is Marcher's own failure *to* love, his forcing of May Bartram into the attitude of a mother.

The Short Story
SEAN O'FAOLAIN*

If there ever was a waste of words here is utter squander. Everything is presented with an air of the greatest subtlety which, since the point is not subtle, can only make any normal reader resent the masculine self-importance of the presumption that we must approach the obvious on tip-toe. . . . I really cannot say which must seem the more humourless, James in recounting (at great length), or I in repeating, that the Horror which this ass—the word is used early and with a brief flash of good-sense that lamentably disappears—has experienced is his failure to love the lady. He makes the momentous discovery in the last lines (about forty pages after the reader has presumed it), flinging himself with an appalling obviousness on his silly face across her tomb. Somebody like Oscar Wilde would have written the fable in a couple of thousand words, perhaps far less, and he would have done it simply by presuming that his readers had at least enough of his own mother-wit to be able to see a haystack without needing to be buried in it.

"Henry James and the Garden of Death"
LOUISE DAUNER†

[With Henry James] the garden is a typical setting for crucial decisions or acts. Thus, it often becomes the ambivalent symbol for a kind of life-death struggle. As such, it inevitably attaches to itself

* Quoted from *The Short Story*, by Sean O'Faolain, published, 1951, by The Devin-Adair Co., New York; Copyright, 1951, by Devin-Adair.
† FROM *The University of Kansas City Review*, XIX (Winter, 1952).

a New Testament connotation, and becomes a symbolic Gethsemane. And, since the renunciation of the heart's desire, of the natural impulse, occurs with disturbing frequency, for the James character, increasingly the garden becomes a garden of death.

[We meet this extraordinary situation] in that painfully ironic and probing tale of egotism and blindness matched by generosity and vision, of adolescent romanticism matched by mature realism, "The Beast in the Jungle." After John Marcher's arid, wasted years have achieved their climax in the death of May Bartram, his secret sharer for so long, . . . her grave becomes for him the only spot on earth of any meaning. . . . "What it all amounted to, oddly enough, was that, in his now so simplified world, this garden of death gave him the few square feet on earth on which he could still most live." And what the garden of death amounts to, finally, for Marcher, is that if it can not give him life, in essence, it does give him the tragic illumination of the meaning of his life—which is to say, of the utter meaninglessness of it. For it is here that the Beast finally springs; and Marcher's flinging of himself face down upon May Bartram's tomb is the signal symbolic act by which he admits his acceptance of his destiny. . . . It is too late for retrieval or redemption; but at least he is granted his heart-breaking benison of knowledge. . . . [It] is the garden—though here a metaphorical garden—which bears the strange fruit of paradox, being both pain and wisdom. (But has not wisdom, since the Garden of Eden, been achieved only at the cost of pain?)

One might speculate, at this point, about a possible echo of Hawthorne's garden of death. . . . It is Rappaccini's scientific pride which allows him to sacrifice Beatrice to his experiment; it is Marcher's self-complacency and utter selfishness which allow him to sacrifice May to his romantic destiny. It is, in both, a Hawthornesque divorce of head from heart.

"James's 'Jungle': The Seasons"

EDWARD STONE*

Let us note, first, that the man is named Marcher. [This could mean either] a marcher, or one advancing in a grave or stately manner, steadily . . . or someone meant to suggest the month of March.

* FROM *The University of Kansas City Review,* XXI (Winter, 1954).

. . . [Notice] next that the heroine is named *May*. Next, that the month which finally and irrevocably comes between them is both as a matter of record and of reiteration the month of *April*. And finally, that both the story and the year begin in autumn. . . . [May] not the calendar in James's tale be observed as a backdrop to James's little play?

If so, then the most important of all is the month of April, for it is being asked to serve as two medians. . . . Can it . . .? Consider first its first function. When, in Part IV, Marcher is finally at the point of thwarting his doom, when the reader is finally led to expect a declaration—to expect the chill of March(er) to be transmuted into the warmth of May (Bartram),—the coldness both of his nature and of April fatally intervenes. For their interview takes place "in that long fresh light of waning April days. . . ." Spring was to have come early that year (March was eventually to have yielded to May). Nevertheless, it had not, and the treachery of Eliot's "cruelest month" emphasizes the egotism or treachery or cruelty or whatever of Marcher, whose heart fails to act at the promptings of his intelligence.

He perceives the "cold meaningless cheer" of May's room for this, "the first time of the year," of all times, "without a fire"; intuits that "it will never see a fire again," that whereas her eyes are still as beautiful as they were many years ago, they are beautiful "with a strange cold light. . . ." Her "cold sweet" eyes are on him as she comes up to him standing by the now fireless chimney-piece, and he knows that "her light might at any instant go out; wherefore he must make the most of it." But he does nothing about it, and so she dies. That is, the chill of his loveless relationship to her kills her, for spring can come early as well as late (April can be an early May or a late March) and in James's parable for once ("that year") spring was to have come early, but May judged wrong in putting out her artificial warmth, for spring came . . . too late. . . . May could not bridge the gap by herself, and we are told that to the very end of his own life he recalls the twilight of "the cold April when, pale, ill, wasted, but all beautiful," she had been "perhaps even then recoverable."

The other season correspondence . . . may also yield an effect. . . . If we discount the first meeting . . . ten years before the story opens . . ., then they meet first at Weatherend, in the autumn. It is an October day that charms him, both because of itself and because of her, and for the same reason . . .: their *light*, their power of illuminating things for him. The charm of Weatherend is "in the way the autumn day looked into the high windows as it waned; the way the red light . . . played over old wainscots, old tapestry, old gold, old colour." And May herself brings back all the details of their first meeting "like the torch of a lamplighter who touches into flame, one by one, a long row of gas jets. . . ." They are truly at the end of the weather during this first autumnal encounter at Weatherend.

But because of Marcher, May moves out of weather's end and *into* the weather: specifically, she sets up in London in order to accompany him on his fantastic quest. Some years later (in Part II) when he brings her the customary birthday present, it is "at a season of thick fog and general outward gloom"—the very day, note, when she foresees her doom and his, but he doesn't. This is, by inference, winter, for it is as a result of her realization (in Part III) that she can no longer meet him anywhere except in front of her fire, to which she now resigns herself more and more. Now it is because of this failure of his to understand that, when April comes, the fire goes out, in both senses. . . . Thus there is nothing in life left for him but to continue to draw breath, now apparently to no purpose. This he does until the final day, which, like the first, is in autumn.

But this one is a "grey afternoon when the leaves were thick in the alleys." . . . Now her two names [on her gravestone] finally illuminate his life as she herself did that first day back at Weatherend, and he sees that May was what he had missed. But this time there is no longer a May Bartram to illuminate this much later autumn, and nothing remains for him but this last, appropriate gesture: to seek in her embrace the light and warmth that she, who had once brought them to him, had taken from him forever.

"The Beast in Henry James"

ROBERT ROGERS[*]

James's writing is full of mother surrogates. The character pattern repeats itself over and over again with only minor variations. Alice Staverton is a mother figure. . . . As a preview to Alice Staverton

[*] FROM *The American Imago*, XIII (Winter, 1956).

let us see what James had to say about her counterpart, May Bartram. John Marcher thinks of her "mercy, sympathy, seriousness, her consent not to regard him as the funniest of the funny." This is an idealized description of motherly care and indulgence. May is his "kind, wise keeper. . . . The rest of the world of course thought him queer, but she, she only, knew how, and above all why, queer." Again, motherly understanding, motherly protection of the helpless child against the rigors of the world. (A relationship of strong dependence always exists between the John Marchers and Spencer Brydons and their mother companions.) Marcher's comment on May Bartram's house is significant: in it "every object was as familiar to him as the things of his own house." It was his house, his mother's house, it occurs to us, and we compare it to the homelike atmosphere of Alice Staverton's house in New York. Late in the story May Bartram "was the picture of a serene and exquisite but impenetrable sphinx, whose head, or indeed all whose person might have been powdered with silver." Again, an idealized mother portrait, this time of old age. Once May Bartram and her counterparts are understood as mother substitutes the question of marriage with them becomes comprehensible. Alluding to the outward appearance that they are having an affair Marcher says to May Bartram, "You help me to pass for a man like another." Remarks like this one in James are loaded comments. This one means just what it says, that is, that Marcher (James) is something less than a man for the very reason that he is not having normal relations with women. Referring to that portentous event, the beast in the jungle, which Marcher tells May he anticipates encountering, she says, "Isn't what you describe perhaps but the expectation—or at any rate the sense of danger, familiar to so many people—of falling in love?" Marcher denies this possibility, intimating that he has already been in love. "It hasn't been overwhelming," he says. "Then it hasn't been love," answers May. And on the question of marrying May, John Marcher thinks, "The real form it should have taken on the basis that stood out large was the form of their marrying. But the devil in this was that the very basis itself put marrying out of the question." Whatever basis Marcher has in mind is never brought out, but the real reason is clear: one cannot marry one's mother.

The Jolly Corner

[1908]

I

"Every one asks me what I 'think' of everything," said Spencer Brydon; "and I make answer as I can—begging or dodging the question, putting them off with any nonsense. It wouldn't matter to any of them really," he went on, "for, even were it possible to meet in that stand-and-deliver way so silly a demand on so big a subject, my 'thoughts' would still be almost altogether about something that concerns only myself." He was talking to Miss Staverton, with whom for a couple of months now he had availed himself of every possible occasion to talk; this disposition and this resource, this comfort and support, as the situation in fact presented itself, having promptly enough taken the first place in the considerable array of rather unattenuated surprises attending his so strangely belated return to America. Everything was somehow a surprise; and that might be natural when one had so long and so consistently neglected everything, taken pains to give surprises so much margin for play. He had given them more than thirty years—thirty-three, to be exact; and they now seemed to him to have organised their performance quite on the scale of that licence. He had been twenty-three on leaving New York—he was fifty-six today: unless indeed he were to reckon as he had sometimes, since his repatriation, found himself feeling; in which case he would have lived longer than is often allotted to man. It would have taken a century, he repeatedly said to himself, and said also to Alice Staverton, it would have taken a longer absence and a more averted mind than those even of which he had been guilty, to pile up the differences, the newnesses, the queernesses, above all the bignesses, for the better or the worse, that at present assaulted his vision wherever he looked.

The great fact all the while however had been the incalcula-
bility; since he *had* supposed himself, from decade to decade, to
be allowing, and in the most liberal and intelligent manner, for
brilliancy of change. He actually saw that he had allowed for nothing; he missed what he would have been sure of finding, he found
what he would never have imagined. Proportions and values were
upside-down; the ugly things he had expected, the ugly things of
his far-away youth, when he had too promptly waked up to a sense
of the ugly—these uncanny phenomena placed him rather, as it
happened, under the charm; whereas the "swagger" things, the
modern, the monstrous, the famous things, those he had more particularly, like thousands of ingenuous enquirers every year, come
over to see, were exactly his sources of dismay. They were as so
many set traps for displeasure, above all for reaction, of which
his restless tread was constantly pressing the spring. It was interesting, doubtless, the whole show, but it would have been too dis-
concerting hadn't a certain finer truth saved the situation. He
had distinctly not, in this steadier light, come over *all* for the monstrosities; he had come, not only in the last analysis but quite on
the face of the act, under an impulse with which they had nothing
to do. He had come—putting the thing pompously—to look at his
"property," which he had thus for a third of a century not been
within four thousand miles of; or, expressing it less sordidly, he
had yielded to the humour of seeing again his house on the jolly
corner, as he usually, and quite fondly, described it—the one in
which he had first seen the light, in which various members of his
family had lived and had died, in which the holidays of his over-
schooled boyhood had been passed and the few social flowers of
his chilled adolescence gathered, and which, alienated then for
so long a period, had, through the successive deaths of his two
brothers and the termination of old arrangements, come wholly
into his hands. He was the owner of another, not quite so "good"
—the jolly corner having been, from far back, superlatively extended and consecrated; and the value of the pair represented his
main capital, with an income consisting, in these later years, of
their respective rents which (thanks precisely to their original excellent type) had never been depressingly low. He could live in
"Europe," as he had been in the habit of living, on the product of
these flourishing New York leases, and all the better since, that of
the second structure, the mere number in its long row, having

within a twelvemonth fallen in, renovation at a high advance had
proved beautifully possible.

These were items of property indeed, but he had found himself
since his arrival distinguishing more than ever between them. The
house within the street, two bristling blocks westward, was already in course of reconstruction as a tall mass of flats; he had ac-
ceded, some time before, to overtures for this conversion—in which,
now that it was going forward, it had been not the least of his as-
tonishments to find himself able, on the spot, and though without
a previous ounce of such experience, to participate with a certain
intelligence, almost with a certain authority. He had lived his
life with his back so turned to such concerns and his face addressed
to those of so different an order that he scarce knew what to make
of this lively stir, in a compartment of his mind never yet penetrated, of a capacity for business and a sense for construction.
These virtues, so common all round him now, had been dormant
in his own organism—where it might be said of them perhaps that
they had slept the sleep of the just. At present, in the splendid
autumn weather—the autumn at least was a pure boon in the
terrible place—he loafed about his "work" undeterred, secretly
agitated; not in the least "minding" that the whole proposition,
as they said, was vulgar and sordid, and ready to climb ladders,
to walk the plank, to handle materials and look wise about them,
to ask questions, in fine, and challenge explanations and really
"go into" figures.

It amused, it verily quite charmed him; and, by the same stroke,
it amused, and even more, Alice Staverton, though perhaps charming her perceptibly less. She wasn't however going to be better off
for it, as *he* was—and so astonishingly much: nothing was now
likely, he knew, ever to make her better off than she found herself,
in the afternoon of life, as the delicately frugal possessor and ten-
ant of the small house in Irving Place to which she had subtly
managed to cling through her almost unbroken New York career.
If he knew the way to it now better than to any other address
among the dreadful multiplied numberings which seemed to him
to reduce the whole place to some vast ledger-page, overgrown,
fantastic, of ruled and criss-crossed lines and figures—if he had
formed, for his consolation, that habit, it was really not a little
because of the charm of his having encountered and recognised,
in the vast wilderness of the wholesale, breaking through the mere

gross generalisation of wealth and force and success, a small still scene where items and shades, all delicate things, kept the sharpness of the notes of a high voice perfectly trained, and where economy hung about like the scent of a garden. His old friend lived with one maid and herself dusted her relics and trimmed her lamps and polished her silver; she stood off, in the awful modern crush, when she could, but she sallied forth and did battle when the challenge was really to "spirit," the spirit she after all confessed to, proudly and a little shyly, as to that of the better time, that of *their* common, their quite far-away and antediluvian social period and order. She made use of the street-cars when need be, the terrible things that people scrambled for as the panic-stricken at sea scramble for the boats; she affronted, inscrutably, under stress, all the public concussions and ordeals; and yet, with that slim mystifying grace of her appearance, which defied you to say if she were a fair young woman who looked older through trouble, or a fine smooth older one who looked young through successful indifference; with her precious reference, above all, to memories and histories into which he could enter, she was as exquisite for him as some pale pressed flower (a rarity to begin with), and, failing other sweetnesses, she was a sufficient reward of his effort. They had communities of knowledge, "their" knowledge (this discriminating possessive was always on her lips) of presences of the other age, presences all overlaid, in his case, by the experience of a man and the freedom of a wanderer, overlaid by pleasure, by infidelity, by passages of life that were strange and dim to her, just by "Europe" in short, but still unobscured, still exposed and cherished, under that pious visitation of the spirit from which she had never been diverted.

She had come with him one day to see how his "apartment-house" was rising; he had helped her over gaps and explained to her plans, and while they were there had happened to have, before her, a brief but lively discussion with the man in charge, the representative of the building-firm that had undertaken his work. He had found himself quite "standing-up" to this personage over a failure on the latter's part to observe some detail of one of their noted conditions, and had so lucidly urged his case that, besides ever so prettily flushing, at the time, for sympathy in his triumph, she had afterwards said to him (though to a slightly greater effect of irony) that he had clearly for too many years neglected a real gift. If he had but stayed at home he would have anticipated the inventor of the sky-scraper. If he had but stayed at home he would have discovered his genius in time really to start some new variety of awful architectural hare and run it till it burrowed in a gold-mine. He was to remember these words, while the weeks elapsed, for the small silver ring they had sounded over the queerest and deepest of his own lately most disguised and most muffled vibrations.

It had begun to be present to him after the first fortnight, it had broken out with the oddest abruptness, this particular wanton wonderment: it met him there—and this was the image under which he himself judged the matter, or at least, not a little, thrilled and flushed with it—very much as he might have been met by some strange figure, some unexpected occupant, at a turn of one of the dim passages of an empty house. The quaint analogy quite hauntingly remained with him, when he didn't indeed rather improve it by a still intenser form: that of his opening a door behind which he would have made sure of finding nothing, a door into a room shuttered and void, and yet so coming, with a great suppressed start, on some quite erect confronting presence, something planted in the middle of the place and facing him through the dusk. After that visit to the house in construction he walked with his companion to see the other and always so much the better one, which in the eastward direction formed one of the corners, the "jolly" one precisely, of the street now so generally dishonoured and disfigured in its westward reaches, and of the comparatively conservative Avenue. The Avenue still had pretensions, as Miss Staverton said, to decency; the old people had mostly gone, the old names were unknown, and here and there an old association seemed to stray, all vaguely, like some very aged person, out too late, whom you might meet and feel the impulse to watch or follow, in kindness, for safe restoration to shelter.

They went in together, our friends; he admitted himself with his key, as he kept no one there, he explained, preferring, for his reasons, to leave the place empty, under a simple arrangement with a good woman living in the neighbourhood and who came for a daily hour to open windows and dust and sweep. Spencer Brydon had his reasons and was growingly aware of them; they seemed to him better each time he was there, though he didn't name them all to his companion, any more than he told her as yet how often,

how quite absurdly often, he himself came. He only let her see for
the present, while they walked through the great blank rooms,
that absolute vacancy reigned and that, from top to bottom, there
was nothing but Mrs. Muldoon's broomstick, in a corner, to tempt
the burglar. Mrs. Muldoon was then on the premises, and she
loquaciously attended the visitors, preceding them from room to
room and pushing back shutters and throwing up sashes—all to
show them, as she remarked, how little there was to see. There was
little indeed to see in the great gaunt shell where the main dis-
positions and the general apportionment of space, the style of an
age of ampler allowances, had nevertheless for its master their
honest pleading message, affecting him as some good old servant's,
some lifelong retainer's appeal for a character, or even for a
retiring-pension; yet it was also a remark of Mrs. Muldoon's that,
glad as she was to oblige him by her noonday round, there was a
request she greatly hoped he would never make of her. If he should
wish her for any reason to come in after dark she would just tell
him, if he "plased," that he must ask it of somebody else.

The fact that there was nothing to see didn't militate for the
worthy woman against what one *might* see, and she put it frankly
to Miss Staverton that no lady could be expected to like, could
she? "craping up to thim top storeys in the ayvil hours." The gas
and the electric light were off the house, and she fairly evoked a
gruesome vision of her march through the great grey rooms—so
many of them as there were too!—with her glimmering taper. Miss
Staverton met her honest glare with a smile and the profession
that she herself certainly would recoil from such an adventure.
Spencer Brydon meanwhile held his peace—for the moment; the
question of the "evil" hours in his old home had already become
too grave for him. He had begun some time since to "crape," and
he knew just why a packet of candles addressed to that pursuit had
been stowed by his own hand, three weeks before, at the back of
a drawer of the fine old sideboard that occupied, as a "fixture," the
deep recess in the dining-room. Just now he laughed at his companions—quickly however changing the subject; for the reason
that, in the first place, his laugh struck him even at that moment
as starting the odd echo, the conscious human resonance (he scarce
knew how to qualify it) that sounds made while he was there alone
sent back to his ear or his fancy; and that, in the second, he
imagined Alice Staverton for the instant on the point of asking him,

with a divination, if he ever so prowled. There were divinations he was unprepared for, and he had at all events averted enquiry by the time Mrs. Muldoon had left them, passing on to other parts.

There was happily enough to say, on so consecrated a spot, that could be said freely and fairly; so that a whole train of declarations was precipitated by his friend's having herself broken out, after a yearning look round: "But I hope you don't mean they want you to pull *this* to pieces!" His answer came, promptly, with his re-awakened wrath: it was of course exactly what they wanted, and what they were "at" him for, daily, with the iteration of people who couldn't for their life understand a man's liability to decent feelings. He had found the place, just as it stood and beyond what he could express, an interest and a joy. There were values other than the beastly rent-values, and in short, in short—! But it was thus Miss Staverton took him up. "In short you're to make so good a thing of your sky-scraper that, living in luxury on *those* ill-gotten gains, you can afford for a while to be sentimental here!" Her smile had for him, with the words, the particular mild irony with which he found half her talk suffused; an irony without bitterness and that came, exactly, from her having so much imagination—not, like the cheap sarcasms with which one heard most people, about the world of "society," bid for the reputation of cleverness, from nobody's really having any. It was agreeable to him at this very moment to be sure that when he had answered, after a brief demur, "Well yes: so, precisely, you may put it!" her imagination would still do him justice. He explained that even if never a dollar were to come to him from the other house he would nevertheless cherish this one; and he dwelt, further, while they lingered and wandered, on the fact of the stupefaction he was already exciting, the positive mystification he felt himself create.

He spoke of the value of all he read into it, into the mere sight of the walls, mere shapes of the rooms, mere sound of the floors, mere feel, in his hand, of the old silver-plated knobs of the several mahogany doors, which suggested the pressure of the palms of the dead; the seventy years of the past in fine that these things represented, the annals of nearly three generations, counting his grandfather's, the one that had ended there, and the impalpable ashes of his long-extinct youth, afloat in the very air like microscopic motes. She listened to everything; she was a woman who answered intimately but who utterly didn't chatter. She scattered abroad therefore no cloud of words; she could assent, she could agree, above all she could encourage, without doing that. Only at the last she went a little further than he had done himself. "And then how do you know? You may still, after all, want to live here." It rather indeed pulled him up, for it wasn't what he had been thinking, at least in her sense of the words. "You mean I may decide to stay on for the sake of it?"

"Well, *with* such a home—!" But, quite beautifully, she had too much tact to dot so monstrous an *i*, and it was precisely an illustration of the way she didn't rattle. How could any one—of any wit—insist on any one else's "wanting" to live in New York?

"Oh," he said, "I *might* have lived here (since I had my opportunity early in life); I might have put in here all these years. Then everything would have been different enough—and, I dare say, 'funny' enough. But that's another matter. And then the beauty of it—I mean of my perversity, of my refusal to agree to a 'deal'—is just in the total absence of a reason. Don't you see that if I had a reason about the matter at all it would *have* to be the other way, and would then be inevitably a reason of dollars? There are no reasons here *but* of dollars. Let us therefore have none whatever—not the ghost of one."

They were back in the hall then for departure, but from where they stood the vista was large, through an open door, into the great square main saloon, with its almost antique felicity of brave spaces between windows. Her eyes came back from that reach and met his own a moment. "Are you very sure the 'ghost' of one doesn't, much rather, serve—?"

He had a positive sense of turning pale. But it was as near as they were then to come. For he made answer, he believed, between a glare and a grin: "Oh ghosts—of course the place must swarm with them! I should be ashamed of it if it didn't. Poor Mrs. Muldoon's right, and it's why I haven't asked her to do more than look in."

Miss Staverton's gaze again lost itself, and things she didn't utter, it was clear, came and went in her mind. She might even for the minute, off there in the fine room, have imagined some element dimly gathering. Simplified like the death-mask of a handsome face, it perhaps produced for her just then an effect akin to the stir of an expression in the "set" commemorative plaster. Yet whatever her impression may have been she produced instead a vague platitude. "Well, if it were only furnished and lived in—!"

She appeared to imply that in case of its being still furnished he might have been a little less opposed to the idea of a return. But she passed straight into the vestibule, as if to leave her words behind her, and the next moment he had opened the house-door and was standing with her on the steps. He closed the door and, while he re-pocketed his key, looking up and down, they took in the comparatively harsh actuality of the Avenue, which reminded him of the assault of the outer light of the Desert on the traveller emerging from an Egyptian tomb. But he risked before they stepped into the street his gathered answer to her speech. "For me it *is* lived in. For me it *is* furnished." At which it was easy for her to sigh "Ah yes—!" all vaguely and discreetly; since his parents and his favourite sister, to say nothing of other kin, in numbers, had run their course and met their end there. That represented, within the walls, ineffaceable life.

It was a few days after this that, during an hour passed with her again, he had expressed his impatience of the too flattering curiosity—among the people he met—about his appreciation of New York. He had arrived at none at all that was socially producible, and as for that matter of his "thinking" (thinking the better or the worse of anything there) he was wholly taken up with one subject of thought. It was mere vain egoism, and it was moreover, if she liked, a morbid obsession. He found all things come back to the question of what he personally might have been, how he might have led his life and "turned out," if he had not so, at the outset, given it up. And confessing for the first time to the intensity within him of this absurd speculation—which but proved also, no doubt, the habit of too selfishly thinking—he affirmed the impotence there of any other source of interest, any other native appeal. "What would it have made of me, what would it have made of me? I keep for ever wondering, all idiotically; as if I could possibly know! I see what it has made of dozens of others, those I meet, and it positively aches within me, to the point of exasperation, that it would have made something of me as well. Only I can't make out *what*, and the worry of it, the small rage of curiosity never to be satisfied, brings back what I remember to have felt, once or twice, after judging best, for reasons, to burn some important letter unopened. I've been sorry, I've hated it—I've never known what was in the letter. You may of course say it's a trifle—!"

"I don't say it's a trifle," Miss Staverton gravely interrupted.

She was seated by her fire, and before her, on his feet and restless, he turned to and fro between this intensity of his idea and a fitful and unseeing inspection, through his single eye-glass, of the dear little old objects on her chimney-piece. Her interruption made him for an instant look at her harder. "I shouldn't care if you did!" he laughed, however; "and it's only a figure, at any rate, for the way I now feel. *Not* to have followed my perverse young course— and almost in the teeth of my father's curse, as I may say; not to have kept it up, so, 'over there,' from that day to this, without a doubt or a pang; not, above all, to have liked it, to have loved it, so much, loved it, no doubt, with such an abysmal conceit of my own preference: some variation from *that*, I say, must have produced some different effect for my life and for my 'form.' I should have stuck here—if it had been possible; and I was too young, at twenty-three, to judge, *pour deux sous*, whether it *were* possible. If I had waited I might have seen it was, and then I might have been, by staying here, something nearer to one of these types who have been hammered so hard and made so keen by their conditions. It isn't that I admire them so much—the question of any charm in them, or of any charm, beyond that of the rank money-passion, exerted by their conditions *for* them, has nothing to do with the matter: it's only a question of what fantastic, yet perfectly possible, development of my own nature I mayn't have missed. It comes over me that I had then a strange *alter ego* deep down somewhere within me, as the full-blown flower is in the small tight bud, and that I just took the course, I just transferred him to the climate, that blighted him for once and for ever."

"And you wonder about the flower," Miss Staverton said. "So do I, if you want to know; and so I've been wondering these several weeks. I believe in the flower," she continued, "I feel it would have been quite splendid, quite huge and monstrous."

"Monstrous above all!" her visitor echoed; "and I imagine, by the same stroke, quite hideous and offensive."

"You don't believe that," she returned; "if you did you wouldn't wonder. You'd know, and that would be enough for you. What you feel—and what I feel *for* you—is that you'd have had power."

"You'd have liked me that way?" he asked.

She barely hung fire. "How should I not have liked you?"

"I see. You'd have liked me, have preferred me, a billionaire!"

"How should I not have liked you?" she simply again asked.

He stood before her still—her question kept him motionless. He took it in, so much there was of it; and indeed his not otherwise meeting it testified to that. "I know at least what I am," he simply went on; "the other side of the medal's clear enough. I've not been edifying—I believe I'm thought in a hundred quarters to have been barely decent. I've followed strange paths and worshipped strange gods; it must have come to you again and again—in fact you've admitted to me as much—that I was leading, at any time these thirty years, a selfish frivolous scandalous life. And you see what it has made of me."

She just waited, smiling at him. "You see what it has made of *me*."

"Oh you're a person whom nothing can have altered. You were born to be what you are, anywhere, anyway: you've the perfection nothing else could have blighted. And don't you see how, without my exile, I shouldn't have been waiting till now—?" But he pulled up for the strange pang.

"The great thing to see," she presently said, "seems to me to be that it has spoiled nothing. It hasn't spoiled your being here at last. It hasn't spoiled this. It hasn't spoiled your speaking—" She also however faltered.

He wondered at everything her controlled emotion might mean. "Do you believe then—too dreadfully!—that I *am* as good as I might ever have been?"

"Oh no! Far from it!" With which she got up from her chair and was nearer to him. "But I don't care," she smiled.

"You mean I'm good enough?"

She considered a little. "Will you believe it if I say so? I mean will you let that settle your question for you?" And then as if making out in his face that he drew back from this, that he had some idea which, however absurd, he couldn't yet bargain away: "Oh you don't care either—but very differently: you don't care for anything but yourself."

Spencer Brydon recognised it—it was in fact what he had absolutely professed. Yet he importantly qualified. "*He* isn't myself. He's the just so totally other person. But I do want to see him," he added. "And I can. And I shall."

Their eyes met for a minute while he guessed from something in hers that she divined his strange sense. But neither of them otherwise expressed it, and her apparent understanding, with no protesting shock, no easy derision, touched him more deeply than anything yet, constituting for his stifled perversity, on the spot, an element that was like breatheable air. What she said however was unexpected. "Well, *I've* seen him."

"You—?"

"I've seen him in a dream."

"Oh a 'dream'—!" It let him down.

"But twice over," she continued. "I saw him as I see you now."

"You've dreamed the same dream—?"

"Twice over," she repeated. "The very same."

This did somehow a little speak to him, as it also gratified him. "You dream about me at that rate?"

"Ah about *him!*" she smiled.

His eyes again sounded her. "Then you know all about him." And as she said nothing more: "What's the wretch like?"

She hesitated, and it was as if he were pressing her so hard that, resisting for reasons of her own, she had to turn away. "I'll tell you some other time!"

II

It was after this that there was most of a virtue for him, most of a cultivated charm, most of a preposterous secret thrill, in the particular form of surrender to his obsession and of address to what he more and more believed to be his privilege. It was what in these weeks he was living for—since he really felt life to begin but after Mrs. Muldoon had retired from the scene and, visiting the ample house from attic to cellar, making sure he was alone, he knew himself in safe possession and, as he tacitly expressed it, let himself go. He sometimes came twice in the twenty-four hours; the moments he liked best were those of gathering dusk, of the short autumn twilight; this was the time of which, again and again, he found himself hoping most. Then he could, as seemed to him, most intimately wander and wait, linger and listen, feel his fine attention, never in his life before so fine, on the pulse of the great vague place: he preferred the lampless hour and only wished he might have prolonged each day the deep crepuscular spell. Later—rarely much before midnight, but then for a considerable vigil—he watched with his glimmering light; moving slowly, holding it high, playing it far, rejoicing above all, as much as he might, in open vistas, reaches of communication between rooms and by passages; the long straight chance or show, as he would have called it, for the revelation he pretended to invite. It was practice he found he could perfectly "work" without exciting remark; no one was in the least the wiser for it; even Alice Staverton, who was moreover a well of discretion, didn't quite fully imagine.

He let himself in and let himself out with the assurance of calm proprietorship; and accident so far favoured him that, if a fat Avenue "officer" had happened on occasion to see him entering at eleven-thirty, he had never yet, to the best of his belief, been noticed as emerging at two. He walked there on the crisp November nights, arrived regularly at the evening's end; it was as easy to do this after dining out as to take his way to a club or to his hotel. When he left his club, if he hadn't been dining out, it was ostensibly to go to his hotel; and when he left his hotel, if he had spent a part of the evening there, it was ostensibly to go to his club. Everything was easy in fine; everything conspired and promoted: there was truly even in the strain of his experience something that glossed over, something that salved and simplified, all the rest of consciousness. He circulated, talked, renewed, loosely and pleasantly, old relations—met indeed, so far as he could, new expectations and seemed to make out on the whole that in spite of the career, of such different contacts, which he had spoken of to Miss Staverton as ministering so little, for those who might have watched it, to edification, he was positively rather liked than not. He was a dim secondary social success—and all with people who had truly not an idea of him. It was all mere surface sound, this murmur of their welcome, this popping of their corks—just as his gestures of response were the extravagant shadows, emphatic in proportion as they meant little, of some game of *ombres chinoises*. He projected himself all day, in thought, straight over the bristling line of hard unconscious heads and into the other, the real, the waiting life; the life that, as soon as he had heard behind him the click of his great house-door, began for him, on the jolly corner, as beguilingly as the slow opening bars of some rich music follows the tap of the conductor's wand.

He always caught the first effect of the steel point of his stick

on the old marble of the hall pavement, large black-and-white
squares that he remembered as the admiration of his childhood
and that had then made in him, as he now saw, for the growth of
an early conception of style. This effect was the dim reverberating
tinkle as of some far-off bell hung who should say where?—in the
depths of the house, of the past, of that mystical other world that
might have flourished for him had he not, for weal or woe, abandoned it. On this impression he did ever the same thing; he put
his stick noiselessly away in a corner—feeling the place once more
in the likeness of some great glass bowl, all precious concave
crystal, set delicately humming by the play of a moist finger round
its edge. The concave crystal held, as it were, this mystical other
world, and the indescribably fine murmur of its rim was the sigh
there, the scarce audible pathetic wail to his strained ear, of all
the old baffled forsworn possibilities. What he did therefore by
this appeal of his hushed presence was to wake them into such
measure of ghostly life as they might still enjoy. They were shy,
all but unappeasably shy, but they weren't really sinister; at least
they weren't as he had hitherto felt them—before they had taken
the Form he so yearned to make them take, the Form he at moments saw himself in the light of fairly hunting on tiptoe, the points
of his evening-shoes, from room to room and from storey to storey.

That was the essence of his vision—which was all rank folly, if
one would, while he was out of the house and otherwise occupied,
but which took on the last verisimilitude as soon as he was placed
and posted. He knew what he meant and what he wanted; it was
as clear as the figure on a cheque presented in demand for cash.
His *alter ego* "walked"—that was the note of his image of him,
while his image of his motive for his own odd pastime was the
desire to waylay him and meet him. He roamed, slowly, warily,
but all restlessly, he himself did—Mrs. Muldoon had been right,
absolutely, with her figure of their "craping"; and the presence
he watched for would roam restlessly too. But it would be as
cautious and as shifty; the conviction of its probable, in fact its
already quite sensible, quite audible evasion of pursuit grew for
him from night to night, laying on him finally a rigour to which
nothing in his life had been comparable. It had been the theory of
many superficially-judging persons, he knew, that he was wasting
that life in a surrender to sensations, but he had tasted of no
pleasure so fine as his actual tension, had been introduced to no

sport that demanded at once the patience and the nerve of this stalking of a creature more subtle, yet at bay perhaps more formidable, than any beast of the forest. The terms, the comparisons, the very practices of the chase positively came again into play; there were even moments when passages of his occasional experience as a sportsman, stirred memories, from his younger time, of moor and mountain and desert, revived for him—and to the increase of his keenness—by the tremendous force of analogy. He found himself at moments—once he had placed his single light on some mantel-shelf or in some recess—stepping back into shelter or shade, effacing himself behind a door or in an embrasure, as he had sought of old the vantage of rock and tree; he found himself holding his breath and living in the joy of the instant, the supreme suspense created by big game alone.

He wasn't afraid (though putting himself the question as he believed gentlemen on Bengal tiger-shoots or in close quarters with the great bear of the Rockies had been known to confess to having put it); and this indeed—since here at least he might be frank!—because of the impression, so intimate and so strange, that he himself produced as yet a dread, produced certainly a strain, beyond the liveliest he was likely to feel. They fell for him into categories, they fairly became familiar, the signs, for his own perception, of the alarm his presence and his vigilance created; though leaving him always to remark, portentously, on his probably having formed a relation, his probably enjoying a consciousness, unique in the experience of man. People enough, first and last, had been in terror of apparitions, but who had ever before so turned the tables and become himself, in the apparitional world, an incalculable terror? He might have found this sublime had he quite dared to think of it; but he didn't too much insist, truly, on that side of his privilege. With habit and repetition he gained to an extraordinary degree the power to penetrate the dusk of distances and the darkness of corners, to resolve back into their innocence the treacheries of uncertain light, the evil-looking forms taken in the gloom by mere shadows, by accidents of the air, by shifting effects of perspective; putting down his dim luminary he could still wander on without it, pass into other rooms and, only knowing it was there behind him in case of need, see his way about, visually project for his purpose a comparative clearness. It made him feel, this acquired faculty, like some monstrous stealthy cat; he wondered if he would have glared at these moments with large shining yellow eyes, and what it mightn't verily be, for the poor hard-pressed *alter ego*, to be confronted with such a type.

He liked however the open shutters; he opened everywhere those Mrs. Muldoon had closed, closing them as carefully afterwards, so that she shouldn't notice: he liked—oh this he did like, and above all in the upper rooms!—the sense of the hard silver of the autumn stars through the window-panes, and scarcely less the flare of the street-lamps below, the white electric lustre which it would have taken curtains to keep out. This was human actual social; this was of the world he had lived in, and he was more at his ease certainly for the countenance, coldly general and impersonal, that all the while and in spite of his detachment it seemed to give him. He had support of course mostly in the rooms at the wide front and the prolonged side; it failed him considerably in the central shades and the parts at the back. But if he sometimes, on his rounds, was glad of his optical reach, so none the less often the rear of the house affected him as the very jungle of his prey. The place was there more subdivided; a large "extension" in particular, where small rooms for servants had been multiplied, abounded in nooks and corners, in closets and passages, in the ramifications especially of an ample back staircase over which he leaned, many a time, to look far down—not deterred from his gravity even while aware that he might, for a spectator, have figured some solemn simpleton playing at hide-and-seek. Outside in fact he might himself make that ironic *rapprochement;* but within the walls, and in spite of the clear windows, his consistency was proof against the cynical light of New York.

It had belonged to that idea of the exasperated consciousness of his victim to become a real test for him; since he had quite put it to himself from the first that, oh distinctly! he could "cultivate" his whole perception. He had felt it as above all open to cultivation—which indeed was but another name for his manner of spending his time. He was bringing it on, bringing it to perfection, by practice; in consequence of which it had grown so fine that he was now aware of impressions, attestations of his general postulate, that couldn't have broken upon him at once. This was the case more specifically with a phenomenon at last quite frequent for him in the upper rooms, the recognition—absolutely unmistakable, and by a turn dating from a particular hour, his resumption of his campaign after a diplomatic drop, a calculated absence of three nights—of his being definitely followed, tracked at a distance carefully taken and to the express end that he should the less confidently, less arrogantly, appear to himself merely to pursue. It worried, it finally quite broke him up, for it proved, of all the conceivable impressions, the one least suited to his book. He was kept in sight while remaining himself—as regards the essence of his position—sightless, and his only recourse then was in abrupt turns, rapid recoveries of ground. He wheeled about, retracing his steps, as if he might so catch in his face at least the stirred air of some other quick revolution. It was indeed true that his fully dislocalised thought of these manœuvres recalled to him Pantaloon, at the Christmas farce, buffeted and tricked from behind by ubiquitous Harlequin; but it left intact the influence of the conditions themselves each time he was re-exposed to them, so that in fact this association, had he suffered it to become constant, would on a certain side have but ministered to his intenser gravity. He had made, as I have said, to create on the premises the baseless sense of a reprieve, his three absences; and the result of the third was to confirm the after-effect of the second.

On his return, that night—the night succeeding his last intermission—he stood in the hall and looked up the staircase with a certainty more intimate than any he had yet known. "He's *there*, at the top, and waiting—not, as in general, falling back for disappearance. He's holding his ground, and it's the first time—which is a proof, isn't it? that something has happened for him." So Brydon argued with his hand on the banister and his foot on the lowest stair; in which position he felt as never before the air chilled by his logic. He himself turned cold in it, for he seemed of a sudden to know what now was involved. "Harder pressed?—yes, he takes it in, with its thus making clear to him that I've come, as they say, 'to stay.' He finally doesn't like and can't bear it, in the sense, I mean, that his wrath, his menaced interest, now balances with his dread. I've hunted him till he has 'turned': that, up there, is what has happened—he's the fanged or the antlered animal brought at last to bay." There came to him, as I say—but determined by an influence beyond my notation!—the acuteness of this certainty; under which however the next moment he had broken into a sweat that he would as little have consented to attribute to fear as he would have dared immediately to act upon it for enterprise. It marked none the less a prodigious thrill, a thrill that represented sudden dismay, no doubt, but also represented, and with the selfsame throb, the strangest, the most joyous, possibly the next minute almost the proudest, duplication of consciousness.

"He has been dodging, retreating, hiding, but now, worked up to anger, he'll fight!"—this intense impression made a single mouthful, as it were, of terror and applause. But what was wondrous was that the applause, for the felt fact, was so eager, since, if it was his other self he was running to earth, this ineffable identity was thus in the last resort not unworthy of him. It bristled there—somewhere near at hand, however unseen still—as the hunted thing, even as the trodden worm of the adage *must* at last bristle; and Brydon at this instant tasted probably of a sensation more complex than had ever before found itself consistent with sanity. It was as if it would have shamed him that a character so associated with his own should triumphantly succeed in just skulking, should to the end not risk the open, so that the drop of this danger was, on the spot, a great lift of the whole situation. Yet with another rare shift of the same subtlety he was already trying to measure by how much more he himself might now be in peril of fear; so rejoicing that he could, in another form, actively inspire that fear, and simultaneously quaking for the form in which he might passively know it.

The apprehension of knowing it must after a little have grown in him, and the strangest moment of his adventure perhaps, the most memorable or really most interesting, afterwards, of his crisis, was the lapse of certain instants of concentrated conscious *combat*, the sense of a need to hold on to something, even after the manner of a man slipping and slipping on some awful incline; the vivid impulse, above all, to move, to act, to charge, somehow and upon something—to show himself, in a word, that he wasn't afraid. The state of "holding-on" was thus the state to which he was momentarily reduced; if there had been anything, in the great vacancy, to seize, he would presently have been aware of having clutched it as he might under a shock at home have clutched the nearest chair-back. He had been surprised at any rate—of this he *was* aware—into something unprecedented since his original appropriation of the place; he had closed his eyes, held them tight, for a long minute, as with that instinct of dismay and that terror of vision. When he opened them the room, the other contiguous rooms, extraordinarily, seemed lighter—so light, almost, that at first he took the change for day. He stood firm, however that might be, just where he had paused; his resistance had helped him—it was as if there were something he had tided over. He knew after a little what this was—it had been in the imminent danger of flight. He had stiffened his will against going; without this he would have made for the stairs, and it seemed to him that, still with his eyes closed, he would have descended them, would have known how, straight and swiftly, to the bottom.

Well, as he had held out, here he was—still at the top, among the more intricate upper rooms and with the gauntlet of the others, of all the rest of the house, still to run when it should be his time to go. He would go at his time—only at his time: didn't he go every night very much at the same hour? He took out his watch—there was light for that: it was scarcely a quarter past one, and he had never withdrawn so soon. He reached his lodgings for the most part at two—with his walk of a quarter of an hour. He would wait for the last quarter—he wouldn't stir till then; and he kept his watch there with his eyes on it, reflecting while he held it that this deliberate wait, a wait with an effort, which he recognised, would serve perfectly for the attestation he desired to make. It would prove his courage—unless indeed the latter might most be proved by his budging at last from his place. What he mainly felt now was that, since he hadn't originally scuttled, he had his dignities—which had never in his life seemed so many—all to preserve and to carry aloft. This was before him in truth as a physical image, an image almost worthy of an age of greater romance. That remark indeed glimmered for him only to glow the next instant with a finer light; since what age of romance, after all, could have matched either the state of his mind or, "objectively," as they said, the wonder of his situation? The only difference would have been that, brandishing his dignities over his head as in a parchment scroll, he might then—that is in the heroic time—have proceeded downstairs with a drawn sword in his other grasp.

At present, really, the light he had set down on the mantel of the next room would have to figure his sword; which utensil, in the course of a minute, he had taken the requisite number of steps to possess himself of. The door between the rooms was open, and from the second another door opened to a third. These rooms, as he remembered, gave all three upon a common corridor as well, but there was a fourth, beyond them, without issue save through the preceding. To have moved, to have heard his step again, was appreciably a help; though even in recognising this he lingered once more a little by the chimney-piece on which his light had rested. When he next moved, just hesitating where to turn, he found himself considering a circumstance that, after his first and comparatively vague apprehension of it, produced in him the start that often attends some pang of recollection, the violent shock of having ceased happily to forget. He had come into sight of the door in which the brief chain of communication ended and which he now surveyed from the nearer threshold, the one not directly facing it. Placed at some distance to the left of this point, it would have admitted him to the last room of the four, the room without other approach or egress, had it not, to his intimate conviction, been closed *since* his former visitation, the matter probably of a quarter of an hour before. He stared with all his eyes at the wonder of the fact, arrested again where he stood and again holding his breath while he sounded its sense. Surely it had been *subsequently* closed—that is it had been on his previous passage indubitably open!

He took it full in the face that something had happened between—that he couldn't not have noticed before (by which he meant on his original tour of all the rooms that evening) that such a barrier had exceptionally presented itself. He had indeed since that moment undergone an agitation so extraordinary that it might have muddled for him any earlier view; and he tried to convince himself that he might perhaps then have gone into the room and, inadvertently, automatically, on coming out, have drawn the door after him. The difficulty was that this exactly was what he never did; it was against his whole policy, as he might have said, the essence of which was to keep vistas clear. He had them from the first, as he was well aware, quite on the brain: the strange apparition, at the far end of one of them, of his baffled "prey" (which had become by so sharp an irony so little the term now to apply!) was the form of success his imagination had most cherished, projecting into it always a refinement of beauty. He had known fifty times the start of perception that had afterwards dropped; had fifty times gasped to himself "There!" under some fond brief hallucination. The house, as the case stood, admirably lent itself; he might wonder at the taste, the native architecture of the particular time, which could rejoice so in the multiplication of doors—the opposite extreme to the modern, the actual almost complete proscription of them; but it had fairly contributed to provoke this obsession of the presence encountered telescopically, as he might say, focussed and studied in diminishing perspective and as by a rest for the elbow.

It was with these considerations that his present attention was charged—they perfectly availed to make what he saw portentous. He *couldn't*, by any lapse, have blocked that aperture; and if he hadn't, if it was unthinkable, why what else was clear but that there had been another agent? Another agent?—he had been catching, as he felt, a moment back, the very breath of him; but when had he been so close as in this simple, this logical, this completely personal act? It was so logical, that is, that one might have *taken* it for personal; yet for what did Brydon take it, he asked himself, while, softly panting, he felt his eyes almost leave their sockets. Ah this time at last they *were*, the two, the opposed projections of him, in presence; and this time, as much as one would, the question of danger loomed. With it rose, as not before, the question of courage—for what he knew the blank face of the door to say to him was "Show us how much you have!" It stared, it glared back at him with that challenge; it put to him the two alternatives: should he just push it open or not? Oh to have this consciousness was to *think*—and to think, Brydon knew, as he stood there, was, with the lapsing moments, not to have acted! Not to have acted— that was the misery and the pang—was even still not to act; was in fact *all* to feel the thing in another, in a new and terrible way. How long did he pause and how long did he debate? There was presently nothing to measure it; for his vibration had already changed—as just by the effect of its intensity. Shut up there, at bay, defiant, and with the prodigy of the thing palpably provably *done*, thus giving notice like some stark signboard—under that accession of accent the situation itself had turned; and Brydon at last remarkably made up his mind on what it had turned to.

It had turned altogether to a different admonition; to a supreme hint, for him, of the value of Discretion! This slowly dawned, no doubt—for it could take its time; so perfectly, on his threshold, had he been stayed, so little as yet had he either advanced or retreated. It was the strangest of all things that now when, by his taking ten steps and applying his hand to a latch, or even his shoulder and his knee, if necessary, to a panel, all the hunger of his prime need might have been met, his high curiosity crowned, his unrest assuaged—it was amazing, but it was also exquisite and rare, that insistence should have, at a touch, quite dropped from him. Discretion—he jumped at that; and yet not, verily, at such a pitch, because it saved his nerves or his skin, but because, much more valuably, it saved the situation. When I say he "jumped" at it I feel the consonance of this term with the fact that—at the end indeed of I know not how long—he did move again, he crossed straight to the door. He wouldn't touch it—it seemed now that he might *if* he would: he would only just wait there a little, to show, to prove, that he wouldn't. He had thus another station, close to the thin partition by which revelation was denied him; but with his eyes bent and his hands held off in a mere intensity of stillness. He listened as if there had been something to hear, but this attitude, while it lasted, was his own communication. "If you won't then—good: I spare you and I give up. You affect me as by the appeal positively for pity: you convince me that for reasons rigid and sublime—what do I know?—we both of us should have suffered. I respect them then, and, though moved and privileged as, I believe, it has never been given to man, I retire, I renounce—never, on my honour, to try again. So rest for ever—and let *me!*"

That, for Brydon was the deep sense of his last demonstration—solemn, measured, directed, as he felt it to be. He brought it to a close, he turned away; and now verily he knew how deeply he had been stirred. He retraced his steps, taking up his candle, burnt, he observed, well-nigh to the socket, and marking again, lighten it as he would, the distinctness of his footfall; after which, in a moment, he knew himself at the other side of the house. He did here what he had not yet done at these hours—he opened half a casement, one of those in the front, and let in the air of the night; a thing he would have taken at any time previous for a sharp rupture of his spell. His spell was broken now, and it didn't matter—broken by his concession and his surrender, which made it idle henceforth that he should ever come back. The empty street—its other life so marked even by the great lamplit vacancy—was within call, within touch; he stayed there as to be in it again, high above it though he was still perched; he watched as for some comforting common fact, some vulgar human note, the passage of a scavenger or a thief, some night-bird however base. He would have blessed that sign of life; he would have welcomed positively the slow approach of his friend the policeman, whom he had hitherto only sought to avoid, and was not sure that if the patrol had come into sight he mightn't have felt the impulse to get into relation with it, to hail it, on some pretext, from his fourth floor.

The pretext that wouldn't have been too silly or too compromising, the explanation that would have saved his dignity and kept his name, in such a case, out of the papers, was not definite to him: he was so occupied with the thought of recording his Discretion— as an effect of the vow he had just uttered to his intimate adversary —that the importance of this loomed large and something had overtaken all ironically his sense of proportion. If there had been a ladder applied to the front of the house, even one of the vertiginous perpendiculars employed by painters and roofers and sometimes left standing overnight, he would have managed somehow, astride of the window-sill, to compass by outstretched leg and arm that mode of descent. If there had been some such uncanny thing as he had found in his room at hotels, a workable fire-escape in the form of notched cable or a canvas shoot, he would have availed himself of it as a proof—well, of his present delicacy. He nursed that sentiment, as the question stood, a little in vain, and even— at the end of he scarce knew, once more, how long—found it, as by the action on his mind of the failure of response of the outer world, sinking back to vague anguish. It seemed to him he had waited an age for some stir of the great grim hush; the life of the town was itself under a spell—so unnaturally, up and down the whole prospect of known and rather ugly objects, the blankness and the silence lasted. Had they ever, he asked himself, the hard-faced houses, which had begun to look livid in the dim dawn, had they ever spoken so little to any need of his spirit? Great builded voids, great crowded stillnesses put on, often, in the heart of cities, for the small hours, a sort of sinister mask, and it was of this large collective negation that Brydon presently became conscious—and the more that the break of day was, almost incredibly, now at hand, proving to him what a night he had made of it.

He looked again at his watch, saw what had become of his time values (he had taken hours for minutes—not, as in other tense situations, minutes for hours) and the strange air of the street was but the weak, the sullen flush of a dawn in which everything was still locked up. His choked appeal from his own open window had been the sole note of life, and he could but break off at last as for a worse despair. Yet while so deeply demoralised he was capable again of an impulse denoting—at least by his present measure—extraordinary resolution; of retracing his steps to the spot where he had turned cold with the extinction of his last pulse of doubt as to there being in the place another presence than his own. This required an effort strong enough to sicken him; but he had his reason, which over-mastered for the moment everything else. There was the whole of the rest of the house to traverse, and how should he screw himself to that if the door he had seen closed were at present open? He could hold to the idea that the closing had practically been for him an act of mercy, a chance offered him to descend, depart, get off the ground and never again profane it. This conception held together, it worked; but what it meant for him depended now clearly on the amount of forbearance his recent action, or rather his recent inaction, had engendered. The image of the "presence," whatever it was, waiting there for him to go— this image had not yet been so concrete for his nerves as when he stopped short of the point at which certainty would have come to him. For, with all his resolution, or more exactly with all his dread, he did stop short—he hung back from really seeing. The risk was too great and his fear too definite: it took at this moment an awful specific form.

He knew—yes, as he had never known anything—that, *should* he see the door open, it would all too abjectly be the end of him. It would mean that the agent of his shame—for his shame was the deep abjection—was once more at large and in general possession; and what glared him thus in the face was the act that this would determine for him. It would send him straight about to the window he had left open, and by that window, be long ladder and dangling rope as absent as they would, he saw himself uncontrollably insanely fatally take his way to the street. The hideous chance of this he at least could avert; but he could only avert it by recoiling in time from assurance. He had the whole house to deal with, this fact was still there; only he now knew that uncertainty alone could start him. He stole back from where he had checked himself— merely to do so was suddenly like safety—and, making blindly for the greater staircase, left gaping rooms and sounding passages behind. Here was the top of the stairs, with a fine large dim descent and three spacious landings to mark off. His instinct was all for mildness, but his feet were harsh on the floors, and, strangely,

when he had in a couple of minutes become aware of this, it
counted somehow for help. He couldn't have spoken, the tone of
his voice would have scared him, and the common conceit or resource of "whistling in the dark" (whether literally or figuratively)
have appeared basely vulgar; yet he liked none the less to hear
himself go, and when he had reached his first landing—taking it
all with no rush, but quite steadily—that stage of success drew
from him a gasp of relief.

The house, withal, seemed immense, the scale of space again
inordinate; the open rooms to no one of which his eyes deflected,
gloomed in their shuttered state like mouths of caverns; only the
high skylight that formed the crown of the deep well created for
him a medium in which he could advance, but which might have
been, for queerness of colour, some watery under-world. He tried
to think of something noble, as that his property was really grand,
a splendid possession; but this nobleness took the form too of the
clear delight with which he was finally to sacrifice it. They might
come in now, the builders, the destroyers—they might come as
soon as they would. At the end of two flights he had dropped to
another zone, and from the middle of the third, with only one more
left, he recognised the influence of the lower windows, of half-
drawn blinds, of the occasional gleam of street-lamps, of the glazed
spaces of the vestibule. This was the bottom of the sea, which
showed an illumination of its own and which he even saw paved—
when at a given moment he drew up to sink a long look over the
banisters—with the marble squares of his childhood. By that time
indubitably he felt, as he might have said in a commoner cause,
better; it had allowed him to stop and draw breath, and the ease
increased with the sight of the old black-and-white slabs. But what
he most felt was that now surely, with the element of impunity
pulling him as by hard firm hands, the case was settled for what he
might have seen above had he dared that last look. The closed
door, blessedly remote now, was still closed—and he had only in
short to reach that of the house.

He came down further, he crossed the passage forming the
access to the last flight; and if here again he stopped an instant
it was almost for the sharpness of the thrill of assured escape. It
made him shut his eyes—which opened again to the straight slope
of the remainder of the stairs. Here was impunity still, but impunity almost excessive; inasmuch as the side-lights and the high

fan-tracery of the entrance were glimmering straight into the hall; an appearance produced, he the next instant saw, by the fact that the vestibule gaped wide, that the hinged halves of the inner door had been thrown far back. Out of that again the *question* sprang at him, making his eyes, as he felt, half-start from his head, as they had done, at the top of the house, before the sign of the other door. If he had left that one open, hadn't he left this one closed, and wasn't he now in *most* immediate presence of some inconceivable occult activity? It was as sharp, the question, as a knife in his side, but the answer hung fire still and seemed to lose itself in the vague darkness to which the thin admitted dawn, glimmering archwise over the whole outer door, made a semicircular margin, a cold silvery nimbus that seemed to play a little as he looked—to shift and expand and contract.

It was as if there had been something within it, protected by indistinctness and corresponding in extent with the opaque surface behind, the painted panels of the last barrier to his escape, of which the key was in his pocket. The indistinctness mocked him even while he stared, affected him as somehow shrouding or challenging certitude, so that after faltering an instant on his step he let himself go with the sense that here *was* at last something to meet, to touch, to take, to know—something all unnatural and dreadful, but to advance upon which was the condition for him either of liberation or of supreme defeat. The penumbra, dense and dark, was the virtual screen of a figure which stood in it as still as some image erect in a niche or as some black-vizored sentinel guarding a treasure. Brydon was to know afterwards, was to recall and make out, the particular thing he had believed during the rest of his descent. He saw, in its great grey glimmering margin, the central vagueness diminish, and he felt it to be taking the very form toward which, for so many days, the passion of his curiosity had yearned. It gloomed, it loomed, it was something, it was somebody, the prodigy of a personal presence.

Rigid and conscious, spectral yet human, a man of his own substance and stature waited there to measure himself with his power to dismay. This only could it be—this only till he recognised, with his advance, that what made the face dim was the pair of raised hands that covered it and in which, so far from being offered in defiance, it was buried as for dark deprecation. So Brydon, before him, took him in; with every fact of him now, in the higher light, hard and acute—his planted stillness, his vivid truth, his grizzled bent head and white masking hands, his queer actuality of evening-dress, of dangling double eye-glass, of gleaming silk lappet and white linen, of pearl button and gold watch-guard and polished shoe. No portrait by a great modern master could have presented him with more intensity, thrust him out of his frame with more art, as if there had been "treatment," of the consummate sort, in his every shade and salience. The revulsion, for our friend, had become, before he knew it, immense—this drop, in the act of apprehension, to the sense of his adversary's inscrutable manœuvre. That meaning at least, while he gaped, it offered him; for he could but gape at his other self in this other anguish, gape as a proof that *he*, standing there for the achieved, the enjoyed, the triumphant life, couldn't be faced in his triumph. Wasn't the proof in the splendid covering hands, strong and completely spread?—so spread and so intentional that, in spite of a special verity that surpassed every other, the fact that one of these hands had lost two fingers, which were reduced to stumps, as if accidentally shot away, the face was effectually guarded and saved.

"Saved," though, *would* it be?—Brydon breathed his wonder till the very impunity of his attitude and the very insistence of his eyes produced, as he felt, a sudden stir which showed the next instant as a deeper portent, while the head raised itself, the betrayal of a braver purpose. The hands, as he looked, began to move, to open; then, as if deciding in a flash, dropped from the face and left it uncovered and presented. Horror, with the sight, had leaped into Brydon's throat, gasping there in a sound he couldn't utter; for the bared identity was too hideous as *his*, and his glare was the passion of his protest. The face, *that* face, Spencer Brydon's?—he searched it still, but looking away from it in dismay and denial, falling straight from his height of sublimity. It was unknown, inconceivable, awful, disconnected from any possibility—! He had been "sold," he inwardly moaned, stalking such game as this: the presence before him was a presence, the horror within him a horror, but the waste of his nights had been only grotesque and the success of his adventure an irony. Such an identity fitted his at *no* point, made its alternative monstrous. A thousand times yes, as it came upon him nearer now—the face was the face of a stranger. It came upon him nearer now, quite as one of those expanding fantastic images projected by the magic lantern of childhood; for the stranger, whoever he might be, evil, odious, blatant, vulgar, had advanced as for aggression, and he knew himself give ground. Then harder pressed still, sick with the force of his shock, and falling back as under the hot breath and the roused passion of a life larger than his own, a rage of personality before which his own collapsed, he felt the whole vision turn to darkness and his very feet give way. His head went round; he was going; he had gone.

III

WHAT HAD next brought him back, clearly—though after how long?—was Mrs. Muldoon's voice, coming to him from quite near, from so near that he seemed presently to see her as kneeling on the ground before him while he lay looking up at her; himself not wholly on the ground, but half-raised and upheld—conscious, yes, of tenderness of support and, more particularly, of a head pillowed in extraordinary softness and faintly refreshing fragrance. He considered, he wondered, his wit but half at his service; then another face intervened, bending more directly over him, and he finally knew that Alice Staverton had made her lap an ample and perfect cushion to him, and that she had to this end seated herself on the lowest degree of the staircase, the rest of his long person remaining stretched on his old black-and-white slabs. They were cold, these marble squares of his youth; but *he* somehow was not, in this rich return of consciousness—the most wonderful hour, little by little, that he had ever known, leaving him, as it did, so gratefully, so abysmally passive, and yet as with a treasure of intelligence waiting all round him for quiet appropriation; dissolved, he might call it, in the air of the place and producing the golden glow of a late autumn afternoon. He had come back, yes—come back from further away than any man but himself had ever travelled; but it was strange how with this sense what he had come back *to* seemed really the great thing, and as if his prodigious journey had been all for the sake of it. Slowly but surely his consciousness grew, his vision of his state thus completing itself: he had been miraculously *carried* back—lifted and carefully borne as from where he had been picked up, the uttermost end of an interminable grey passage. Even with this he was suffered to rest, and what had now brought him to knowledge was the break in the long mild motion.

It had brought him to knowledge, to knowledge—yes, this was

the beauty of his state; which came to resemble more and more that of a man who has gone to sleep on some news of a great inheritance, and then, after dreaming it away, after profaning it with matters strange to it, has waked up again to serenity of certitude and has only to lie and watch it grow. This was the drift of his patience—that he had only to let it shine on him. He must moreover, with intermissions, still have been lifted and borne; since why and how else should he have known himself, later on, with the afternoon glow intenser, no longer at the foot of his stairs—situated as these now seemed at that dark other end of his tunnel—but on a deep window-bench of his high saloon, over which had been spread, couch-fashion, a mantle of soft stuff lined with grey fur that was familiar to his eyes and that one of his hands kept fondly feeling as for its pledge of truth. Mrs. Muldoon's face had gone, but the other, the second he had recognised, hung over him in a way that showed how he was still propped and pillowed. He took it all in, and the more he took it the more it seemed to suffice: he was as much at peace as if he had had food and drink. It was the two women who had found him, on Mrs. Muldoon's having plied, at her usual hour, her latch-key—and on her having above all arrived while Miss Staverton still lingered near the house. She had been turning away, all anxiety, from worrying the vain bell-handle—her calculation having been of the hour of the good woman's visit; but the latter, blessedly, had come up while she was still there, and they had entered together. He had then lain, beyond the vestibule, very much as he was lying now—quite, that is, as he appeared to have fallen, but all so wondrously without bruise or gash; only in a depth of stupor. What he most took in, however, at present, with the steadier clearance, was that Alice Staverton had for a long unspeakable moment not doubted he was dead.

"It must have been that I *was*." He made it out as she held him. "Yes—I can only have died. You brought me literally to life. Only," he wondered, his eyes rising to her, "only, in the name of all the benedictions, how?"

It took her but an instant to bend her face and kiss him, and something in the manner of it, and in the way her hands clasped and locked his head while he felt the cool charity and virtue of her lips, something in all this beatitude somehow answered everything. "And now I keep you," she said.

"Oh keep me, keep me!" he pleaded while her face still hung over him: in response to which it dropped again and stayed close, clingingly close. It was the seal of their situation—of which he tasted the impress for a long blissful moment in silence. But he came back. "Yet how did you know—?"

"I was uneasy. You were to have come, you remember—and you had sent no word."

"Yes, I remember—I was to have gone to you at one today." It caught on to their "old" life and relation—which were so near and so far. "I was still out there in my strange darkness—where was it, what was it? I must have stayed there so long." He could but wonder at the depth and the duration of his swoon.

"Since last night?" she asked with a shade of fear for her possible indiscretion.

"Since this morning—it must have been: the cold dim dawn of today. Where have I been," he vaguely wailed, "where have I been?" He felt her hold him close, and it was as if this helped him now to make in all security his mild moan. "What a long dark day!"

All in her tenderness she had waited a moment. "In the cold dim dawn?" she quavered.

But he had already gone on piecing together the parts of the whole prodigy. "As I didn't turn up you came straight—?"

She barely cast about. "I went first to your hotel—where they told me of your absence. You had dined out last evening and hadn't been back since. But they appeared to know you had been at your club."

"So you had the idea of *this*—?"

"Of what?" she asked in a moment.

"Well—of what has happened."

"I believed at least you'd have been here. I've known, all along," she said, "that you've been coming."

" 'Known' it—?"

"Well, I've believed it. I said nothing to you after that talk we had a month ago—but I felt sure. I knew you *would*," she declared.

"That I'd persist, you mean?"

"That you'd see him."

"Ah but I didn't!" cried Brydon with his long wail. "There's somebody—an awful beast; whom I brought, too horribly, to bay. But it's not me."

At this she bent over him again, and her eyes were in his eyes. "No—it's not you." And it was as if, while her face hovered, he might have made out in it, hadn't it been so near, some particular meaning blurred by a smile. "No, thank heaven," she repeated— "it's not you! Of course it wasn't to have been."

"Ah but it *was*," he gently insisted. And he stared before him now as he had been staring for so many weeks. "I was to have known myself."

"You couldn't!" she returned consolingly. And then reverting, and as if to account further for what she had herself done, "But it wasn't only *that,* that you hadn't been at home," she went on. "I waited till the hour at which we had found Mrs. Muldoon that day of my going with you; and she arrived, as I've told you, while failing to bring any one to the door, I lingered in my despair on the steps. After a little, if she hadn't come, by such a mercy, I should have found means to hunt her up. But it wasn't," said Alice Staverton, as if once more with her fine intention—"it wasn't only that."

His eyes, as he lay, turned back to her. "What more then?"

She met it, the wonder she had stirred. "In the cold dim dawn, you say? Well, in the cold dim dawn of this morning I too saw you."

"Saw *me*—?"

"Saw *him*," said Alice Staverton. "It must have been at the same moment."

He lay an instant taking it in—as if he wished to be quite reasonable. "At the same moment?"

"Yes—in my dream again, the same one I've named to you. He came back to me. Then I knew it for a sign. He had come to you."

At this Brydon raised himself; he had to see her better. She helped him when she understood his movement, and he sat up, steadying himself beside her there on the window-bench and with his right hand grasping her left. "*He* didn't come to me."

"You came to yourself," she beautifully smiled.

"Ah I've come to myself now—thanks to you, dearest. But this brute, with his awful face—this brute's a black stranger. He's none of *me*, even as I *might* have been," Brydon sturdily declared.

But she kept the clearness that was like the breath of infallibility. "Isn't the whole point that you'd have been different?"

He almost scowled for it. "As different as *that*—?"

Her look again was more beautiful to him than the things of this world. "Haven't you exactly wanted to know *how* different? So this morning," she said, "you appeared to me."

"Like *him?*"

"A black stranger!"

"Then how did you know it was I?"

"Because, as I told you weeks ago, my mind, my imagination, had worked so over what you might, what you mightn't have been—to show you, you see, how I've thought of you. In the midst of that you came to me—that my wonder might be answered. So I knew," she went on; "and believed that, since the question held you too so fast, as you told me that day, you too would see for yourself. And when this morning I again saw I knew it would be because you had—and also then, from the first moment, because you somehow wanted me. *He* seemed to tell me of that. So why," she strangely smiled, "shouldn't I like him?"

It brought Spencer Brydon to his feet. "You 'like' that horror—?"

"I *could* have liked him. And to me," she said, "he was no horror. I had accepted him."

"'Accepted'—?" Brydon oddly sounded.

"Before, for the interest of his difference—yes. And as *I* didn't disown him, as *I* knew him—which you at last, confronted with him in his difference, so cruelly didn't, my dear—well, he must have been, you see, less dreadful to me. And it may have pleased him that I pitied him."

She was beside him on her feet, but still holding his hand—still with her arm supporting him. But though it all brought for him thus a dim light, "You 'pitied' him?" he grudgingly, resentfully asked.

"He has been unhappy; he has been ravaged," she said.

"And haven't I been unhappy? Am not I—you've only to look at me!—ravaged?"

"Ah I don't say I like him *better*," she granted after a thought. "But he's grim, he's worn—and things have happened to him. He doesn't make shift, for sight, with your charming monocle."

"No"—it struck Brydon: "I couldn't have sported mine 'downtown.' They'd have guyed me there."

"His great convex pince-nez—I saw it, I recognised the kind—is for his poor ruined sight. And his poor right hand—!"

"Ah!" Brydon winced—whether for his proved identity or for

his lost fingers. Then, "He has a million a year," he lucidly added. "But he hasn't you."

"And he isn't—no, he isn't—*you!*" she murmured as he drew her to his breast.

STUDY

❧

The Notebooks of Henry James
F. O. Matthiessen and Kenneth B. Murdock (eds.)*
[Undated entry]

The most intimate idea of ["The Jolly Corner"] is that my hero's adventure there takes the form so to speak of his turning the tables . . . on a "ghost" or whatever, a visiting or haunting apparition otherwise qualified to appal *him;* and thereby winning a sort of victory by the appearance, and the evidence, that this personage or presence was more overwhelmingly affected by him than he by *it.*

The Altar of the Dead and Other Tales
Henry James†
Preface [1907–1909]

[About] the composition of ["The Jolly Corner"] there would be more to say than my space allows; almost more in fact than categorical clearness might see its way to. A very limited thing being on this occasion in question, I was moved to adopt as my motive an analysis of some one of the conceivably rarest and intensest grounds for an "unnatural" anxiety, a *malaise* so incongruous and discordant, in the given prosaic prosperous condition, as almost to be compromising. Spencer Brydon's adventure how-

---

ever is one of those finished fantasies that . . . speak best even to
the critical sense for themselves. . . .

The Triple Thinkers
EDMUND WILSON*

[T]he whole development of American society during [James's]
absence is implied in [James's] later books.

Now when he returns—late in the day though it is for him—he
reacts strongly and reports vividly what he finds.

The returning New Yorker of "The Jolly Corner" encounters the
apparition of himself as he would have been if he had stayed in
America: "Rigid and conscious, spectral yet human, a man of his
own substance and stature waited there to measure himself with
his power to dismay."

"The Ghost of Henry James: A Study in Thematic Apperception"
SAUL ROSENZWEIG†

In general . . . the impression seems sustained that Henry James's
visit to America in 1904–1905, after twenty years of absence, was
largely actuated by an impulse to repair, if possible, the injury and
to complete the unfinished experience of his youth. He was, as it
were, haunted by the ghost of his own past and of this he wished to
disabuse his mind before actual death overtook him. Since the Civil
War had played so vital a part in his early blight, he now visited
the South for the first time and received there those impressions
which bear so strong a mark of personal projection.

The plausibility of this reconstruction and of the preceding interpretation of "The Story of a Year" [above] is strengthened by a
psychological reading of the later supernatural tales, especially
"The Jolly Corner." . . .

The specter in this tale is typical of Henry James. Unlike the
ghosts of other writers, the creatures of James's imagination represent not the shadows of lives once lived, but the immortal impulses

* (New York, Oxford University Press, Inc., 1938). By permission of publisher and author.

† FROM *Journal of Personality,* XII (December, 1943).

of the unlived life. In the present story the ghost of Spencer Brydon is obviously his rejected self. Moreover, an injury—the two lost fingers—here stands in some relation to the fact that the life was not lived or that, in other words, a kind of psychological death had occurred. Finally, the injury and the related incompletion have entailed an unfulfilled love. The hero has fled the heroine because he could not face himself.

At this point one is obviously but a step from "The Story of a Year," written forty years earlier . . .: with the death of John Ford the ghost of Spencer Brydon came into existence. The story of the latter is a complement to that of the former. As Henry James—or Ford—left America to reside abroad Brydon returns to confront his former self. The identity of the characters is established by the injuries each suffered—James's "obscure hurt," Ford's wounds, and Brydon's missing fingers. But like James during his visit in 1904–1905, Brydon is obviously attempting to rectify the past—to face it again and test the answer previously given. There is thus represented here not merely a harking back with vain regrets but an obvious effort to overcome old barriers and pass beyond them. It is in this spirit that the woman in the case, Alice Staverton, now likewise appears as a complement to Elizabeth Crowe. Whereas Elizabeth had been faithless, Alice is ever faithful and still ready to accept her lover both as he was and as he is. Even the device of the dream recurs—the dream of Elizabeth having presaged her abandonment of Ford, while that of Alice brings her through her empathy to the scene of Brydon's overwhelming encounter with his ghost.

The complementary relationship of these two tales, standing at the very beginning and all but the end of James's creative work, is so striking that one is impelled to believe that the second was intentionally written as a counterpart to the first.

"The Merciful Fraud in Three Stories by James"
EDWIN HONIG[*]

In his discussion of the Dionysus myth, Frazer remarks on the substitute sacrifice of an animal for a human being as "part of a pious

[*] FROM *The Tiger's Eye*, I, No. 9 (October, 1949).

and merciful fraud." . . . The abrupt similarity between the Thracian-Greek legend and American master's stories occurs through the visible transformation in both from what we are first *given* as the myth to what we presently see *enacted* as the ritual.

Most varieties of the Dionysus legend have at least three features in common. They all tell us that Dionysus was a Zeus-engendered god who, having aroused the jealousy of the other gods, first took refuge in the shape of a succeeding variety of animals, and finally, in the disguise of a bull or a goat, was discovered and torn to pieces by the deities. The three facts inherent in the myth . . . all give way before a fourth, upon which the ritual was established —the fact of Dionysus's resurrection. . . . When the details of "his sufferings, death and resurrection were enacted in his sacred rites," Dionysus was celebrated in the form of his disguise, as an animal, and in that form was symbolically torn apart and the parts offered to his own image by the celebrants. Among some primitive tribes, a royally descended human being, instead of the animal, was used as the sacrificial victim. Either form, however, was a manifestation of the god's mythical disguise. But whatever the form of the sacrifice, it was still the embodiment of a former self which the god was offered. 'Thus," as Frazer concludes,

> we have the strange spectacle of a god sacrificed to himself on the ground that he is his own enemy. And as the deity is supposed to partake of the victim offered to him, it follows that, when the victim is the god's old self, the god eats of his own flesh.

Now the corresponding transformation in James's stories from what we are given to begin with (the *donnée*, as James calls it) to what is presented in the action approaching its climax may be put generally in the following terms. In ["The Jolly Corner," "The Beast in the Jungle," and "The Altar of the Dead"] there is a framing of the problem: the desire of the central character to realize total self-hood by discovering or rediscovering the value of the self in some other than its present form. The means by which this is done involves an active communion with another person from whom the self elicits a disguise with which to enact the role of the ideally projected or mysteriously potential other self. The sympathetic person is a woman who, because she helps to identify the other self, becomes identified with it as an heroic substitute-agent. The climax of the action, through which the sought self is encountered, invariably produces a "merciful fraud." That is to say, either some disguise of the total self or the substitute-agent is sacrificed, released or destroyed, as a less worthy victim in the act of reaching the complete consciousness of self. In banal terms: "One always kills the thing one loves," i.e., there is no cheaper way of gaining self-knowledge than the necessary tearing to pieces, the dismantling and transfiguration of the self by its idealized or potential image. . . .

[Brydon] senses that the house on "the jolly corner" represents his deepest consciousness, his refuge from the hint of a gregarious, profitmaking self. But even there, while on its consecrated premises, he is pulled up short by Miss Staverton's further irony and his own unlooked-for admission. To her statement, "But I hope you don't mean they want you to pull *this* to pieces!" he answers "promptly, with his re-awakened wrath: it was of course exactly what they wanted, and what they were 'at' him for daily, with the iteration of people who couldn't for their life understand a man's liability to decent feelings." The decency amounts to his feeling that there are "values other than beastly rent-values" and that "there are no reasons here *but* of dollars. Let us therefore have none whatever—not the ghost of one." To Brydon's dismay, Miss Staverton's reply unearths the ambiguity of such "decency" and floods his conscience with the real accusation he has been avoiding: "Are you very sure the 'ghost' of one doesn't much rather, serve—?" That is to say, it is not they, the building contractors, who want to pull his consciousness to pieces. It is not only the vulgar world outside which is so impervious to "A man's liability to decent feelings"; it is much rather the vulgar world in himself to which he must look either for his own destruction or his own salvation.

How well directed he is he discovers only later when, on the highest floor of his house, where he can stand confident and god-like, feeling he has tracked down the "monster," he is suddenly challenged by that very monster, that other god-like presence waiting for him. And when he knows the split totality of himself, being at once the thing feared and the thing fearing, the hunter and the hunted both, the hideous certainty presents itself: either one or the other must emerge to be sacrificed. But the ultimate strength in Brydon is Discretion, a courage upheld by reason and taste. To step beyond that, to force the closed door, is no longer to challenge but to merge with the characterless presence of his "rejected" self; it is, in fact to walk into madness. . . . Escaping madness, . . . he turns to descend. . . . For Brydon it is there below, "on the old marble of the hall pavement, large black-and-white squares that he remembered as the admiration of his childhood and that had then made in him, as he now saw, for the growth of an early conception of style." Brydon's *style,* of course, has been precisely the accession of taste and reason, the choice of good and evil. It is here that "the black stranger" (the vision of unrelieved evil for him— because tied up with the curse that environment can inflict—and the vision of defeated, and hence acceptable, evil, for Miss Staverton) uncovers itself as "one of those expanding fantastic images projected by the magic lantern of childhood," and in this form is irrevocably returned to silence and death. Now it is possible to let the undertakers, the finally subdued world, the contractors, in on the sacrifice. . . . It is this sacrifice, this ritual death of "the black stranger," from which he is awakened, lying "on his old black-and-white slabs," his head on Miss Staverton's lap, to the joy of complete self-recognition.

The return to childhood (the idyllic scene of the hero's resurrection) and the sensual identity of the god with his worshipper, the fertile force (Miss Staverton), provide an amazing illustration of one of Frazer's further observations. "On a red-figured vase the god is portrayed as a calf-headed child seated in a woman's lap." No small part of the ritual, the event of Brydon's "rebirth" depends on the maternal-romantic role of Miss Staverton. For it is she, as the fruitful mother-substitute, who has induced the growth of Brydon's search through the dark womb of the past, the passages from which he emerges reborn. And it is she, as the prize of love, his lady, to whom he returns with the dragon head of his worldly self dangling from his consciousness. When he takes his reward in the end by drawing her to his breast, it is only after she has becalmed his jealousy and admitted that "the black stranger," the slain god (whom she had accepted in her dreams because, as she says, "I *could* have liked him," as another Brydon), is actually no longer part of Brydon: "And he isn't—no, he isn't—*you!*" Only then is the "merciful fraud" consummated: the animal, the beastly self, has been offered as a substitute sacrifice for the human self—the god has eaten of himself so that his cause, his vindicated standards, might flourish.

The American Novels and Stories of Henry James

F. O. MATHIESSEN (ed.)*

[James's] pictorial skills reached one of their summits in "The Jolly Corner," in his presentation of the interior of his hero's old house, at his moment of crisis, solely by means of the light that flickers in from the street to heighten the mystery and terror of his ghostly encounter. . . . [Here] the presence that Spencer Brydon stalks down is James's means of symbolizing another aspect of the past and present of New York. . . . Once here, [Brydon] begins to speculate on what he might have been if, instead of spending what he knows to be deemed a frivolous idle life, he had stayed at home and gone into business and become "one of those types who have been hammered so hard and made so keen by their conditions." He gets his answer in his horrified vision of his *alter ego*, whose mutilated hand drops to reveal his "evil, odious, blatant, vulgar" face, and thus becomes a sign of his crippled spirit.

"The Mothers of Henry James"

JOHN W. SCHROEDER†

["The Beast in the Jungle," "The Jolly Corner," and "Crapy Cornelia"] have enough surface resemblances in common to justify our treating them as a group. And the most striking of these unifying resemblances is the peculiar and stereotyped relation of the male protagonist, typically a mature, sensitive gentleman, to the principal female protagonist, typically a mature, sensitive gentlewoman. . . .

[We note that in "The Great Good Place" the protagonist George Dane] returns, symbolically, to the maternal depths, dropping his burden, as he returns, both by transferring it to the young visitor and by relapsing into a condition of what we might describe as

* (New York, Alfred A. Knopf, Inc., 1951).
† FROM *American Literature*, XXII (January, 1951).

foetal dependence. Subsequently, Dane permits himself to be re-born without his burden.

Now it is my suspicion that the symbolic component of this whole process was placed in the tale consciously. The various details—the loss of identity, the presence of "Brothers" only, the gradual dawn of sense, the imagery of submersion, the image of the "great mild invisible mother," the images of death and childhood, the arch [were consciously inserted].

Attacked with the key [of interpretation] of "The Great Good Place," [the three above-mentioned stories] assume a measure of co-herency. The fables of Marcher . . . and Brydon represent . . . the intensification of Dane's symbolic quest for the reviving deeps. The quest and the quest's object admit of wide variation. . . . Marcher's quest, which is never completed, is for revelation—a revelation somehow open to—indeed, incorporated in—the am-biguous May. And Brydon's quest, finally, is also for revelation, and here again the mother-symbol, Alice Staverton, is somehow possessed of the illumination for which Brydon yearns. And the re-turn to the mothers, the symbolized quest for a condition of release and security, promises at once . . . the evasion of Marcher's destiny, the revelation of Brydon's hidden hurt, and the trans-ference of the burdens represented by these men. The mothers, fortuitously returned out of the shadowy past, offer the advantages of a "general refuge" to each of our sensitive gentlemen. . . .

Brydon, in his final nocturnal visit to the "jolly corner," envisions himself in some "watery underworld." He is, indeed, at "the bottom of the sea, which showed an illumination of its own and which he even saw paved . . . with the marble squares of his childhood." Outside, Brydon glimpses the "thin admitted dawn, glimmering archwise over the whole outer door." And, finally and inevitably, he finds himself, after the period of unconsciousness which followed his encounter with his alter ego . . . cradled in Alice's lap; she has, he observes, "brought me literally to life. . . . Now [the passionate play which follows] of course, is in some degree the way of a maid with a man; it is also, however, the way of a mother with a babe. And Brydon's exclamations ["O keep me, keep me!"] seem designedly more infantile than adult.

In . . . "The Great Good Place" and "The Jolly Corner," the progression of quest, return, and rebirth is complete upon both narrative and symbolic levels. . . . And in . . . "The Beast in the Jungle," the progression is implied and subsequently frustrated. . . . The case of Marcher and Miss Bartram is more difficult [than the other two cases]. However, I can point to May's omniscience . . ., to May's protective and overly self-renunciative care of Marcher, and to Marcher's symptomatic inability to wed May. . . . May as "kind keeper" assumes a potential mythic stature in the light of what we have seen before in this study, and the . . . passage ["She was dying and he would lose her; she was dying and his life would end"] hints even at a mother-child interdependency. But these various clues, I repeat, do not make the presence of the symbolic mother an established fact, and I must be content here merely to observe the possibility of her presence. If this tale should finally be ruled out, we still have three definite examples of the archetypal mother-quest as an integrative symbolic element in the work of Henry James. . . . Even if [the theme] was not . . . employed [with full consciousness on James's part] of course, the problem for criticism would not be altered.

"Symbol and Image in the Later Work of Henry James"

MIRIAM ALLOTT*

[This] story . . . closes on a note of acceptance, an attitude carrying comparatively little conviction after the *tour de force* of [Brydon's] experiences and their horrifying climax. . . . In seeking to recall his early memories, at first merely with a pleasurable nostalgia, this Europeanized American gradually undergoes a sense of oppression, which changes into fear when he understands that . . . instead of the seeker he is now the sought. . . . In the moment of victory, . . . when the being at last materializes and raises its tormented head from its maimed hands, Brydon has to recognize that the face, though horribly altered and ravaged, is indeed his own. . . . The maimed hand which the figure draws from its face suggests heaven knows what degree of violence and passion in the hard struggle for easy money. . . . For "The Jolly Corner" also derives its quality from another of James's obsessional

* FROM *Essays in Criticism*, III (July, 1953).

themes, the violence which lies behind the "golden display" of great possessions.

"The Turned Back of Henry James"

Maurice Beebe[*]

Although one need not accept [Dr. Saul Rosenzweig's] idea that "The Jolly Corner" is a complement to "The Story of a Year" . . . it is impossible to disagree with the contention that the story deals with an attempt to face the rejected self. That is the surface theme of the story. And James himself could scarcely deny that the story was suggested by his own return to America.

But does it deal with an attempt to "rectify the past"? Brydon discovers in himself the presence of an alter ego, a split in personality. . . . Both Brydons are within the one man. . . . When Brydon tells Alice Staverton that he will never consent to the desecration of the Jolly Corner property, she replies, "In short you're to make so good a thing of your skyscraper that, living in luxury on *those* ill-gotten gains, you can afford for a while to be sentimental here!" The compromise thus suggested is proof that Brydon is both the detached and passive observer and the aggressive participant. He is somewhat taken aback by Alice Staverton's remark, but the story concludes with his reconciliation with his other self. The love of Alice, demonstrated by her willingness to accept both Brydons, permits him to overcome his horror and to recognize the other self. . . . The emphasis on sight placed conspicuously in [the] concluding passage is not, I think, accidental. We noted earlier that much is made of vision in James's stories of artists and detached observers, and if Brydon is a symbolic representation of James himself, the "poor ruined sight" of the other self is a more important injury than the mutilated fingers. But the two go together: the eyes that see, the hand that writes. It had occurred to Brydon on facing a closed door that he could not have closed it because "it was against his whole policy . . . the essence of which was to keep vistas clear. He had them from the first, as he was well aware, on the brain," says Alice Staverton. "The Jolly Corner" certainly represents a confronting of the rejected self, but it is less an attempt

[*] From *The South Atlantic Quarterly*, LIII (October, 1954).

to rectify the past than to justify the present. And Spencer Brydon
discovers something that James had known for a long time.

"The Beast in Henry James"

Robert Rogers*

It is not surprising, then, that early in "The Jolly Corner" Brydon
reflects that the house which represents home and childhood
security "had, through the sucessive deaths of his two brothers
and the termination of old arrangements, come wholly into his
hands." It follows that this house, the boyhood home where Brydon received the lavish care, warmth, and attention of his loving
mother, represents in actuality the mother herself. Houses are
commonly feminine symbols in dreams. . . . Brydon's return to
the home of his childhood is a return to the womb in phantasy. He
has his mother's womb all to himself: the brothers and father have
all been killed off. The architectural symbol as it will be seen to
function in this story is perhaps one of the most extraordinary examples of symbolic association to be found anywhere in literature.

The American Henry James

Quentin Anderson†

The Jolly Corner has been treated as a venture in the supernatural,
and an unwitting betrayal of James's own psychic wounds, but it
is something much more important than a remnant of uncontrolled
experience or a mere fictional device. It is a parable which employs
James's "ideal limits" of moral and aesthetic motion as characters. . . .

We have fallen into James's trap in reading this story as that of
a man who discovers what he *would have been*. What Spencer
Brydon really discovers is what he *has been*. It is this discovery
that enables him to recognize Alice Staverton's love. This is one
of James's pretty inversions or equivalences—there is no moral
distinction between the greed of the American expatriate and
that of the American millionaire. . . .

Spencer Brydon . . . undergoes what [James's father] had re-

* From *The American Imago*, XIII (Winter, 1956).
† (New Brunswick, Rutgers University Press, 1957).

ferred to in his own case as "My Moral Death and Burial." He confronts the awful creature, "to advance upon which was the condition for him either of liberation or of supreme defeat." The man he sees is presented with more "shade and salience" than any "portrait" could have given him. Brydon's whole being revolts; he asserts the total *otherness* of the creature in evening dress with his two amputated fingers—and dies to self-hood. (The reader will find this a useful instance of the portrait theme. To accept this presentment as one's self is to be damned; when Alice Staverton encounters this creature in her dream of the same hour, she in effect replaces him. What has become *other* for Brydon does so at the moment he is prepared to accept Alice Staverton's version of life and reject the one he has so long cherished.) His "early conception of style" had been nothing less than a love of the images of life for the sake of life itself which had been represented by the persons whose love had filled the house. . . .

At one end of the "interminable grey passage" there had stood the other self. Now "*carried* back" from "the dark other end of his tunnel," he finds himself possessed of a wonderful fullness of "knowledge." Directly, this is of Alice Staverton's love, an "inheritance" no less than infinite. . . . Love has borne Brydon back a third of a century and given him an actual second chance; not a supernatural glimpse of what he might have been, but a chance to become what his inordinately extended "middle years" had not made him—the inheritor of the house of life, delightedly dependent on fostering love. . . . [The] protagonist in the story is not an artist, but a dilettante, a redeemed appropriator, who stands, morally speaking, much closer to [the sculptor] William Wetmore Story [the expatriate American whose biography James had recently written] than he does to Henry James, who has so contrived the situation that the real sinner is the expatriate, not the American he might have been.

"Henry James's 'The Jolly Corner'"

Floyd Stovall[*]

There is in Spencer Brydon a double consciousness, but I cannot agree that it is explained as the selfish and selfless aspects of Bry-

[*] From *Nineteenth-Century Fiction*, XII (June, 1957. Published by The University of California Press).

don's soul. The ghost, or alter ego, is indeed himself as he might have been if he had remained in New York. Brydon does not see it and has only a vague idea of it; hence he mistakenly supposes the apparition of the entrance hall is the same ghost and it has come from behind the closed door and gone down before him. The ghost prefers the back rooms of the fourth floor because they are most remote from actuality. The apparition, on the contrary, is himself as he actually is; it very properly seems to come from without through the vestibule doors and is seen by the dim light of breaking day. Brydon is puzzled by the apparition because he expects it to be his alter ego and therefore recognizable, yet the face is so horrible that he rejects it with loathing. For thirty-three years he has been false to his true self without realizing it. It is this false self that is revealed to him, as symbolized by the removal of the covering hands, though he does not yet recognize it as his.

Brydon is evidently confused by the working of his double consciousness: the consciousness of his actual self—which is the false self, the mask that he has worn during his European years—and the consciousness of his ghostly self—which is the self that might have been, the self that has been evoked by the strong sense of the past that he feels while in the house. The consciousness of the actual self belongs to the world outside, whereas the consciousness of the self that might have been is inseparable from the old house and is particularly strong in the back rooms of the fourth floor farthest removed from the street. The combat that occurs within Brydon as he starts to mount the stairs on that last night of the story is the struggle between these two consciousnesses. He has an impulse to flee, which is the consequence of his fear of being lost to actuality and pulled into the ghostly world of his alter ego, but he conquers it for the moment. The reason James does not describe how Brydon gets to the fourth floor is that he wishes us to have the impression that the consciousness of actuality, the false self, remains below and the consciousness of himself as he might have been, the ghostly self, remains at the top. In the interval, the time during which he mounts the stairs, he is in effect without an operative consciousness, since the consciousness of his true self— so long buried under the consciousness of the actual self—has not yet been released. So it seems; yet the consciousness of actuality is never wholly lost, and even the consciousness of his true self, so long buried, has already begun to revive although Brydon does not yet realize what is happening to him. The crisis for him comes when he stands so long, unconscious of time, before the door of the innermost room, and finally abandons forever his pursuit of his alter ego and begs it not to trouble him further.

During the hours of this strange experience, Brydon's consciousness of his true self is struggling to emerge and has so far succeeded that when at last he does go downstairs the consciousness of actuality seems to rise before him in the apparition as something monstrous. This apparition is not a ghost in the sense that the alter ego on the fourth floor is a ghost. The false self, which he now sees in the apparition, has actually existed, whereas the self that might have been obviously has not except in his imagination. That the apparition belongs to the world without the house is symbolized by the fact that it is seen against the background of the open vestibule doors. The ghost, it will be remembered, remained unseen behind the door of the innermost room of the top floor, and there is no evidence that it comes out at all, though Brydon at first supposes that the apparition and the ghost are the same because he simply cannot otherwise account for what he sees, being still incompletely aware of his false self as false. The closed door above, which is not really closed, and the open doors below, which are not really open, are a part of his hallucination, but for the reader they are important symbolic keys to James's meaning.

Brydon does not recognize himself in the apparition with its evening dress, its double eyeglass, its two missing fingers, and its hideous face because it is the confused projection of his double consciousness. The symbols of both consciousnesses appear in the figure and contradict one another. The evening dress could belong to either, but the double eyeglass suggests to him that the apparition is himself as he would have become if he had remained in America. He actually uses a single eyeglass, but Americans prefer the double eyeglass. On the other hand, the missing fingers identify the apparition as himself as he actually is, his physical self. He has been an adventurer, a big-game hunter. If he had remained in New York he probably would not have lost the fingers. Brydon himself is not fully aware, as the reader is, of the workings of his double consciousness and quite naturally supposes the apparition to be the ghost that he had hoped would remain behind the closed door upstairs. When he sees the face, however, he cannot admit that his could ever have been so horrible. Neither is he ready to admit that it is himself as he actually is, in spite of the missing fingers. Yet when he rejects it, it becomes aggressive. This aggressiveness suggests that Brydon does recognize, after a moment, that the face is his own; that he continues to try to deny it to himself, but is no longer wholly self-deceived by such denial.

Alice Staverton understands him better than he understands himself. She has seen the face of the apparition in a dream at the very moment it appeared to Brydon, and she had also seen it twice before in dreams, recognizing it at once as his false self. Their mutual love (though he has not until then acknowledged it) has produced for them a common psychic experience; indeed it is the power of Alice's love, which is wholly unselfish, that has determined the character of Brydon's strange adventure. It is she who saves him from the ghostly past and later releases his buried self. It is worthwhile to quote James's description of Brydon's feelings after he regains consciousness:

> It had brought him to knowledge, to knowledge—yes, this was the beauty of his state; which came to resemble more and more that of a man who has gone to sleep on some news of a great inheritance, and then, after dreaming it away, after profaning it with matters strange to it, has waked up again to serenity of certitude and has only to lie and watch it grow.

He still does not know how he has come to possess knowledge— the knowledge both of his true self and of his false—but he is at peace. He tells Alice that he must have died and she brought him to life again. Alice says, as I have mentioned already, that he has come to himself. She must mean, or James must mean, that Brydon has passed through an experience somewhat like religious conversion that is symbolized by death and resurrection. He has been blind all these years—as the double eyeglass symbolically suggests—to the truth about himself and the love she has been waiting to give him when he should realize his need of it.

When Alice Staverton tells Brydon that he "came to himself" her words have a double meaning. To Brydon they mean simply that he has recovered consciousness. To the reader they are intended to mean that Alice understands that Brydon has seen himself as he has lived during his European years. The double eyeglass, Alice says, is for his "poor ruined sight," clearly symbolic of Brydon's blindness to the true state of things. There are then three "selves" in the story: the real self that is released by Alice's love, the self that she has believed in throughout; the false self that for thirty-three years has overlaid Brydon's true self and caused him to refuse to acknowledge his love for Alice; and the self that might have been had he never left New York, which is the ghost of the back rooms on the fourth floor of the house on the jolly corner.

The Image of Europe in Henry James

CHRISTOF WEGELIN*

The theme of the American's return now replaces his earlier theme of the American pilgrim to Europe. One of these stories reads in fact like a symbolical rendering of James's own return and the revelation it brought him. For the reactions of Spencer Brydon . . . can be documented almost point by point with James's letters. In the case of the disfigurement of Brydon's American alter ego by the pursuit of "a million a year" this may not be surprising, but the "muffled vibrations" with which the Europeanized Brydon responds to the appeal of "business," too, have their origin in James's own experience. He too could "vibrate" momentarily. For his lecture on "The Lesson of Balzac," he wrote excitedly to Edmund Gosse, "Indianapolis offers £100 for 50 minutes!" and to somebody else a few days later, "a pound a minute—like Patti!" In America even he could make money, and if he preferred nevertheless to "live a beggar at Lamb House," at least he wanted his biographer to "recall the solid sacrifice" involved.

This may be written with tongue in cheek, but no reader of *The Ambassadors* can doubt that James knew well enough how much the "helpless jelly" of his consciousness had been molded by Europe. In this sense, "The Jolly Corner" can quite properly be spoken of as autobiographical and the final note of pity for Brydon's disfigured alter ego as an expression of James's own sense that the ravaged businessman is no less victim of his conditions and therefore no less worthy of sympathy than an Isabel Archer or a Strether. Nevertheless, the man Brydon would have been had he stayed in America is "grim," "worn," "ruined" despite his "million a year"; he appeals to the lady's sympathy; the man he has become by

* (Dallas, Southern Methodist University Press, 1958).

living in Europe charms her. Her choice is as clear as James's
own choice of Lamb House. If the contrast of values remains undefined, it is because the values themselves are neither clearly
moral nor clearly intellectual or aesthetic, though all of these somehow hover in the story as possibilities. "The Jolly Corner" is another
example of James's refusal to oppose one cultural value to another,
and the most that can be said is that, if the European Brydon has
it over the American, it is because the civilization which formed
him has more charm—morally, intellectually, aesthetically in one
—than that which might have formed him in America.

TOPICS FOR FURTHER READING
AND WRITING

"Europe"
FADIMAN, Clifton (ed.), *The Short Stories of Henry James* (New York, The Modern Library), p. 383.

The Liar
KANE, Robert J., "Hawthorne's 'Prophetic Pictures' and James's 'The Liar,' " *Modern Language Notes,* LXV (April, 1950), 257–258.

The Real Thing
ANDERSON, Quentin, "Henry James and the New Jerusalem," *The Kenyon Review,* VIII (Autumn, 1946), 539.

ANDERSON, Quentin, "The Two Henry Jameses," *Scrutiny,* XIV (September, 1947), 249.

HAFLEY, James, "Malice in Wonderland," *Arizona Quarterly,* XV (Spring, 1959), 8–11.

KENTON, Edna (ed.), *Eight Uncollected Tales of Henry James* (New Brunswick, Rutgers University Press, 1950), p. 5.

RICHARDSON, Lyon (ed.), *Henry James* (New York, American Book Company, American Writers Series, 1941), p. 489.

RODITI, Edouard, *Oscar Wilde* (Norfolk, Connecticut, New Directions Books, 1947), pp. 104–107.

The Pupil
FADIMAN, Clifton (ed.), *The Short Stories of Henry James* (New York, The Modern Library), p. 272.

The Beast in the Jungle
BAILEY, Dorothy Dee, "Study of Theme in *The Beast in the Jungle,*" *Exercise Exchange,* VI (December, 1958—February, 1959), 4–5.

DEATON, Mary B., "From *Ethan Brand* to *The Stranger* . . . ," *Exercise Exchange,* VII (April, 1960), 4–5.

LUCKE, Jessie R., "The Inception of 'The Beast in the Jungle,' " *The New England Quarterly,* XXVI (December, 1953), 529–532.

MILLER, Betty, "Miss Savage and Miss Bartram," *The Nineteenth Century*, CXLIV (November, 1948), 285–292.

RAHV, Philip (ed.), *The Great Short Novels of Henry James* (New York, Dial Press, Inc., 1944), pp. 751–752.

TATE, Allen, "Three Commentaries: Poe, James, and Joyce," *The Sewanee Review*, LVIII (Winter, 1950), 1–15.

The Jolly Corner
MATTHIESSEN, F. O., and MURDOCK, Kenneth (eds.), *The Notebooks of Henry James*, pp. 361–369.